ASIAN MITIGATION
Insights, Mitigation Actions, Strategies
and Policies for Asian Economies

World Scientific Series on Environmental, Energy and Climate Economics

Series Editor: Richard S J Tol (*University of Sussex, UK*)

Published

Vol. 4 *Sustainable Growth and Green Policies: Navigating Energy and Environmental Challenges*
edited by Farhad Taghizadeh-Hesary, Naoyuki Yoshino, Nawazish Mirza and Muhammad Mohsin

Vol. 3 *Asian Mitigation: Insights, Mitigation Actions, Strategies and Policies for Asian Economies*
edited by Hongbo Duan

Vol. 2 *Climate Change Economics: Commemoration of Nobel Prize for William Nordhaus*
edited by Robert Mendelsohn

Vol. 1 *Climate and Development*
edited by Anil Markandya and Dirk T G Rübbelke

Volume 3 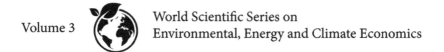 World Scientific Series on
Environmental, Energy and Climate Economics

ASIAN MITIGATION

Insights, Mitigation Actions, Strategies
and Policies for Asian Economies

Editor

Hongbo Duan
University of Chinese Academy of Sciences, China

NEW JERSEY • LONDON • SINGAPORE • BEIJING • SHANGHAI • TAIPEI • CHENNAI

Published by

World Scientific Publishing Co. Pte. Ltd.
5 Toh Tuck Link, Singapore 596224
USA office: 27 Warren Street, Suite 401-402, Hackensack, NJ 07601
UK office: 57 Shelton Street, Covent Garden, London WC2H 9HE

British Library Cataloguing-in-Publication Data
A catalogue record for this book is available from the British Library.

World Scientific Series on Environmental, Energy and Climate Economics — Vol. 3
ASIAN MITIGATION
Insights, Mitigation Actions, Strategies and Policies for Asian Economies

Copyright © 2025 by World Scientific Publishing Co. Pte. Ltd.

All rights reserved. This book, or parts thereof, may not be reproduced in any form or by any means, electronic or mechanical, including photocopying, recording or any information storage and retrieval system now known or to be invented, without written permission from the publisher.

For photocopying of material in this volume, please pay a copying fee through the Copyright Clearance Center, Inc., 222 Rosewood Drive, Danvers, MA 01923, USA. In this case permission to photocopy is not required from the publisher.

ISBN 978-981-98-1225-7 (hardcover)
ISBN 978-981-98-1226-4 (ebook for institutions)
ISBN 978-981-98-1227-1 (ebook for individuals)

For any available supplementary material, please visit
https://www.worldscientific.com/worldscibooks/10.1142/14285#t=suppl

Desk Editor: Venkatesh Sandhya

Typeset by Stallion Press
Email: enquiries@stallionpress.com

PREFACE

The Paris Agreement set an ambitious target that global average temperature not exceed 2°C. In order to meet this goal, countries around the world must reduce their future Greenhouse Gas emissions effectively to zero in the next thirty years. This will be a serious challenge for all but a handful of countries with substantial renewable energy resources. However, the challenge is especially great for Asian economies that are expected to generate more than half of future global GDP. The global target will not be met without Asian success.

This book illustrates the number of ways that Asia is planning on tackling mitigation. There are new ideas about organizing value chains, about national regulations, ways to change the power sector, adjusting the textile industry, sharing responsibility across nations, redesigning cities, and mixing taxes and subsidies. Every chapter in this book explores some way that Asia can address mitigation and move Asian mitigation towards the Paris goals. Implementing all of these ideas will not be easy but the book makes clear that Asia is actively engaged in the global mitigation effort.

Robert Mendelsohn
Yale University

CONTENTS

Preface   v

Introduction: What Mitigation Can Asia Contribute to the Paris Agreement Goals?   1
   H. Duan, J. Pan, T. G. Tsvetanov and B. Zhang

The Regional Roles Alongside the Evolution of Carbon Transfer Structure Within China: A Perspective from the National Value Chain   9
   S. Wang, J. Wu and G. Xu

Plant-Level Evaluation of China's National Emissions Trading Scheme: Benchmark Matters   41
   R. Ma and H. Qian

The Distributional Effect of Inter-Regional Transmission Grid Expansion on China's Power Industry   67
   X. Tan, S. Lin and B.-C. Xie

Assessing Strategies for Reducing the Carbon Footprint of Textile Products in China Under the Shared Socioeconomic Pathways Framework   93
   S.-Y. Peng, J.-Y. Liu and Y. Geng

Exploring Fair and Ambitious Mitigation Contributions of Asian Economies for the Global Warming Limit Under the Paris Agreement   113
   X. Li, X. Jiang and Y. Xia

How the Satellite City Is Affecting CO_2 Emissions   129
   D. Liao, L. Guo, G. Liu, F. Wu, C. Chen, X. Yin,
   J. Xue, Q. Yang, H. Li and M. Casazza

Analysis of the Synergistic Effect of Carbon Taxes and Clean Energy Subsidies: An Enterprise-Heterogeneity E-DSGE Model Approach   163
   Q. Tu and Y. Wang

A Bootstrap Assessment of the Shadow Prices of CO_2 for the Industrial Sector in China's Key Cities   191
   M. Yang, J. Xu, M. Li and H. Duan

© 2025 World Scientific Publishing Company
https://doi.org/10.1142/9789819812264_0001

INTRODUCTION: WHAT MITIGATION CAN ASIA CONTRIBUTE TO THE PARIS AGREEMENT GOALS?[||]

HONGBO DUAN[*], JIAHUA PAN[†,‡], TSVETAN G. TSVETANOV[§]
and BING ZHANG[¶]

[*]*School of Economics and Management*
University of Chinese Academy of Sciences
Beijing 100190, P. R. China

[†]*Institute for Eco-Civilization Studies*
Beijing University of Technology
Beijing 100710, P. R. China

[‡]*Research Centre for Sustainable Development*
Chinese Academy of Social Sciences
Beijing 100732, P. R. China

[§]*Department of Economics University of Kansas*
Lawrence, KS 66045, USA

[¶]*School of Environment, Nanjing University*
Nanjing 210023, P. R. China
[*]hbduan@ucas.ac.cn

Asia, particularly China, has been a story of rapid economic growth, rising to a prominent position in the global economy. Continued rapid growth suggests that Asia will be a source of substantial future greenhouse gas (GHG) emissions as well. Despite modest declines in emissions in industrialized countries, such as the United States and the European Union (EU), global emissions will not come close to meeting the Paris targets without substantial mitigation actions in Asian areas. In this regard, we initiated this topical issue and tried to study how Asia can contribute to the global effort to meet the 1.5°C and 2°C targets, from both national and industrial levels. The papers accepted bring insightful understandings and fresh perspectives to policy making and climate governance in Asian economies. We believe that these studies well contribute to the extant literature on both climate economic methodologies and regional climate policy research.

Keywords: Carbon mitigation; Paris Agreement; Climate economics research; Asia.

1. Introduction

Since the industrial revolution, carbon emissions from human activities have accumulated to a substantial degree. With the growing risk of social-ecological system

---

[*]Corresponding author.
[||]This chapter was originally published in Climate Change Economics, Vol. 13, No. 1 (2022), published by World Scientific Publishing, Singapore. Reprinted with permission.

deterioration and collapse (Magnan *et al.*, 2021), global warming could reach as high as 5.7°C by 2100 in the worst case (IPCC, 2021). Effective abatement designs that reduce greenhouse gas emissions rapidly and at scale are capable of substantially improving the chances of meeting the Paris Agreement targets to keep global warming well below 2°C or even 1.5°C relative to pre-industrial levels (Duan *et al.*, 2021; Ou *et al.*, 2021). It is therefore of great necessity to determine the optimal mitigation pathways, strategies and policies for sustainable development of economies at various development stages.

Home to more than half the world's population, Asia's energy demand is constantly growing in recent years, resulting in massive carbon emissions (Steckel *et al.*, 2021). With Regional Comprehensive Economic Partnership (RCEP) agreement entering into force, the yearly growth rate of CO_2 emissions from fossil fuel combustion in Asia will increase (Yang *et al.*, 2020; Tian *et al.*, 2022). Meanwhile, Asia is more vulnerable to climate change due to geographical factors and socioeconomic situations (Mei and Xie, 2016; Kraaijenbrink *et al.*, 2017; Chevuturi *et al.*, 2018). On the other hand, owing to different mitigation ambitions (Tørstad *et al.*, 2020), existing nationally determined contributions (NDCs) of Asian nations and regions would struggle to limit temperature rise to 2°C (Gambhir *et al.*, 2022). Therefore, coherence between climate actions and decarbonization objectives in Asia is a key issue.

Climate governance necessitates well-thought-out plans and practices. Sustainable strategy and policy design rely on effective cost-benefit analysis and pathway planning, which can be fulfilled using equilibrium models (Peng *et al.*, 2022; Tan *et al.*, 2022; Tu and Wang, 2022), Long-range Energy Alternatives Planning (LEAP) models (Liao *et al.*, 2021), input–output approaches (Wang *et al.*, 2022) and integrated assessment models (Duan *et al.*, 2019; Riahi *et al.*, 2021). In the face of varying heterogeneity, complexity and uncertainty, models should be updated so that they can be assessed at the regional, industry and enterprise levels under numerous scenarios.

To enrich research on mitigation contributions of Asia to meet the Paris Agreement targets, this special issue aims to provide new theoretical and practical ideas for decarbonization and sustainable development of Asian economies at the regional, sectoral and firm levels. The accepted papers covered several subtopics from regional contributions to effective climate governance, distribution effects of industry strategies to policy efficacy for low-carbon transformation of enterprises in Asian economies.

2. Climate Governance and Regional Role

Whether the temperature control targets committed in the Paris Agreement can be achieved is contingent on regional actions and decisions. Three papers deal with regional contributions to meet the goal of warming limit from national, inter-provincial and city perspectives. Targeting 14 Asian economies, Li *et al.* (2021) estimated allowable emission quotas based on effort-sharing approaches to limit global warming below 2°C. By examining the unconditional and conditional NDCs, they assessed the emissions gap between the NDCs and the cumulative emissions budgets of Asian economies to reach the Paris climate mitigation goals. The results reveal that the Equal-Per-Capita and Grandfathering criteria would be preferred by most emerging Asian economies, allowing them to earn higher emission quotas. Contrary to Asian developed economies, official mitigation promises represented by NDCs are insufficient for the developing economies, since their emission trajectories under NDCs considerably exceed the optimum routes under all effort-sharing approaches.

Wang *et al.* (2022) integrated trade in value-added (TiVA) accounting framework to track the evolution of the inter-regional carbon transfer network along the national value chain (NVC) within China. They further investigated the changing roles of each region in China participating in the carbon emissions transfer network from 2007 to 2017. The research finds that the inter-regional carbon emissions transfer structure has altered from "transferring from interior areas to developed areas" to a "carbon emissions transfer network with the Yangtze River Delta and the Central region as pivots." This study provides valuable insights into China's efforts to achieve carbon neutrality by striking a balance between economic development and environmental protection across regions.

Since cities' emissions account for the vast majority of the country's total, reaching carbon neutrality requires coordinated development of low-carbon cities. Liao *et al.* (2021) employed a LEAP model to assess satellite cities' involvement in alleviating the demographic and environmental pressures on the major city. Xiong'an New District, an area extending from Hebei province (China) and supporting the development of Beijing, is discussed as an example. The research shows that increased population and construction area would result in a considerable rise in GHG emissions from residential consumption in Hebei province, whereas modestly lowering GHG emissions in Beijing. Faced with this situation, green planning, such as improvements in industrial structure and industrial transformation, can compensate for GHG emissions rise in Hebei province due to population migration.

3. Sector-Level Mitigation Strategies and Distribution Effects

Considering the input–output structure of industries, market-oriented mitigation strategies would have distribution effects throughout the whole supply chains and even the entire society. In this volume, Peng *et al.* (2022) focused on the textile industry and looked at how socioeconomic factors and climate policies may assist China to reduce greenhouse gas emissions of textile goods. They first use life cycle assessment (LCA) to calculate the current GHG emissions of textile types and discover that polyethylene terephthalate yarn (PET) and cotton yarn have the highest GHG emissions in the raw material and processing stages. By introducing Shared Socio-economic Pathways (SSPs) into the Asia-Pacific Integrated Model/Computable General Equilibrium (AIM/CGE) model, they show that a combination of socioeconomic conditions and climate policies could reduce annual carbon emissions by 89% and cumulative emissions by

34.3% by 2050. The study identified key strategies that exhibited great potential for lowering emissions, including energy decarbonization and power conservation.

Inspired by Limpaitoon et al. (2014) and Tan et al. (2020), Tan et al. (2022) applied the electricity market equilibrium model to evaluate the extent that ultra-high voltage (UHV) lines affect the distributional effects of the power industry in China. They employed the mixed complementarity problems (MCPs) method to quantitatively examine the distributional effect of UHV lines in terms of power deployment, carbon emissions and producer surplus. The results reveal that the distribution effect of the UHV transmission line has substantially lessened. At the same time, the environmental and economic distribution effect of the UHV transmission network among provinces was not sensitive to load expansion.

4. Firm Heterogeneity and Policy Effectiveness

To achieve low-carbon transformation of enterprises, it is vital to take into account the firm heterogeneity and focus on the synergistic effects of structural environmental policies. The objective of Tu and Wang (2022) was to determine the synergistic effects of structural carbon taxes and clean energy subsidies in low carbon transition. By developing a heterogeneous Environmental Dynamic Stochastic General Equilibrium (E-DSGE) model with firm heterogeneity, they explore pollution accumulation and economic growth under the effects of the aforementioned two policies. The simulation results demonstrate that policies aimed at reducing structural carbon emissions have synergistic effects and can effectively balance the relationship between energy demand and economic growth. Furthermore, distinguishing production technology and green innovation technology can aid in the growth of energy-efficient and environmentally friendly businesses while also improving the industrial structure.

Given the scarce *ex-ante* evaluation for China's national emission trading scheme (ETS) at the micro level in previous literature (Yan et al., 2020; Qian et al., 2021), Ma and Qian (2022) used plant-level data to assess the impacts of various permit allocation designs. The findings demonstrate that the national ETS's current benchmark standards would result in an oversupply of permits. Only when benchmark standards are set as high as the top 2% efficiency levels will the entire carbon market achieve market clearance. The entire market size will dramatically grow if an auction mechanism is used, with overall revenue reaching 600 billion yuan once all permits are auctioned.

5. Conclusion

The papers accepted in this special issue present in-depth understanding and fresh perspectives on optimal mitigation actions, strategies and policies in Asian economies using a set of quantitative models, such as CGE models, DSGE model, LEAP models, LCA approaches and input–output analysis. We believe that these studies should have value added to the existing literature for actions oriented towards implementation of

Paris goals and shed light on new research avenues. Looking ahead, in terms of model construction, more consideration should be given to the bilateral coupling between human and natural systems, and the interaction between energy and climate, which is necessary for the planning of climate strategies; more attention should also be made to the coordinated reduction of CO_2 and non-CO_2 greenhouse gases, as well as the fulfillment of family and individual demands; the evaluation of mitigation policies should place a greater emphasis on policy justice and human well-being. Further, to cope with the economic uncertainties on mitigation policy assessment, particularly in the longer run, more robust approaches are urgent to develop, such as multi-model comparisons (Duan *et al.*, 2021). Last but not the least, critical economics of net zero emissions is indicated to generate new theoretical foundations for a shift of development paradigm from conventional utilitarian profit maximization approach to a nature-based man-and-nature in harmony solution as countries in the region including China, India and Japan have pledged the carbon neutrality targets (Pan, 2019, 2022).

Acknowledgments

Financial support from the National Natural Science Foundation of China (72325008; 72274188), the National Key Research and Development Program of China (2020YFA0608603), and the MOE Philosophy and Social Sciences Innovative Group on "Complex Systems Modeling in Economic Management in the Era of Digital Intelligence" are greatly acknowledged.

References

Chevuturi, A, NP Klingaman, AG Turner and S Hannah (2018). Projected changes in the Asian-Australian monsoon region in 1.5°C and 2.0°C global-warming scenarios. *Earth's Future*, 6, 339–358, https://doi.org/10.1002/2017EF000734.

Duan, HB, GP Zhang, SY Wang and Y Fan (2019). Integrated benefit-cost analysis of China's optimal adaptation and targeted mitigation. *Ecological Economics*, 160, 76–86, https://doi.org/10.1016/j.ecolecon.2019.02.008.

Duan, HB, S Zhou, KJ Jiang, C Bertram, M Harmsen, E Kriegler, DP van Vuuren, SY Wang, S Fujimori, M Tavoni, X Ming, K Keramidas, G Iyer and J Edmonds (2021). Assessing China's efforts to pursue the 1.5°C warming limit. *Science*, 372(6540), 378–385, https://www.science.org/doi/abs/10.1126/science.aba8767.

Gambhir, A, M George, H McJeon, NW Arnell, D Bernie, S Mittal, AC Köberle, J Lowe, J Rogelj and S Monteith (2022). Near-term transition and longer-term physical climate risks of greenhouse gas emissions pathways. *Nature Climate Change*, 12, 88–96, https://doi.org/10.1038/s41558-021-01236-x.

Intergovernmental Panel on Climate Change (IPCC) (2021). Climate Change 2021: The Physical Science Basis. Contribution of Working Group I to the Sixth Assessment Report of the Intergovernmental Panel on Climate Change. Cambridge University Press, https://www.ipcc.ch/report/ar6/wg1/.

Kraaijenbrink, PDA, MFP Bierkens, AF Lutz and WW Immerzeel (2017). Impact of a global temperature rise of 1.5 degrees Celsius on Asia's glaciers. *Nature*, 549(7671), 257–260, https://doi.org/10.1038/nature23878.

Li, XR, XM Jiang and Y Xia (2021). Exploring fair and ambitious mitigation contributions of Asian economies for the global warming limit under the Paris Agreement. *Climate Change Economics*, 13(1), 2240002, https://doi.org/10.1142/S2010007822400024.

Liao, DQ, LS Guo, GY Liu, F Wu, CC Chen, XA Yin, HM Zheng, JY Xue, Q Yang, H Li and M Casazza (2021). How the satellite city is affecting CO2 emissions. *Climate Change Economics*, 13(1), 2240001, https://doi.org/10.1142/S2010007822400012.

Limpaitoon, T, Y Chen and SS Oren (2014). The impact of imperfect competition in emission permits trading on oligopolistic electricity markets. *Energy Journal*, 35, 145–168, https://doi.org/10.5547/01956574.35.3.7.

Magnan, AK, HO Pörtner, VK Duvat, M Garschagen, VA Guinder, Z Zommers, OH Guldberg and JP Gattuso (2021). Estimating the global risk of anthropogenic climate change. *Nature Climate Change*, 11, 879–885, https://doi.org/10.1038/s41558-021-01156-w.

Ma, R and HQ Qian (2022). Plant-level evaluation of China's National Emissions Trading Scheme: Benchmark matters. *Climate Change Economics*, 13(1), 2240009.

Mei, W and SP Xie (2016). Intensification of landfalling typhoons over the northwest Pacific since the late 1970s. *Nat. Geosci.*, 9, 753–757, https://doi.org/10.1038/ngeo2792.

Ou, Y, G Iyer, L Clarke, J Edmonds, AA Fawcett, N Hultman, JR Mcfarland, M Binsted, R Cui, C Fyson, A Geiges, S Gonzales-Zuñiga, MJ Gidden, N Höhne, L Jeffery, T Kuramochi, J Lewis, M Meinshausen, Z Nicholls, P Patel, S Ragnauth, J Rogelj, S Waldhoff, S Yu and H McJeon (2021). Can updated climate pledges limit warming well below 2°C? *Science*, 374(6568), 693–695, https://www.science.org/doi/abs/10.1126/science.abl8976.

Pan, J (2019). From ecological imbalance to ecological civilization: The process of China's Green transformation over 40 years of reform and opening up and its outlook. *Chinese Journal of Urban and Environmental Studies*, 7(3), 1950007, doi.org/10.1142/S2345748119500076.

Pan, J (2022). A thift of development paradigm brought by carbon neutrality revolution and overall coordination. *Yuejiang Academic Journal*, 2022(1), 21–35.

Peng, SY, JY Liu and Y Geng (2022). Assessing strategies for reducing the carbon footprint of textile products in China under the Shared Socioeconomic Pathways framework. *Climate Change Economics*, 13(1) 2240004.

Qian, HQ, SD Xu, J Cao, FZ Ren, WD Wei, J Meng and LB Wu (2021). Air pollution reduction and climate co-benefits in China's industries. *Nature Sustainability*, 4(5), 417–425, https://doi.org/10.1038/s41893-020-00669-0.

Riahi, K, C Bertram, D Huppmann, J Rogelj, V Bosetti, AM Cabardos, A Deppermann, L Drouet, S Frank, O Fricko, S Fujimori, M Harmsen, T Hasegawa, V Krey, G Luderer, L Paroussos, R Schaeffer, M Weitzel, BVD Zwaan, Z Vrontisi, FD Longa, J Després, F Fosse, K Fragkiadakis, M Gusti, F Humpenöder, K Keramidas, P Kishimoto, E Kriegler, M Meinshausen, LP Nogueira, K Oshiro, A Popp, PRR Rochedo, G Ünlü, BV Ruijven, J Takakura, M Tavoni, DV Vuuren and B Zakeri (2021). Cost and attainability of meeting stringent climate targets without overshoot. *Nature Climate Change*, 11, 1063–1069, https://doi.org/10.1038/s41558-021-01215-2.

Steckel, JC, II Dorband, L Montrone, H Ward, L Missbach, F Hafner, M Jakob and S Renner (2021). Distributional impacts of carbon pricing in developing Asia. *Nature Sustainability*, 4, 1005–1014, https://doi.org/10.1038/s41893-021-00758-8.

Tan, X, S Lin, YL Liu and BC Xie (2020). Has the inter-regional transmission grid promoted clean power development? A quantitative assessment on China's electricity sector. *Journal of Cleaner Production*, 269, 122370, https://doi.org/10.1016/j.jclepro.2020.122370.

Tan, X, S Lin and BC Xie (2022). The distributional effect of inter-regional transmission grid expansion on China's power industry. *Climate Change Economics*, 13(1) 2240005.

Tian, KL, Y Zhang, YZ Li, X Ming, SY Jiang, HB Duan, CH Yang and SY Wang (2022). Regional trade agreement burdens global carbon emissions mitigation. *Nature Communications*, 13, 1–12, https://doi.org/10.1038/s41467-022-28004-5.

Tu, QY and Y Wang (2022). Analysis of the synergistic effect of carbon taxes and clean energy subsidies — An enterprise-heterogeneity E-DSGE model approach. *Climate Change Economics*.

Tørstad, V, H Sælen and LS Bøyum (2020). The domestic politics of international climate commitments: Which factors explain cross-country variation in NDC ambition?. *Environmental Research Letters*, 15, 024021, https://iopscience.iop.org/article/10.1088/1748-9326/ab63e0.

Wang, SY, J Wu and GX Xu (2022). The regional roles alongside the evolution of carbon transfer structure within China: A perspective from the national value chain. *Climate Change Economics*, 13(1) 2240011.

Yang, L, YT Wang, RR Wang, JJ Klemeš, CMVB de Almeida, MZ Jin, XZ Zheng and YB Qiao (2020). Environmental-social-economic footprints of consumption and trade in the Asia-Pacific region. *Nature Communications*, 11, 1–9, https://doi.org/10.1038/s41467-020-18338-3.

Yan, K, W Zhang and DH Shen (2020). Stylized facts of the carbon emission market in China. *Physica A: Statistical Mechanics and its Applications*, 555, 124739, https://doi.org/10.1016/j.physa.2020.124739.

© 2025 World Scientific Publishing Company
https://doi.org/10.1142/9789819812264_0002

THE REGIONAL ROLES ALONGSIDE THE EVOLUTION OF CARBON TRANSFER STRUCTURE WITHIN CHINA: A PERSPECTIVE FROM THE NATIONAL VALUE CHAIN[§]

SHUYU WANG[*], JIE WU[*,‡] and GUOXIANG XU[*,†]

[*]*School of Statistics and Management*
Shanghai University of Finance and Economics
Shanghai 200433, P. R. China

[†]*Branch Center of Shanghai University of*
Finance and Economics
Shanghai Social Survey and Research Center (SSSRC)
Shanghai 200433, P. R. China
[‡]*wu.jie@mail.shufe.edu.cn*

To strengthen the national efforts to meet Paris Agreement Targets, China has announced its carbon neutrality goal in 2020 and launched the national carbon market in 2021. Regional carbon emissions accounting is important for the allocation of regional mitigation targets and emission allowances in the policy-making of the national carbon market. This paper integrates the trade in value-added (TiVA) accounting method to comprehensively analyze the evolution of the carbon emissions transfer network in China along the national value chain (NVC) and further clarifies the changing roles of regions participating in the network during 2007–2017. The results indicate that the inter-regional carbon emissions transfer structure in China has changed from the pattern of "transferring from inland areas to developed areas" to a new pattern of a "carbon emissions transfer network with the Yangtze River Delta and the Central regions as pivots". This paper provides insightful results for China to strike a balance between economic development and environmental governance among regions in achieving carbon neutrality.

Keywords: Carbon emissions transfer effects; national value chain (NVC); embodied emissions; trade in value-added (TiVA).

1. Introduction

Change in climate has brought human and natural systems additional risks such as more frequent extreme weather, food and water shortages, health damage, and economic retardation (IPCC, 2018). Without effective controls on greenhouse gas emissions, the global society may suffer severe climate change damage, especially in less developed and climate-vulnerable countries (Duan *et al.*, 2021; Mora *et al.*, 2018;

[‡]Corresponding author.
[§]This chapter was originally published in Climate Change Economics, Vol. 13, No. 1 (2022), published by World Scientific Publishing, Singapore. Reprinted with permission.

Wang *et al.*, 2020). To strengthen the national efforts to meet the Paris Agreement Targets, China has announced the carbon neutrality goal in 2020 and a national carbon market was launched in 2021 (Mo *et al.*, 2021; Wang *et al.*, 2021). As such market-based policy provides a platform for different regions to cooperatively implement the national mitigation goal, the regional burden-sharing regime for the allocation of emission reduction obligations has become an important concern for policymakers (Edmonds *et al.*, 2021; Kober *et al.*, 2014). For that reason, accurate accounting of inter-regional carbon emissions is a prerequisite for the allocation of regional mitigation targets and emission allowances. In this context, clarifying the inter-regional emissions transfer structure and the role of regions in the evolution of the carbon transfer network is essential for the policy-making of the national carbon market in China.

Similar to the fact that international trade is one of the most important drivers of global carbon emissions (Davis and Caldeira, 2010; Liu *et al.*, 2016), inter-regional trade within China is the main cause of regional carbon emissions. Faced with the external environment of de-globalization and the COVID-19 pandemic, China has proposed the establishment of a "dual circulation" pattern led by the national value chain (NVC) (Bekkers, 2019; Robinson and Thierfelder, 2019). Since high-tech products with high-value-added in developed regions usually show excessive dependence on carbon-intensive products with low-value-added in less developed regions, the rapid growth of inter-regional trade may reallocate and complicate carbon emissions embodied in trade through the NVC (Cui *et al.*, 2019; Feng *et al.*, 2020; Guo *et al.*, 2021).

In the measurement of carbon emission transfers, the input–output theory has been widely adopted due to its elaborate depiction of economic relationships among entities in the value chain (Daudin *et al.*, 2011; Hertwich and Peters, 2009). And most existing studies were conducted with a production- or consumption-based accounting framework (Peters, 2008; Shigeto *et al.*, 2012). From the perspective of forward-linkage, the production-based accounting framework traces where the emissions generated by a source region are absorbed; while the consumption-based accounting framework is from a backward-linkage perspective, which traces back to how the final demands of a terminal region induce emissions from the associated production segments (including itself) (Andrew and Peter, 2013; Hasegawa *et al.*, 2015). For example, Arto and Dietzenbacher (2014) found that developed countries in international carbon emission transfers appeared to be net importers with higher consumption-based emissions than production-based emissions due to outsourcing of the high-carbon industries. Although the consumption-based accounting framework is considered to be fairer in identifying differentiated emission responsibilities shared by regions (Girod *et al.*, 2014; Jakob *et al.*, 2014), the two frameworks provide different perspectives and cannot be substituted for each other when describing the emissions transfer structure (Xia and Tang, 2017).

However, the deepening of vertical specialization in inter-regional trade has led to an increase in carbon emissions transferred through trade in intermediate products, resulting in double counting of emissions embodied in gross trade (Johnson and Noguera, 2012; Timmer et al., 2014). In order to calculate the double counting value-added in the gross exports, a framework of trade in value-added (TiVA) accounting was first proposed by Koopman et al. (2014), which could trace the value-added from both perspectives of forward and backward linkages. By integrating the concept of TiVA and embodied emissions in trade, the carbon emissions transfer effects in the global value chain (GVC) have been widely explored (Meng et al., 2018). Compared with the production- or consumption-based accounting frameworks, the TiVA accounting framework provides a way to decompose the carbon emissions embodied in gross exports and trace the carbon transfers along the value chains. Nevertheless, the former two frameworks could not be replaced by the TiVA framework as it cannot deal with issues such as how much emissions in a region are sorted as self-responsibility, or the extent to which the final demand of a region induces emissions from upstream production.

In the context of China, most of the existing literature focuses on the national carbon emission transfers in the international trade from a GVC perspective (Levitt et al., 2019; Mi et al., 2017; Su and Thomson, 2016; Yan et al., 2020). Few literature works that investigated the carbon emission transfers among regions in China use either a production-based framework or a consumption-based framework. From a perspective of backward linkage, Duan et al. (2018) and Tang et al. (2019) found that the developed regions in eastern China appeared to outsource emissions to the central and western regions. With the carbon transfers showing a direction from less developed and heavy chemo-industrial or energy-intensive areas to developed areas (Zhou et al., 2018), developed provinces (e.g., Guangdong, Zhejiang, and Jiangsu) presented a higher degree of centrality in the energy flow network (Tang et al., 2014). By comparing the carbon emissions of different regions in 2017 and 2010, the results in Shao et al. (2018) revealed that less developed regions have experienced a faster increase in carbon emissions than developed regions, whether from the perspective of forward or backward linkage. However, the above-mentioned studies conducted with the production- or consumption-based approach have abstracted from the value-added embodied in trade, which might magnify the disparities in regional emissions. In addition, the expanding scale of carbon emission transfers caused by the deeper participation of the southwest and central regions in the NVC has further aggravated the complexity of China's carbon transfer network (Lv et al., 2019; Zheng et al., 2020). Therefore, it is of great significance to explore the structure of inter-regional emissions transfer from a perspective of TiVA and to identify the role of regions in the evolution of the carbon transfer network within China.

Against this background, this paper contributes to the existing literature by tracing carbon transfers along the NVC within China from a perspective of TiVA, as a supplement to the perspectives of forward and backward linkages. Based on the TiVA framework, this study extends the frameworks in Wang et al. (2015) and Meng et al. (2018) at the NVC level, so as to be able to identify the emissions sourced from local, direct trade regions or third regions in intermediate products trade. On the other hand, by comparisons during the 2007–2017 period, this study further analyzes the evolution of the inter-regional emissions transfer structure and identifies the role of regions in the evolution.

The remainder of this paper is organized as follows: Sec. 2 introduces the integrated accounting framework and data. Section 3 presents empirical results, and Sec. 4 concludes.

2. Methodology and Data

2.1. *Accounting frameworks*

The accounting framework for carbon emission transfers presented in this paper originated in the input–output theory put forward by Leontief (1936), which demonstrates complex input–output linkages among economic entities using the input–output table. Based on China's multi-regional input–output (MRIO) table, the 30 provinces are considered as an economic system in this study, with other territories and countries externalized. By integrating the carbon emission intensity with the input–output models from the perspectives of forward-linkage, backward-linkage and TiVA, we achieve to estimate the inter-regional carbon emission transfers along the NVC in China. Detailed derivation processes of the three accounting frameworks are presented in Supplementary Material.

The forward-linkage-based accounting framework decomposes carbon emissions produced by the source region into nine distinct routes (Table 1), traces carbon emission transfers from upstream to downstream and identifies the self-responsibility of the source region. The decomposition is conducted to figure out how and where the emissions generated by the source region are absorbed.

As presented in Table 1, the sum of the first three routes (Routes 1–3) represents the carbon emissions of a region to satisfy its final demand. In particular, Route 1 indicates emissions in products totally produced and consumed in a region without any participation in inter-regional trade, which could be considered pure self-responsibility of this region. Routes 4 and 5 express the carbon emissions of a region to satisfy the final demand of the region's direct trade partner, and Route 6 denotes carbon emissions to satisfy the final demand of third regions in the economic system. The sum of Routes 7–9 marks the carbon emissions exported. As a result, the sum of Routes 2–6 measures the carbon emissions embodied in bilateral trade in the NVC, while Routes 7–9 indicate the emissions associated with the GVC.

The backward-linkage-based accounting framework traces upstream emissions in other regions induced by local final demand (Table 2), and the decomposition under this framework is to figure out where the emissions caused by local final demand are generated in regions within China. Note that the first route of the backward-linkage-based accounting framework is equivalent to the sum of Routes 1, 2, 4, 7 and 8 in the forward-linkage-based accounting framework. In addition, the energy structure of

Table 1. Description of carbon transfer routes decomposed with the forward-linkage-based framework.

Routes	Description
Route 1	Local carbon emissions for local demands are completely not involved in the NVC and the GVC
Route 2	Carbon emissions in intermediate products produced in the region that return to the home region after the multi-stage NVC to produce local-consumed final products
Route 3	Carbon emissions in intermediate products produced in the region that are used by partner regions to produce final products shipped back to the home region
Route 4	Carbon emissions in final products produced in the region absorbed by partner regions
Route 5	Carbon emissions in intermediate products produced in the region that are used by partner regions to produce final products absorbed there
Route 6	Carbon emissions in intermediate products produced in the region that are used by partner regions to produce final products absorbed by third regions
Route 7	Carbon emissions in exports produced in the region not involved in the NVC
Route 8	Carbon emissions in intermediate products produced in the region that return to the home region after the multi-stage NVC to produce exports
Route 9	Carbon emissions in intermediate products produced in the region that are used by partner regions to produce exports there

Table 2. Description of carbon transfer routes decomposed with the backward-linkage-based framework.

Routes	Description
Route 1	Carbon emissions generated locally induced by local final demand
Route 2	Carbon emissions generated in upstream stages by sectors in other regions induced by local final demand

carbon transfers could be measured by adopting the carbon emission intensity of different energy types (mainly coal and petroleum mentioned in this paper).

Linking the forward and backward linkages, the TiVA-based accounting framework focuses on carbon emissions embodied in the value chain of inter-regional trade. By extending the gross trade accounting method (Wang *et al.*, 2015) to the level of the NVC and integrating it with carbon emissions accounting, this paper develops a TiVA-based accounting framework to trace emission transfers along the NVC in China. Based on the share matrixes of value-added and import, the sectoral output in different regions could be completely decomposed into value-added sourced from regions within China and abroad, so as to further identify the double counting terms and import-associated terms in the TiVA-based accounting framework. Note that these terms (double counting and import-associated) are excluded in the accounting of inter-regional carbon emission transfers within China. Therefore, the decomposition of TiVA-based framework figures out how the emissions are transferred along the NVC in the gross export production from the source region to partner regions (Table 3).

Table 3. Description of carbon transfer routes decomposed with the TiVA-based framework.

Routes	Description
Route 1	Carbon emissions of the home region embodied in final products absorbed by a partner region
Route 2	Carbon emissions of the home region embodied in intermediate products used by a partner region to produce a final product absorbed there
Route 3	Carbon emissions of the home region embodied in intermediate products used by a partner region to produce final products absorbed by third regions
Route 4	Carbon emissions of the home region embodied in intermediate products used by a partner region to produce final products shipped back to the home region
Route 5	Carbon emissions of the home region embodied in intermediate products used by a partner region to produce exports or intermediate products reshipped to third regions to produce exports
Route 6	Carbon emissions of a direct partner region embodied in final products absorbed by a partner region
Route 7	Carbon emissions of a direct partner region embodied in intermediate products used by a partner region to produce final products absorbed there
Route 8	Carbon emissions of a direct partner region embodied in intermediate products used by a partner region to produce exports
Route 9	Carbon emissions of third regions embodied in final products absorbed by a direct partner region
Route 10	Carbon emissions of third regions embodied in intermediate products used by a direct partner region to produce final products absorbed there
Route 11	Carbon emissions of third regions embodied in intermediate products used by a direct partner region to produce exports

Sorting out the 11 routes above, we obtain that the sum of Routes 1–5 represents local carbon emissions embodied in TiVA from the source region to a partner region. The sum of Routes 6–8 indicates carbon emissions reshipped to a partner region, and the sum of the last three routes reflects carbon emissions of third regions embodied in TiVA from the source region to a partner region.

2.2. Data

The data in this paper are sourced from China MRIO tables during the 2007–2017 period. There are 30 provinces[1] (see Table A.1), and each province has 30 sectors. According to the geographic position and the regional integration strategies in China, the 30 provinces are classified into nine regions as shown in Fig. 1 for comprehensive analysis of carbon transfer structure in the NVC.[2]

---

[1]The word "province" in this paper is used to represent 22 provinces, 4 municipalities and 4 autonomous regions in China's MRIO tables mentioned subsequently.

[2]To better capture the carbon emissions transfer structure among regions in China, the classification principle in this paper is slightly different from that in previous studies (Feng *et al.*, 2020; Shao *et al.*, 2018; Zhou *et al.*, 2018). On one hand, considering Anhui has fully joined the strategy for integrated development of the Yangtze River Delta (YRD) during 2007–2017, we re-classify Anhui as part of the YRD region rather than keep it in the Central region (Mid); on the other hand, considering the differences in economic development and degree of inter-provincial integration, we classify Sichuan and Chongqing as the region Sichuan-Chongqing (C&Y), and classify Yunnan, Guizhou and Guangxi as members of the Southwest (SW) region.

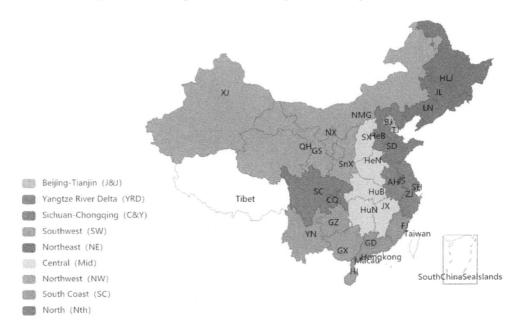

Figure 1. Nine regions and the 30 provinces.

3. Empirical Analysis

Based on the above accounting frameworks, we analyze the evolution of the inter-regional carbon emissions transfer structure in China during the period of 2007–2017. From the perspectives of forward linkages, backward linkages and TiVA, we further explore the changing roles of different provinces in the evolution of carbon transfer networks. In addition, this study takes the electricity sector as an example to explore the sector-level transfer of carbon emissions among provinces from the TiVA perspective.

3.1. Evolution of the inter-regional carbon emissions transfer structure

As total carbon emissions in China increased from 6.29Gt to 10.48Gt during 2007–2012 and then decreased to 9.41Gt in 2017, we first analyze the changes in regional emissions during the period 2007–2017 based on the forward-linkage and backward-linkage frameworks. Figure 2 provides a comparison of carbon emissions decomposed by forward- and backward-linkage frameworks, regardless of the pure self-sufficient emissions, namely, emissions that are completely not involved in the NVC. Results show that while both forward-linkage and backward-linkage emissions in most regions increase gradually during 2007–2017, emissions in the regions North (Nth), Beijing-Tianjin (J&J), and Yangtze River Delta (YRD) present inflection points in 2012 or 2015. Compared with 2012, the emissions of these three regions in 2017 decrease by 8%, 21%, and 4% from the perspective of forward linkage, respectively, and by 37%, 1%, and 21% from the perspective of backward linkage.

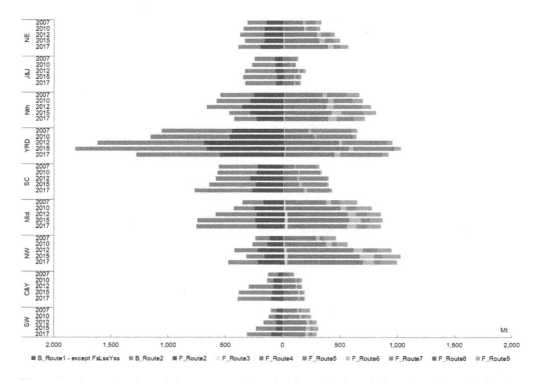

Figure 2. Forward-linkage (right) and backward-linkage (left) emissions in regions during the period 2007–2017.

The inter-regional carbon emissions transfer structure shows significant absorption effects in developed regions such as Beijing-Tianjin, Yangtze River Delta, South Coast, and Sichuan-Chongqing, while the Northeast, Central, North, and Northwest regions present carbon radiation effects. With higher backward-linkage emissions than forward-linkage emissions, the regions Beijing-Tianjin, Yangtze River Delta, South Coast, and Sichuan-Chongqing perform as net carbon importers. However, net carbon inflows in these regions have declined after 2015. For example, the net carbon inflow in Yangtze River Delta decreases by 55% during 2015–2017 after an increase of 92% during 2007–2015. The main reason of the net carbon inflow increase during 2007–2015 is the rapid growth in local final demand and emissions embodied in value-added transfers from carbon-intensive regions. However, the implementation of climate mitigation policies has slowed down the growth of carbon emission transfers based on backward linkages in developed regions since 2012.

Figure 3 presents heatmaps of TiVA-based carbon emission transfers throughout the NVC at the regional level during the period 2007–2017, where the vertical axis represents source regions and the horizontal axis represents trade partner regions. Results show that the total emission transfers throughout the NVC in 2015 are 1.75 times that of 2007 and reduce by 5% in 2017 compared with 2015 (Fig. 3(1a)–3(5a)). While the Yangtze River Delta remains the largest emissions importer during the entire

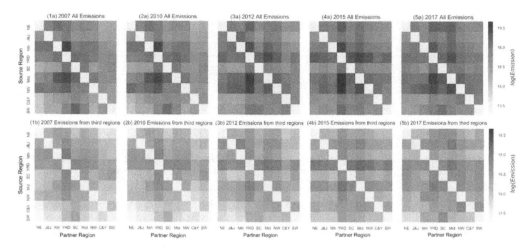

Figure 3. Heatmaps of TiVA-based carbon emissions transfer throughout the NVC at the regional level in the period 2007–2017.

period 2007–2017, the Yangtze River Delta, Northwest, and Central regions have replaced the North as the largest three emissions exporters in 2017.

As to the inter-regional carbon emissions transfer structure during the period 2007–2017, it has gradually changed from the pattern of "transferring from inland areas to developed areas" to a new pattern of a "carbon emissions transfer network with the Yangtze River Delta and the Central region as pivots". Figure 3 shows that from 2007 to 2015, the carbon emission transfers between the Yangtze River Delta and the Central region increase in both directions (from YRD to Mid: 216%; from Mid to YRD: 85%). In particular, the emission transfers between the two regions and the Northwest, Southwest and Northeast regions have increased significantly with considerable non-local emissions embodied in TiVA from upstream regions (Fig. 3(1b)–3(5b)), which makes the Yangtze River Delta and the Central region impressive as pivots in the inter-regional carbon transfer network.

As the increasing participation in the NVC has led to increases in emission transfers between the Northwest, Northwest regions and other regions, it is further indicated that the carbon emission transfers network along the NVC in China is more complex. Results in Fig. 3 show that the local emissions embodied in TiVA in the Northwest region toward the Southwest, Sichuan-Chongqing, and South Coast regions experience significant increases (5.78, 6.02, and 3.28 times larger than in 2007, respectively), whereas the nonlocal emission transfers toward the Sichuan-Chongqing, Southwest, Yangtze River Delta, and Central regions also increase considerably (by 199%, 353%, 15%, and 97%, respectively). At the same time, more in-depth participation in the NVC has made the increase in carbon inflows (3.14 times) in the Southwest region significantly higher than carbon outflows (1.73 times) during the period 2007–2017. As a result, the Southwest region has turned to be a net carbon importer in 2015, and the net carbon inflows in 2017 have further increased by 140%.

18   S. Wang et al.

Table 4. The discrepancies of net carbon transfers estimation measured by forward- and backward-linkage-based accounting.

Region	2007	2010	2012	2015	2017
Northeast	24.97%	−32.34%	−61.44%	−52.84%	16.71%
Beijing-Tianjin	22.79%	8.82%	15.58%	32.62%	−15.01%
North	31.35%	31.06%	−9.48%	−5.32%	−26.06%
Yangtze River Delta	−3.20%	−21.78%	−63.63%	−65.52%	−34.92%
South Coast	9.61%	9.53%	21.56%	35.00%	12.81%
Central	−5.97%	−7.21%	−37.06%	−35.89%	−91.03%
Northwest	5.98%	−20.91%	−28.09%	−23.01%	−2.95%
Sichuan-Chongqing	−62.64%	61.61%	−37.10%	−24.93%	−45.76%
Southwest	−14.88%	−41.02%	−78.51%	0.00%	321.59%

Note: Negative values indicate overestimation, and positive ones indicate underestimation.

The estimation of net carbon transfers in regions from perspectives of forward- and backward linkages presents significant differences with that from TiVA perspective (Table 4), which indicates that the participation in the NVC brings complexity to the inter-regional carbon transfer network. For example, carbon inflows of the regions presenting as pivots in the carbon transfer network might be re-exported to other regions, thus the net carbon transfers of such regions are more likely to be over-estimated by forward- and backward-linkage accounting frameworks. As presented in Table 4, the net inflows in the Yangtze River Delta region during 2007–2017 are overestimated by 3.20–65.52% based on the forward- and backward-linkage accounting frameworks.

3.2. Provincial roles from the forward-linkage perspective versus the backward-linkage perspective

From the forward-linkage perspective, carbon emissions produced by a province are to be absorbed by itself, other provinces in China, or abroad. Figure 4 shows the forward-linkage carbon emission transfers that are decomposed through different routes in 2017, illustrating "who produces emissions for whom". Based on the proportion of carbon emissions induced by self-final demand (Route 1+ Route 2+ Route 3 in Table 1), provinces with such proportion exceeding 50% are classified as self-sufficient carbon emitters (bold-italic labeled in Fig. 4), and others are classified as export-oriented carbon emitters.

Results show that most of the self-sufficient carbon-emitting provinces are in regions such as the Central, Southwest, and Sichuan-Chongqing regions; and the export-oriented carbon emitters are mostly developed or energy-intensive provinces located in the eastern coastal regions. Among the export-oriented carbon-emitting provinces, Guangdong presents the highest proportion (35%) of carbon emissions exported to foreign regions, owing to its large export with geographic and factor

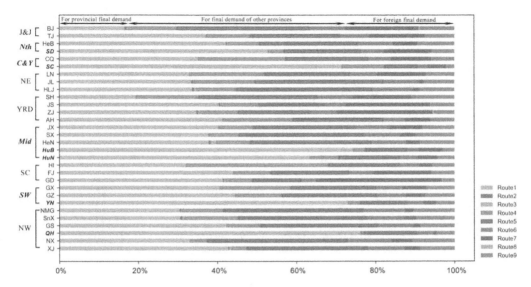

Figure 4. Carbon emissions decomposed with the forward-linkage-based framework in 2017.

endowment advantages. As the carbon emissions induced by the final demand of other domestic provinces account for more than 50%, Hainan, Jilin, Beijing, Inner Mongolia, Shaanxi, Ningxia, Shanghai, and Heilongjiang act as domestic-transfer-oriented emitters. Comparing the carbon emissions export structure (Routes 7–9), developed and coastal provinces (e.g., Guangdong and Zhejiang) show a higher proportion of carbon emissions export (Route 7) without any participation in the NVC, while inland and energy-intensive provinces (e.g., Inner Mongolia and Ningxia) present a higher share through the NVC embodied in intermediate products trade (Route 9).

The changes in the structure of the forward-linkage-based emissions in nine regions (Table 5), as well as in 30 provinces (see Table A.2), indicate that the carbon emission transfers in China have gradually shifted from abroad to the NVC within China. Results show that the average proportion of carbon emissions induced by domestic final demand in China increases by 11% during 2007–2017, and the proportion of carbon emissions induced by foreign final demand has decreased in all regions.

To identify the shared responsibility of carbon emissions between local production and upstream production in other provinces, decomposition of provincial carbon emissions in 2017 based on the backward-linkage accounting framework is shown in Fig. 5. Results show that developed provinces with lower carbon intensity have a higher proportion of carbon emissions (60–86%) from upstream provinces, especially in Beijing, Zhejiang and Chongqing. Besides the lower carbon intensity, an important reason is the high proportion of intermediate inputs supplied by other provinces, which may lead to more carbon emissions in the upstream provinces for local production of final products.

Figure 5 also shows the energy structure of different routes, which indicates that the use of coal accounts for the majority of carbon emissions. Regarding total emissions

Table 5. The structure of the forward-linkage-based emissions in nine regions during 2007–2017.

Region	Carbon emissions induced by local final demand (%) 2007	2012	2017	Carbon emissions induced by final demand of other domestic regions (%) 2007	2012	2017	Carbon emissions induced by final demand of foreign territories (%) 2007	2012	2017
Northeast	**51.61**	**59.95**	39.25	27.55	29.28	46.74	20.84	10.77	14.01
Beijing-Tianjin	34.00	32.54	23.67	33.10	48.66	52.15	32.90	18.81	24.18
North	41.86	**58.08**	**52.27**	32.98	23.73	30.95	25.16	18.19	16.78
Yangtze River Delta	44.10	44.87	44.18	20.05	29.47	29.63	35.85	25.67	26.19
South Coast	39.99	49.51	44.55	20.14	17.44	26.47	39.87	33.05	28.98
Central	48.99	**58.61**	**53.64**	32.28	30.43	34.30	18.74	10.95	12.06
Northwest	38.00	44.16	41.25	42.79	40.51	46.60	19.21	15.33	12.15
Sichuan-Chongqing	**63.40**	**66.50**	**55.74**	24.90	25.35	33.73	11.70	8.14	10.52
Southwest	41.05	**56.49**	**54.31**	34.26	34.48	34.68	24.68	9.03	11.01
AVG	44.78	52.30	45.43	29.78	31.04	37.25	25.44	16.66	17.32

Notes: The highlighted text denotes that the region is classified as a self-sufficient carbon emitter; AVG denotes the average percentage.

induced by local final demand, the emissions caused by the use of coal in most provinces exceed 50% (excluding Beijing, Yunnan, Sichuan, and Shanghai). For example, 79% of the local emissions induced by final demand in Ningxia are caused by the use of coal. In the evolution of backward-linkage-based emissions during 2007–2017, carbon emissions sourced from upstream provinces present rapid growths in Zhejiang, Henan, Jiangxi, Guangdong, Guizhou, and Qinghai (Fig. 6). Such change

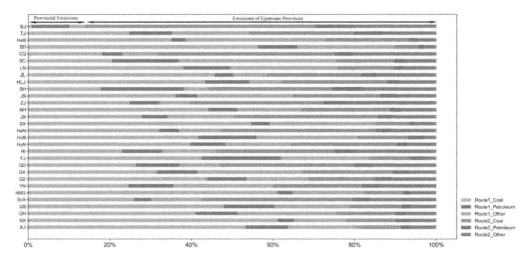

Figure 5. Structure of emissions decomposed by the backward-linkage-based framework in 2017.

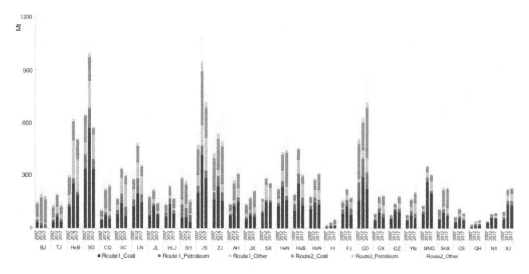

Figure 6. Evolution of the backward-linkage-based emissions during 2007–2017.

mostly ascribes to the emissions from the use of coal; namely, provinces with a more rapid increase in coal-based emissions sourced from other regions present a more rapid increase in backward-linkage-based emissions.

3.3. *Provincial roles from the TiVA perspective*

Figure 7 presents how carbon emissions transfer through 11 routes in the NVC, which corresponds to the TiVA-based accounting framework. The results illustrate that energy-intensive and less-developed provinces exhibit a higher proportion of local carbon emissions embodied in inter-provincial trade. For example, the local carbon emissions embodied in TiVA throughout the NVC (Routes 1–5) account for 94% of the total

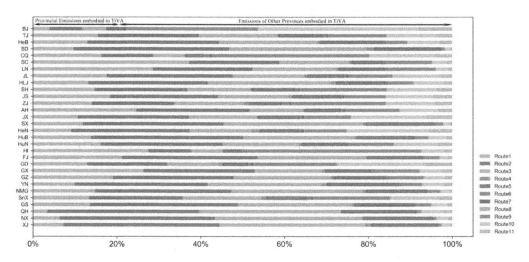

Figure 7. Carbon emissions decomposed by the TiVA-based framework in 2017.

emissions in Inner Mongolia, while it accounts for only 21% in Beijing. In addition, carbon emission transfers embodied in high-carbon intermediate products in energy-intensive provinces present a longer path in the NVC. In Fig. 7, the local emissions embodied in multi-stage intermediate trade (Route 3+ Route 4) make up more than 30% of the carbon emissions in Shanxi, Inner Mongolia, Ningxia, Xinjiang, Qinghai, Shandong, and Heilongjiang. However, the proportions of the carbon emissions shipped back via the NVC (Route 4) are very low in all provinces.

At the same time, developed provinces show high dependence on high-carbon products from other provinces (Routes 6–11). For example, the nonlocal carbon emissions account for a large proportion (more than 40%) of the total emissions in Chongqing and Zhejiang. The main reason is that the production of inter-provincial trade and export products in these provinces is highly dependent on high-carbon inputs from other provinces.

Figure 8 describes the TiVA-based carbon emission transfers throughout the NVC in 2007 and 2017, where the upper two graphs represent all emissions transferring throughout the NVC, and the lower two graphs represent the carbon emissions sourced from third provinces embodied in inter-provincial trade. Figures 8(1a) and 8(2a) show that in the energy-intensive and manufacturing provinces, the carbon emission transfers through the NVC present gradually increasing radiation effects. In 2017, the total outflows from these provinces (including Inner Mongolia, Henan, Hebei, Jiangsu, Liaoning, Shanxi, Shandong, Guangdong, and Shaanxi) account for 51% of the total carbon emission outward transfers in China, showing strong carbon radiation effects. While most carbon emissions embodied in TiVA are absorbed by developed regions, results in Figs. 8(1b) and 8(2b) also show increasing absorption effects in developed provinces. For example, the carbon emissions absorbed by Zhejiang, Jiangsu, Guangdong, and Beijing, account for more than 34% of the total emissions embodied in TiVA throughout the NVC, showing strong carbon absorption effects.

In addition, the emissions sourced from third provinces embodied in inter-provincial trade have increased significantly during 2007–2017, indicating a more complex carbon transfer network throughout the NVC in China (Figs. 8(1b) and 8(2b)). In the pivot regions, provinces in Yangtze River Delta contribute equally to the re-exporting emissions imported from third provinces; but in the Central region, Henan and Jiangxi contribute particularly impressively as pivots. Besides, it is worth noting that developed provinces, such as Beijing, Guangdong, Chongqing, and Shaanxi, have grown into sub-pivots of the inter-provincial carbon transfer network during 2007–2017.

In terms of the provincial role of net carbon exporter and importer,[3] results indicate that most developed provinces remain performing as net carbon importers, and Hebei, Shanxi, and Inner Mongolia perform as net carbon exporters during 2007–2017. However, deep participation in the more complex NVC has turned Henan and Yunnan

---

[3]Detailed values of TiVA-based net carbon transfers are presented in Table A.3.

The Regional Roles Alongside the Evolution of Carbon Transfer Structure within China 23

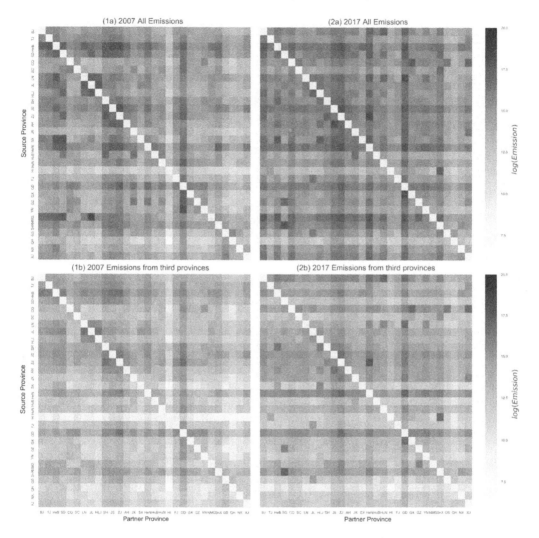

Figure 8. Comparison of heatmaps of the TiVA-based carbon emissions transferring throughout the NVC in 2007 (left) and 2017 (right).

into net carbon importers, while Shandong, Anhui, and Fujian have become net carbon exporters.

3.4. *Inter-provincial carbon emission transfers in the electricity sector*

The electricity sector plays a crucial role in carbon emission transfers, which, on average, accounts for 47% of carbon emissions throughout the NVC in China in 2017; in some provinces, this proportion is more than 70%. Therefore, we further analyze the roles of different provinces in the carbon emissions transfer network of the electricity sector in 2017.

Figure 9 shows the TiVA-based inter-provincial carbon emission transfers of the electricity sector in 2007 and 2017, both of which present a transfer direction from the

24 S. Wang et al.

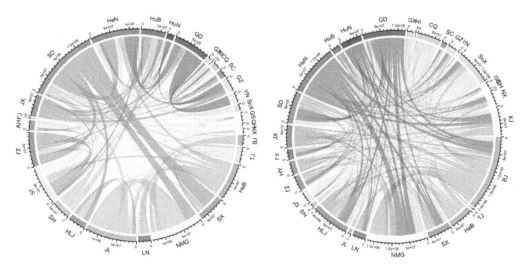

Figure 9. Comparison of TiVA-based inter-provincial carbon emission transfers of the electricity sector in 2007 (left) and 2017 (right).

northern provinces to the southern provinces. Concluding from the comparison between 2007 and 2017, the pattern of carbon transfer in the electricity sector has shifted from inter-regional to extensive inter-provincial transferring along the NVC. In 2017, the total carbon emissions transferred from all provinces embodied in TiVA are 946.07 Mt, accounting for 92% of all TiVA-based emissions throughout the NVC in China. Among the 30 provinces, Inner Mongolia, Shandong, Xinjiang, Heilongjiang, and Shanxi present carbon radiation effects; Beijing, Henan, Guangdong, Hebei, Chongqing, Jiangxi, Shaanxi, and Hunan illustrate carbon absorption effects with larger carbon emission inflows embodied in TiVA. Moreover, Beijing and Shaanxi have simultaneously shown significant emission inflows and outflows in TiVA, which act as pivots of the inter-provincial carbon transfer network in the electricity sector.

3.5. Enlightenment of carbon emissions accounting to the carbon market in China

Analyses above have unveiled the inter-regional carbon emissions transfer pattern along the NVC in China, which provide the basis for the emission allowances allocation of the national carbon market in China and mitigation targets setting in regions from the perspective of TiVA. Therefore, the enlightenment of emissions accounting under the TiVA-based accounting framework to the carbon market is discussed below.

Since the TiVA-based accounting framework provides a more accurate approach to identify the self-responsibility and the responsibilities of others in the total emissions of the region, co-responsibilities shared by different regions should be considered from the TiVA perspective in the emission allowances allocation. For example, regions act as pivots in the carbon transfer network are highly dependent on intermediate inputs along the NVC and thus have a higher proportion of emissions sourced from other regions in total emissions, which are usually ignored in the allocation of emission allowances. In fact, net carbon exporters based on the TiVA accounting framework should undertake more responsibilities for carbon mitigation.

In the setting of regional mitigation targets, changes in local final demand should be considered in the self-sufficient carbon-emitting regions, as most of the total emissions in these regions are induced by local final demand. In addition, the results in this study show that emissions in coal-based energy-intensive regions are mainly caused by final demand from other regions, providing clues for policymakers to consider mitigation costs sharing in setting regional mitigation targets.

In conclusion, the allocation of emission allowances makes carbon emissions a scarce resource, indicating that the national carbon market is essential for the inter-regional wealth transfer in China. Reasonable emission allowances allocation could reduce regional mitigation costs and promote the effectiveness of wealth allocation and regional coordinated development, which might turn out to be an important path for China to achieve common prosperity.

4. Conclusions

Along with rapid economic development, the increasing inter-regional trade linkages complicate the accounting of regional carbon emissions embodied in trade within China, and the deepening of vertical specialization in the NVC leads to the reshaping of the inter-regional carbon transfer network in China. By developing an integrated accounting framework that could decompose carbon emission transfers into various routes along the NVC from the perspective of TiVA, we explore the evolution of carbon emissions transfer structure in China and investigate how each region and province in China participate in the carbon emissions transfer network during the period of 2007–2017. Our main findings are as follows.

The inter-regional carbon emissions transfer structure within China has changed from the pattern of "transferring from inland areas to developed areas" to a new pattern of a "carbon emissions transfer network with the Yangtze River Delta and the Central region as pivots". During 2007–2017, the nonlocal emissions sourced from upstream regions embodied in trade from the two pivots toward the Northwest, Southwest, and Northeast regions have increased considerably.

In addition, the emissions sourced from third provinces embodied in inter-provincial trade have increased significantly during 2007–2017, indicating a more complex carbon transfer network throughout the NVC in China. Participation in the NVC brings changes in regional roles alongside the evolution of the carbon transfer network, the carbon emission transfers through the NVC present gradually increasing radiation effects in the energy-intensive and manufacturing provinces, and absorption effects in developed provinces.

The following policy recommendations can be inferred from our findings. The complexity of participation in the NVC, as well as the level of regional economic development, should be considered in the setting of distinctive emission mitigation targets for different regions in China. As the Northwest and Southwest regions experience increasing participation in the NVC, environmental regulations should be strengthened in these regions to avoid excessive outward transfers of carbon emissions. In addition, it is of great importance to consider regional roles in the carbon transfer network along the NVC in the allocation of emission allowances in China's national carbon market.

Acknowledgments

The authors would like to acknowledge the financial support from the National Natural Science Foundation of China under grant No. 71704100, the Shanghai Pujiang Program under grant No. 2019PJC048, and the Innovative Research Team of Shanghai University of Finance and Economics under grant No. 2020110930.

Appendix A

Table A.1. Provinces listed in the paper and the corresponding abbreviations used in figures in this paper.

Order	Province	Abbr.	Order	Province	Abbr.
1	Beijing	BJ	16	Henan	HeN
2	Tianjin	TJ	17	Hubei	HuB
3	Hebei	HeB	18	Hunan	HuN
4	Shandong	SD	19	Hainan	HI
5	Chongqing	CQ	20	Fujian	FJ
6	Sichuan	SC	21	Guangdong	GD
7	Liaoning	LN	22	Guangxi	GX
8	Jilin	JL	23	Guizhou	GZ
9	Heilongjiang	HLJ	24	Yunnan	YN
10	Shanghai	SH	25	Inner-Mongolia	NMG
11	Jiangsu	JS	26	Shaanxi	SnX
12	Zhejiang	ZJ	27	Gansu	GS
13	Anhui	AH	28	Qinghai	QH
14	Jiangxi	JX	29	Ningxia	NX
15	Shanxi	SX	30	Xinjiang	XJ

Table A.2. The structure of the forward-linkage-based emissions in 30 provinces during 2007–2017.

Region	Province	Carbon emissions induced by local final demand (%) 2007	2012	2017	Carbon emissions induced by final demand of other provinces (%) 2007	2012	2017	Carbon emissions induced by final demand of foreign territories (%) 2007	2012	2017
Beijing-Tianjin	BJ	42.53	19.69	17.34	30.69	61.75	55.05	26.78	18.57	27.61
	TJ	20.16	43.92	37.40	40.78	35.95	41.11	39.06	20.13	21.48
North	HeB	22.79	42.34	42.60	51.86	43.22	41.79	25.35	14.44	15.61
	SD	50.06	66.09	53.43	23.36	12.59	28.71	26.59	21.32	17.86
Sichuan-Chongqing	CQ	57.87	47.07	35.48	30.23	47.05	48.46	11.90	5.88	16.06
	SC	63.40	76.81	71.68	24.92	13.36	21.62	11.68	9.83	6.70
Northeast	LN	40.43	47.04	33.27	34.97	39.57	47.22	24.60	13.39	19.51
	JL	33.98	54.90	33.98	50.50	39.81	57.06	15.52	5.28	8.96
	HLJ	42.36	55.90	34.62	42.03	36.10	54.98	15.61	8.00	10.40
Yangtze River Delta	SH	25.58	27.55	19.82	25.33	44.94	54.42	49.09	27.51	25.76
	JS	34.64	38.34	40.90	31.13	34.67	31.60	34.23	26.99	27.50
	ZJ	40.64	43.93	35.56	24.26	25.24	34.64	35.10	30.82	29.80
	AH	44.14	31.95	41.52	38.05	54.47	45.90	17.81	13.58	12.58
Central	JX	69.80	53.04	40.48	16.36	33.66	43.11	13.84	13.30	16.41
	SX	38.96	44.12	38.23	38.65	43.63	48.17	22.39	12.25	13.60
	HeN	32.28	49.62	39.65	48.34	41.13	48.05	19.38	9.25	12.30
	HuB	56.92	80.12	74.44	27.11	9.27	16.51	15.96	10.62	9.05
	HuN	54.36	58.20	63.64	28.17	34.53	27.10	17.47	7.27	9.25
South Coast	HI	61.92	41.63	32.10	17.98	48.26	59.12	20.10	10.11	8.79
	FJ	48.41	56.12	44.05	15.92	17.43	35.46	35.67	26.46	20.49
	GD	37.12	46.65	42.06	22.41	17.14	22.84	40.47	36.21	35.11
Southwest	GX	46.54	58.53	41.10	30.95	32.19	45.76	22.52	9.29	13.14
	GZ	34.08	45.25	44.85	45.34	45.28	42.78	20.58	9.46	12.37
	YN	32.66	51.70	73.41	35.49	40.51	18.69	31.85	7.79	7.89
Northwest	NMG	23.08	29.29	30.91	59.74	51.54	56.69	17.18	19.18	12.41
	SnX	33.83	36.53	31.62	46.94	47.51	55.47	19.22	15.96	12.91
	GS	43.56	46.11	42.58	35.70	45.56	47.08	20.75	8.34	10.34
	QH	55.81	72.12	76.23	27.01	19.66	18.38	17.18	8.22	5.39
	NX	43.22	40.67	33.23	38.72	48.36	50.76	18.05	10.96	16.00
	XJ	43.83	53.20	43.50	33.74	34.04	43.75	22.43	12.76	12.75
Average		42.50	48.61	42.99	33.89	36.61	41.41	23.61	14.77	15.60

Table A.3. Dynamic changes of net carbon emission transfers at the provincial level measured by TiVA accounting method (Mt).

Order	Province	2007	2012	2017	Order	Province	2007	2012	2017
1	BJ	−113.84	−336.41	−333.39	16	HeN	88.67	−59.66	−255.30
2	TJ	−111.99	−100.22	−43.69	17	HuB	25.24	−39.47	−34.54
3	HeB	56.35	149.55	93.28	18	HuN	6.46	−49.96	−106.59
4	SX	121.27	157.38	196.72	19	GD	−315.36	−259.53	−562.12
5	NMG	183.66	287.28	321.42	20	GX	2.64	−35.25	−10.24
6	LN	24.97	8.83	113.72	21	HI	0.72	−21.02	−18.38
7	JL	−109.71	−44.59	−10.97	22	CQ	−28.26	−104.34	−195.00
8	HLJ	−14.83	−49.91	−26.08	23	SC	−9.66	−41.83	−39.73
9	SH	−195.90	−119.16	−52.91	24	GZ	54.27	55.34	−9.94
10	JS	−124.19	−317.50	−132.59	25	YN	37.43	−15.17	−113.38
11	ZJ	−270.79	−218.02	−388.96	26	SnX	−30.92	−108.77	−133.99
12	AH	−6.39	−16.97	12.67	27	GS	1.18	12.57	31.88
13	FJ	−40.96	−0.88	43.83	28	QH	−9.09	−7.03	−7.60
14	JX	−64.77	−54.34	−83.22	29	NX	13.07	53.35	54.27
15	SD	−53.34	−120.45	113.26	30	XJ	6.12	23.53	81.07

Note: Positive values indicate net carbon export, while negative values indicate net carbon import.

Supplementary Material

To make it clear how we build carbon emissions accounting frameworks rooted in the work of Leontief from the forward-linkage, backward-linkage and TiVA perspectives, we provide the derivation processes in the following section.

S.1. *Forward-linkage-based accounting framework*

Without loss of generality, we assume an economic system composed of G regions and N sectors. Its input–output structure is represented by the inter-region input–output model in Table S1.

Table S1. General inter-region input–output table.

Inputs \ Outputs		Intermediate use				Final demand				Total output	
		R1	R2	...	RG	R1	R2	...	RG	Export	
Intermediate input	R1	X^{11}	X^{12}	...	X^{1G}	Y^{11}	Y^{12}	...	Y^{1G}	Ex^1	X^1
	R2	X^{21}	X^{22}	...	X^{2G}	Y^{21}	Y^{22}	...	Y^{2G}	Ex^2	X^2
	...	...	...		...	...	...		...	...	...
	RG	X^{G1}	X^{G2}	...	X^{GG}	Y^{G1}	Y^{G2}	...	Y^{GG}	Ex^G	X^G
Import		M^1	M^2	...	M^G						
Value-added		V^1	V^2	...	V^G						
Total input		$X^{1'}$	$X^{2'}$	...	$X^{G'}$						

In the table, $\mathbf{X}^{ij}$ is an $N \times N$ matrix of intermediate flows that are produced in region i and used in region j; $\mathbf{Y}^{ij}$ is an $N \times 1$ vector giving final demands of region j that are produced in region i; $\mathbf{Ex}^i$ represents an $N \times 1$ vector expressing exports of N sectors in region i; $\mathbf{M}^i$ denotes a $1 \times N$ vector of imports in region i; and $\mathbf{V}^i$ is a $1 \times N$ vector giving value-added of N sectors in region i. Letting the $N \times N$ matrix $\mathbf{A}^{ij}$ denote the input–output coefficient matrix of region i to region j, we obtain the following total outputs X:

$$\begin{bmatrix} X^1 \\ \cdots \\ X^G \end{bmatrix} = \begin{bmatrix} A^{11} & \cdots & A^{1G} \\ \cdots & \cdots & \cdots \\ A^{G1} & \cdots & A^{GG} \end{bmatrix} \begin{bmatrix} X^1 \\ \cdots \\ X^G \end{bmatrix} + \begin{bmatrix} \sum_{t=1}^{G} Y^{1t} + Ex^1 \\ \cdots \\ \sum_{t=1}^{G} Y^{Gt} + Ex^G \end{bmatrix}. \qquad (1)$$

According to Eq. (1), we can decompose the total outputs in region s based on the forward-linkage perspective as follows:

$$X^s = A^{ss}X^s + Y^{ss} + \sum_{t \neq s}^{G} A^{st}X^t + \sum_{t \neq s}^{G} Y^{st} + Ex^s, \qquad (2)$$

where $A^{ss}X^s + Y^{ss}$ represents the portion of products produced and used in region s; and $\sum_{t \neq s}^{G} A^{st}X^t + \sum_{t \neq s}^{G} Y^{st}$ describes the portion of products produced in region s and used by other regions in the economic system. In addition, $A^{ss}X^s + \sum_{t \neq s}^{G} A^{st}X^t$ denotes intermediate flows, while $Y^{ss} + \sum_{t \neq s}^{G} Y^{st} + Ex^s$ presents the overall final use in region s denoted by Y^s.

Rearranging Eq. (1), we have

$$\begin{bmatrix} X^1 \\ \cdots \\ X^G \end{bmatrix} = \begin{bmatrix} I - A^{11} & \cdots & -A^{1G} \\ \cdots & \cdots & \cdots \\ -A^{G1} & \cdots & I - A^{GG} \end{bmatrix}^{-1} \begin{bmatrix} Y^1 \\ \cdots \\ Y^G \end{bmatrix} = \begin{bmatrix} B^{11} & \cdots & B^{1G} \\ \cdots & \cdots & \cdots \\ B^{G1} & \cdots & B^{GG} \end{bmatrix} \begin{bmatrix} Y^1 \\ \cdots \\ Y^G \end{bmatrix}, \qquad (3)$$

where matrix B denotes the Leontief inverse matrix, with $N \times N$ dimensions for each sub-matrix B^{ij}; that is, $B^{ij} = [b_{pq}^{ij}], (p, q = 1, 2, \ldots, N)$, in which b_{pq}^{ij} denotes the intermediate inputs in region i sector p needed to produce one-unit final products in region j sector q. Similarly, the total outputs in region s can be decomposed as follows:

$$X^s = B^{ss}Y^{ss} + \sum_{r \neq s}^{G} B^{ss}Y^{sr} + B^{ss}Ex^s + \sum_{r \neq s}^{G} B^{sr}Y^{rs} + \sum_{r \neq s}^{G} B^{sr}Y^{rr}$$

$$+ \sum_{r \neq s}^{G} B^{sr} \sum_{t \neq s, r}^{G} Y^{rt} + \sum_{r \neq s}^{G} B^{sr}Ex^r. \qquad (4)$$

In particular, B^{ss} in the equation above differs from the local Leontief inverse matrix L^{ss}, namely, $B^{ss} \neq L^{ss} = (I - A^{ss})^{-1}$. To completely decompose the outputs of region s along the NVC, we further break up the first and third terms in Eq. (4). For $L^{ss} \sum_{r \neq s}^{G} A^{sr} B^{rs} = B^{ss} - L^{ss}$ (Wang et al., 2018), we rearrange Eq. (4) to yield the following:

$$X^s = L^{ss} Y^{ss} + \left(L^{ss} \sum_{r \neq s}^{G} A^{sr} B^{rs} \right) Y^{ss} + \sum_{r \neq s}^{G} B^{sr} Y^{rs} + \sum_{r \neq s}^{G} B^{ss} Y^{sr} + \sum_{r \neq s}^{G} B^{sr} Y^{rr}$$

$$+ \sum_{r \neq s}^{G} B^{sr} \sum_{t \neq s, r}^{G} Y^{rt} + L^{ss} Ex^s + \left(L^{ss} \sum_{r \neq s}^{G} A^{sr} B^{rs} \right) Ex^s + \sum_{r \neq s}^{G} B^{sr} Ex^r. \quad (5)$$

Define $f_j^s = \text{emis}_j^s / X_j^s$ as the direct carbon emission intensity of region s sector j, where emis_j^s denotes total carbon emissions in region s sector j and X_j^s represents total outputs in region s sector j. Given $F^s = (f_1^s, f_2^s, \ldots, f_N^s)'$ as a vector of the direct carbon emission intensity of N sectors in region s, the carbon emission transfers from region s from a forward-linkage perspective can be decomposed as follows:

$$\text{emis\_forward}^s = \hat{F}^s X^s$$

$$= \underbrace{\hat{F}^s L^{ss} Y^{ss}}_{(1)} + \underbrace{\hat{F}^s \left(L^{ss} \sum_{r \neq s}^{G} A^{sr} B^{rs} \right) Y^{ss}}_{(2)} + \underbrace{\hat{F}^s \sum_{r \neq s}^{G} B^{sr} Y^{rs}}_{(3)} + \underbrace{\hat{F}^s \sum_{r \neq s}^{G} B^{ss} Y^{sr}}_{(4)}$$

$$+ \underbrace{\hat{F}^s \sum_{r \neq s}^{G} B^{sr} Y^{rr}}_{(5)} + \underbrace{\hat{F}^s \sum_{r \neq s}^{G} B^{sr} \sum_{t \neq s, r}^{G} Y^{rt}}_{(6)} + \underbrace{\hat{F}^s L^{ss} Ex^s}_{(7)}$$

$$+ \underbrace{\hat{F}^s \left(L^{ss} \sum_{r \neq s}^{G} A^{sr} B^{rs} \right) Ex^s}_{(8)} + \underbrace{\hat{F}^s \sum_{r \neq s}^{G} B^{sr} Ex^r}_{(9)}. \quad (6)$$

There are nine terms in Eq. (6), each representing carbon emissions generated by region s in their production to satisfy distinct kinds of downstream demands along the NVC.

Term (1): Carbon emissions generated by region s when locally producing final products which are directly consumed in region s without any association with other regions.

Term (2): Carbon emissions generated by region s when producing intermediate products used by partner regions to produce intermediate products shipped back to region s and consumed there.

Term (3): Carbon emissions generated by region s when producing intermediate products used by partner regions to produce final products shipped back to region s and consumed there.

Term (4): Carbon emissions generated by region s when producing final products which are consumed by partner regions.

Term (5): Carbon emissions generated by region s when producing intermediate products used by partner regions for the production of final products consumed there.

Term (6): Carbon emissions generated by region s when producing intermediate products used by partner regions for the production of intermediate products which are used by third regions to produce final products consumed there

Term (7): Carbon emissions generated by region s when producing products directly exported to regions outside the economic system without any association within the NVC.

Term (8): Carbon emissions generated by region s when producing intermediate products used by partner regions to produce intermediate products shipped back to region s and used to produce exports to regions outside the economic system.

Term (9): Carbon emissions generated by region s when producing intermediate products used by partner regions to produce their exports to regions outside the economic system.

Equation (6) presents the forward-linkage-based accounting framework through which we could trace carbon emission transfers from upstream to downstream. Note that each term of the right side of Eq. (6) sequentially corresponds to a carbon transfer route described in Table 1 in Sec. 2.1.

S.2. Backward-linkage-based accounting framework

Then we introduce how we decompose carbon emissions from backward-linkage perspective. Similar to the Armington assumption, we assume that locally produced products cannot be completely substituted by those imported from other regions and that production in different regions and sectors stands for different stages in a value chain. To decompose the inputs for the final demands of a region and sector, we rearrange Eq. (3) as follows:

$$B\hat{Y} = \begin{bmatrix} B^{11} & B^{12} & \cdots & B^{1G} \\ B^{21} & B^{22} & \cdots & B^{2G} \\ \cdots & \cdots & \cdots & \cdots \\ B^{G1} & B^{G2} & \cdots & B^{GG} \end{bmatrix} \begin{bmatrix} \hat{Y}^1 & & & \\ & \hat{Y}^2 & & \\ & & \cdots & \\ & & & \hat{Y}^G \end{bmatrix}$$

$$= \begin{bmatrix} B^{11}\hat{Y}^1 & B^{12}\hat{Y}^2 & \cdots & B^{1G}\hat{Y}^G \\ B^{21}\hat{Y}^1 & B^{22}\hat{Y}^2 & \cdots & B^{2G}\hat{Y}^G \\ \cdots & \cdots & \cdots & \cdots \\ B^{G1}\hat{Y}^1 & B^{G2}\hat{Y}^2 & \cdots & B^{GG}\hat{Y}^G \end{bmatrix}, \quad (7)$$

in which $\hat{Y}^j (j = 1, 2, \ldots, G)$ denotes an $N \times N$ diagonal matrix; that is, $\hat{Y}^j = \text{diag}(Y_1^j, Y_2^j, \ldots, Y_N^j)$. The terms on the right side of Eq. (7) represent the use of inputs for separate stages of production. Thus, the carbon emissions structure can be expressed with the following equation:

$$\hat{F}B\hat{Y} = \begin{bmatrix} \hat{F}^1 B^{11} \hat{Y}^1 & \hat{F}^1 B^{12} \hat{Y}^2 & \cdots & \hat{F}^1 B^{1G} \hat{Y}^G \\ \hat{F}^2 B^{21} \hat{Y}^1 & \hat{F}^2 B^{22} \hat{Y}^2 & \cdots & \hat{F}^2 B^{2G} \hat{Y}^G \\ \cdots & \cdots & \cdots & \cdots \\ \hat{F}^G B^{G1} \hat{Y}^1 & \hat{F}^G B^{G2} \hat{Y}^2 & \cdots & \hat{F}^G B^{GG} \hat{Y}^G \end{bmatrix}, \qquad (8)$$

where the elements in the columns reflect carbon emissions in upstream regions and sectors needed by a corresponding region and sector to produce final products. In detail, $f_p^i b_{pq}^{ij} Y_q^j$ denotes carbon emissions in region i sector p for the final use of region j sector q. Moreover, the number of nonzero elements in the columns indicates the length of the production value chain associated with a specific final product, while the summation of the elements in a column represents the total carbon emissions in all intermediate inputs for a specific final product. Then, the backward-linkage-based decomposition of carbon transfers is as follows:

$$\text{emis\_backward}^s = \underbrace{\hat{F}^s B^{ss} \hat{Y}^s}_{(1)} + \underbrace{\sum_{r \neq s}^{G} \hat{F}^r B^{rs} \hat{Y}^s}_{(2)}. \qquad (9)$$

There are two terms in Eq. (9) representing whether the production of final products causes local carbon emissions or emissions from upstream regions.

Term (1): Carbon emissions generated in the production process of region s for local final demand.

Term (2): Carbon emissions generated in upstream stages by other regions and sectors induced by final demand of region s.

Equation (9) presents the backward-linkage-based accounting framework through which we could trace carbon emission transfers from downstream to upstream. Note that each term of the right side of Eq. (9) sequentially corresponds to a carbon transfer route described in Table 2 in Sec. 2.1.

S.3. *TiVA-based accounting framework*

In the following, we present how to obtain the TiVA-based accounting framework. We first extend the gross trade accounting method (Wang *et al.*, 2015) to the level of the NVC to give a full view of the TiVA structure in the economic system. Then we integrated the accounting of carbon emissions in trade to obtain a unified accounting framework to trace emission transfers in TiVA.

We begin with a presentation on how to extend the gross trade accounting framework to the NVC level. For a G-region N-sector economic system, the input–output linkage is presented in Eq. (1). Thus, for region j, we have $X^j = A^{jj}X^j + Y^{jj} + \sum_{t \neq j}^{G} A^{jt}X^t + \sum_{t \neq j}^{G} Y^{jt} + Ex^j$, rearranging it as

$$X^j = (I - A^{jj})^{-1} \left(Y^{jj} + \sum_{t \neq j}^{G} A^{jt}X^t + \sum_{t \neq j}^{G} Y^{jt} + Ex^j \right). \quad (10)$$

Defining inter-regional trade within China for region j as $T^j = \sum_{t \neq j}^{G} A^{jt}X^t + \sum_{t \neq j}^{G} Y^{jt} (j = 1, 2, \ldots, G)$, Eq. (1) could be rewritten as

$$\begin{bmatrix} X^1 \\ X^2 \\ \ldots \\ X^G \end{bmatrix} = \begin{bmatrix} L^{11} & & & \\ & L^{22} & & \\ & & \ldots & \\ & & & L^{GG} \end{bmatrix} \begin{bmatrix} Y^{11} + T^1 + Ex^1 \\ Y^{22} + T^2 + Ex^2 \\ \ldots \\ Y^{GG} + T^G + Ex^G \end{bmatrix}$$

$$= \begin{bmatrix} L^{11}Y^{11} + L^{11}T^1 + L^{11}Ex^1 \\ L^{22}Y^{22} + L^{22}T^2 + L^{22}Ex^2 \\ \\ L^{GG}Y^{GG} + L^{GG}T^G + L^{GG}Ex^G \end{bmatrix}. \quad (11)$$

From Eq. (11), intermediate trade from region i to region j is expressed as

$$Z^{ij} = A^{ij}X^j = A^{ij}L^{jj}Y^{jj} + A^{ij}L^{jj}T^j + A^{ij}L^{jj}Ex^j. \quad (12)$$

Given that $X^j = \sum_{r=1}^{G} B^{jr} \sum_{t=1}^{G} Y^{rt} + \sum_{r=1}^{G} B^{jr}Ex^r$ by Eq. (3), intermediate trade from region i to region j could also be presented as

$$Z^{ij} = A^{ij}X^j = A^{ij} \left(\sum_{r=1}^{G} B^{jr} \sum_{t=1}^{G} Y^{rt} + \sum_{r=1}^{G} B^{jr}Ex^r \right)$$

$$= A^{ij} \left(B^{ji} \left(Y^{ii} + Y^{ij} + \sum_{t \neq i,j}^{G} Y^{it} \right) + B^{jj} \left(Y^{ji} + Y^{jj} + \sum_{t \neq i,j}^{G} Y^{jt} \right) \right.$$

$$\left. + \sum_{r \neq i,j}^{G} B^{jr} \left(Y^{ri} + Y^{rj} + \sum_{t \neq i,j}^{G} Y^{rt} \right) + \sum_{r=1}^{G} B^{jr}Ex^r \right)$$

$$= A^{ij}B^{ji}Y^{ii} + A^{ij}B^{ji}Y^{ij} + A^{ij}B^{ji} \sum_{t \neq i,j}^{G} Y^{it} + A^{ij}B^{ji}Ex^i + A^{ij}B^{jj}Y^{ji}$$

$$+ A^{ij}B^{jj}Y^{jj} + A^{ij}B^{jj} \sum_{t \neq i,j}^{G} Y^{jt} + A^{ij}B^{jj}Ex^j + A^{ij} \sum_{r \neq i,j}^{G} B^{jr}Y^{ri}$$

$$+ A^{ij} \sum_{r \neq i,j}^{G} B^{jr}Y^{rj} + A^{ij} \sum_{r \neq i,j}^{G} B^{jr} \sum_{t \neq i,j}^{G} Y^{rt}$$

$$+ A^{ij} \sum_{r \neq i,j}^{G} B^{jr}Ex^r. \quad (13)$$

Using va_i^s to denote the value added of region s sector i, we define the direct value-added coefficient as $v_i^s = va_i^s/X_i^s$, that is, the value added of region s sector i generated by a one-unit output. Similarly, with imp_i^s representing the imports of region s sector i, we define the coefficient of the import inputs as $m_i^s = imp_i^s/X_i^s$, namely, imported products used as intermediate inputs needed to produce a one-unit output. Then multiplying direct value-added coefficient matrix V with Leontief inverse B produces value-added share matrix VB as follows:

$$VB = \left[\sum_{j=1}^{G} V^j B^{j1}, \sum_{j=1}^{G} V^j B^{j2}, \ldots, \sum_{j=1}^{G} V^j B^{jG} \right]. \tag{14}$$

Moreover, import inputs share matrix MB can be derived in the same way as follows:

$$MB = \left[\sum_{j=1}^{G} M^j B^{j1}, \sum_{j=1}^{G} M^j B^{j2}, \ldots, \sum_{j=1}^{G} M^j B^{jG} \right]. \tag{15}$$

The dimensions of VB and MB are both $1 \times$ GN. As any unit of output can be completely decomposed into value-added sourced from all regions and sectors within and outside the economic system, it is obvious that $VB + MB = u, (u = [1, 1, \ldots, 1]_{1 \times GN})$. For region i, we have

$$V^i B^{ii} + V^j B^{ji} + \sum_{t \neq i,j}^{G} V^t B^{ti} + M^i B^{ii} + M^j B^{ji} + \sum_{t \neq i,j}^{G} M^t B^{ti} = u(u = [1, 1, \ldots, 1]_{1 \times N}). \tag{16}$$

Combining Eqs. (12), (13) with (16), the trade from region i to region j can be completely decomposed as follows:

$$\text{trans}^{ij} = Y^{ij} + A^{ij} X^j$$

$$= \left(V^i B^{ii} + V^j B^{ji} + \sum_{t \neq i,j}^{G} V^t B^{ti} + M^i B^{ii} + M^j B^{ji} + \sum_{t \neq i,j}^{G} M^t B^{ti} \right)' \otimes Y^{ij}$$

$$+ \left(V^i B^{ii} + V^j B^{ji} + \sum_{t \neq i,j}^{G} V^t B^{ti} + M^i B^{ii} + M^j B^{ji} + \sum_{t \neq i,j}^{G} M^t B^{ti} \right)' \otimes A^{ij} X^j$$

$$= \underbrace{(V^i B^{ii})' \otimes Y^{ij}}_{(1)} + \underbrace{(V^i L^{ii})' \otimes A^{ij} B^{jj} Y^{ij}}_{(2)} + \underbrace{(V^i L^{ii})' \otimes A^{ij} \sum_{r \neq i,j}^{G} B^{jr} \sum_{t \neq i,j}^{G} Y^{rt}}_{(3)}$$

$$+ \underbrace{(V^i L^{ii})' \otimes A^{ij} B^{jj} \sum_{t \neq i,j}^{G} Y^{jt}}_{(4)} + \underbrace{(V^i L^{ii})' \otimes A^{ij} \sum_{r \neq i,j}^{G} B^{jr} Y^{rj}}_{(5)}$$

$$+ \underbrace{(V^i L^{ii})' \otimes A^{ij} B^{jj} Y^{ji}}_{(6)} + \underbrace{(V^i L^{ii})' \otimes A^{ij} \sum_{r \neq i,j}^{G} B^{jr} Y^{ri}}_{(7)} + \underbrace{(V^i L^{ii})' \otimes A^{ij} B^{ji} Y^{ii}}_{(8)}$$

$$+ (V^i L^{ii})' \otimes A^{ij} B^{ij} Ex^j + (V^i L^{ii})' \otimes A^{ij} \sum_{r \neq i,j}^{G} B^{jr} Ex^r$$

$$\quad\quad (9) \quad\quad\quad\quad\quad\quad\quad\quad (10)$$

$$+ (V^i L^{ii})' \otimes \left[A^{ij} B^{ji} \left(Y^{ij} + \sum_{t \neq i,j}^{G} Y^{it} + Ex^i \right) \right] + (V^i B^{ii} - V^i L^{ii})' \otimes (A^{ij} X^j)$$

$$\quad\quad\quad\quad\quad (11) \quad\quad\quad\quad\quad\quad\quad\quad\quad\quad\quad\quad (12)$$

$$+ (M^i B^{ii})' \otimes Y^{ij} + (M^i B^{ii})' \otimes (A^{ij} X^j) + (V^j B^{ii})' \otimes Y^{ij}$$

$$\quad (13) \quad\quad\quad\quad\quad (14) \quad\quad\quad\quad\quad (15)$$

$$+ (V^j B^{ii})' \otimes (A^{ij} L^{jj} Y^{jj}) + (V^j B^{ii})' \otimes (A^{ij} L^{jj} T^j) + (V^j B^{ii})' \otimes (A^{ij} L^{jj} Ex^j)$$

$$\quad\quad\quad (16) \quad\quad\quad\quad\quad\quad\quad (17) \quad\quad\quad\quad\quad\quad\quad (18)$$

$$+ (M^j B^{ji})' \otimes Y^{ij} + (M^j B^{ji})' \otimes (A^{ij} X^j) + \left(\sum_{t \neq i,j}^{G} V^t B^{ti} \right)' \otimes Y^{ij}$$

$$\quad (19) \quad\quad\quad\quad\quad (20) \quad\quad\quad\quad\quad\quad (21)$$

$$+ \left(\sum_{t \neq i,j}^{G} V^t B^{ti} \right)' \otimes (A^{ij} L^{jj} Y^{jj}) + \left(\sum_{t \neq i,j}^{G} V^t B^{ti} \right)' \otimes (A^{ij} L^{jj} T^j)$$

$$\quad\quad\quad\quad (22) \quad\quad\quad\quad\quad\quad\quad\quad\quad (23)$$

$$+ \left(\sum_{t \neq i,j}^{G} V^t B^{ti} \right)' \otimes (A^{ij} L^{jj} Ex^j) + \left(\sum_{t \neq i,j}^{G} M^t B^{ti} \right)' \otimes Y^{ij}$$

$$\quad\quad\quad\quad (24) \quad\quad\quad\quad\quad\quad\quad\quad (25)$$

$$+ \left(\sum_{t \neq i,j}^{G} M^t B^{ti} \right)' \otimes (A^{ij} X^j),$$

$$\quad\quad\quad (26) \quad\quad\quad\quad\quad\quad\quad\quad\quad\quad\quad\quad\quad\quad\quad (17)$$

in which terms (11), (12), (17) and (23) are marked as double counting terms, while (13), (14), (19), (20), (25) and (26) are terms associated with imports. Double counting terms indicate inter-regional trade overestimation caused by intermediate products reshipped back and then reexported. Thus, these double counting terms were excluded in the corresponding carbon emissions accounting framework to ensure the accuracy of carbon emission transfers measurement. Moreover, terms associated with imports indicate the value sourced from outside the economic system, which were excluded in the corresponding carbon emissions accounting framework for two reasons: on one hand, we could hardly assess foreign carbon emission intensity treating other territories and countries outside the 30-province MRIO table as a whole; on the other hand, this paper mainly focused on carbon emissions generated in the process of domestic production segments.

Reorganizing the remaining terms according to where the value added is sourced from, namely, local value-added, the value-added of direct trade partners and the value-added of third regions and sectors, we then integrate the direct carbon emission intensity F and obtain the decomposition of carbon emission transfers from region i to region j in the NVC without any double counting as follows:

$$\text{emis\_trans}^{ij} = \underbrace{(F^i B^{ii})' \otimes Y^{ij}}_{(1)} + \underbrace{(F^i L^{ii})' \otimes A^{ij} B^{jj} Y^{jj}}_{(2)} + (F^i L^{ii})'$$

$$\otimes \underbrace{\left[A^{ij} B^{jj} \sum_{t \neq i,j}^{G} Y^{jt} + A^{ij} \sum_{r \neq i,j}^{G} B^{jr} Y^{rr} + A^{ij} \sum_{r \neq i,j}^{G} \left(\sum_{t \neq i,j}^{G} B^{jr} Y^{rt} \right) \right]}_{(3)}$$

$$+ \underbrace{(F^i L^{ii})' \otimes A^{ij} \sum_{r \neq i,j}^{G} B^{jr} Y^{ri}}_{(4)}$$

$$+ \underbrace{\left[(F^i L^{ii})' \otimes A^{ij} B^{jj} Ex^j + (F^i L^{ii})' \otimes A^{ij} \sum_{r \neq i,j}^{G} B^{jr} Ex^r \right]}_{(5)}$$

$$+ \underbrace{(F^j B^{ji})' \otimes Y^{ij}}_{(6)} + \underbrace{(F^j B^{ji})' \otimes (A^{ij} L^{jj} Y^{jj})}_{(7)} + \underbrace{(F^j B^{ji})' \otimes (A^{ij} L^{jj} Ex^j)}_{(8)}$$

$$+ \underbrace{\left(\sum_{t \neq i,j}^{G} F^t B^{ti} \right)' \otimes Y^{ij}}_{(9)} + \underbrace{\left(\sum_{t \neq i,j}^{G} F^t B^{ti} \right)' \otimes (A^{ij} L^{jj} Y^{jj})}_{(10)}$$

$$+ \underbrace{\left(\sum_{t \neq i,j}^{G} F^t B^{ti} \right)' \otimes (A^{ij} L^{jj} Ex^j)}_{(11)}. \tag{18}$$

Equation (18)[4] presents the TiVA-based accounting framework which decomposes total carbon emissions generated in the production of gross exports from region i to region j into 11 terms.

Term (1): Carbon emissions generated in region i in the production of final products consumed by partner region j.

---

[4]Notice that V in Eq. (17) is used to decompose source of value added embodied in trade which helps trace source emissions embodied in trade. Since V denotes value added generated by one-unit output and F denotes emissions generated by one-unit output, we should replace coefficient V by F to obtain Eq. (18) after removing the mentioned terms in Eq. (17).

Term (2): Carbon emissions generated in region i in the production of intermediate products used by partner region j to produce final products consumed there.

Term (3): Carbon emissions generated in region i in the production of intermediate products used by partner region j to produce final products consumed by third regions.

Term (4): Carbon emissions generated in region i in the production of intermediate products used by partner region j to produce final products shipped back to region i.

Term (5): Carbon emissions generated in region i in the production of intermediate products used by partner region j to produce exports or intermediate products reshipped to third regions to produce exports to regions outside the economic system.

Term (6): Carbon emissions generated in partner region j in region i's production of final products consumed by region j.

Term (7): Carbon emissions generated in partner region j in region i's production of intermediate products used by region j to produce final products consumed there.

Term (8): Carbon emissions generated in partner region j in region i's production of intermediate products used by region j to produce exports to regions outside the economic system.

Term (9): Carbon emissions generated in third regions in region i's production of final products consumed by region j.

Term (10): Carbon emissions generated in third regions in region i's production of intermediate products used by region j to produce final products consumed there.

Term (11): Carbon emissions generated in third regions in region i's production of intermediate products used by region j to produce exports to regions outside the economic system.

Equation (18) presents the TiVA-based accounting framework through which we could trace carbon emission transfers embodied in gross exports. Note that each term of the right side of Eq. (18) sequentially corresponds to a carbon transfer route described in Table 3 in Sec. 2.1.

References

Andrew, RM and GP Peters (2013). A multi-region input–output table based on the Global Trade Analysis Project Database (GTAP-MRIO). *Economic Systems Research*, 25(1), 99–121.

Arto, I and E Dietzenbacher (2014). Drivers of the growth in global greenhouse gas emissions. *Environmental Science & Technology*, 48(10), 5388–5394.

Bekkers, E (2019). Challenges to the trade system: The potential impact of changes in future trade policy. *Journal of Policy Modeling*, 41(3), 489–506.

Cui, LB, RJ Li, ML Song and L Zhu (2019). Can China achieve its 2030 energy development targets by fulfilling carbon intensity reduction commitments?*Energy Economics*, 83, 61–73.

Daudin, G, C Rifflart and D Schweisguth (2011). Who produces for whom in the world economy. *Canadian Journal of Economics*, 44(4), 1403–1437.

Davis, SJ and K Caldeira (2010). Consumption-based accounting of CO2 emissions. *Proceedings of the National Academy of Sciences of USA*, 107, 5687–5692.

Duan, C et al. (2018). Inter-regional carbon flows of China. *Applied Energy*, 227, 342–352.

Duan, HB et al. (2021). Assessing China's efforts to pursue the 1.5°C warming limit. *Science*, 372(6540), 378–385.

Edmonds, J et al. (2021). How much could Article 6 enhance nationally determined contribution ambition toward Paris Agreement goals through economic efficiency?*Climate Change Economics*, 21(2), 2150007.

Feng, T et al. (2020). Carbon transfer within China: Insights from production fragmentation. *Energy Economics*, 86, 104647.

Girod, B, DP Van Vuuren and EG Hertwich (2014). Climate policy through changing consumption choices: Options and obstacles for reducing greenhouse gas emissions. *Global Environmental Change*, 25, 5–15.

Guo, JJ, Y Zhou, S Ali, U Shahzad and LB Cui (2021). Exploring the role of green innovation and investment in energy for environmental quality: An empirical appraisal from provincial data of China. *Journal of Environmental Management*, 292(1), 112779.

Hasegawa, R, S Kagawa and M Tsukui (2015). Carbon footprint analysis through constructing a multi-region input-output table: A case study of Japan. *Economic Structures*, 4(1), 5.

Hertwich, EG and GP Peters (2009). Carbon footprint of nations: A global, trade-linked analysis. *Environmental Science & Technology*, 43(16), 6414–6420.

IPCC (2018). Summary for policymakers. In *Global Warming of 1.5°C*. V Masson Delmotte, P Zhai and D Roberts et al. (eds.). Geneva, Switzerland: World Meteorological Organization.

Jakob, M, JC Steckel and O Edenhofer (2014). Consumption-versus production-based emission policies. *Annual Review of Environment and Resources*, 6, 297–318.

Johnson, R and G Noguera (2012). Accounting for intermediates: Production sharing and trade in value added. *Journal of International Economics*, 86, 224–236.

Kober, T, BCC Van Der Zwaan and H Rösler (2014). Emission certificate trade and costs under regional burden-sharing regimes for a 2°C climate change control target. *Climate Change Economics*, 5(1), 1440001.

Koopman, R, Z Wang and SJ Wei (2014). Tracing value-added and double counting in gross exports. *American Economic Review*, 104(2), 459–494.

Leontief, W, (1936). Quantitative input and output relations in the economic system of the United States. *Review of Economic and Statistics*, 18, 105–125.

Levitt, C, M Saaby and A Sorensen (2019). The impact of China's trade liberalisation on the greenhouse gas emissions of WTO countries. *China Economic Review*, 54, 113–134.

Liu, Z et al. (2016). Targeted opportunities to address the climate-trade dilemma in China. *Nature Climate Change*, 6, 201–206.

Lv, K et al. (2019). A study on embodied carbon transfer at the provincial level of China from a social network perspective. *Journal of Cleaner Production*, 225, 1089–1104.

Meng, B, GP Peters, Z Wang and M Li (2018). Tracing CO_2 emissions in global value chains. *Energy Economics*, 73, 24–42.

Mi, Z et al. (2017). Chinese CO_2 emission flows have reversed since the global financial crisis. *Nature Communications*, 8(1), 1–10.

Mo, JL et al. (2021). The role of national carbon pricing in phasing out China's coal power. *iScience*, 24(6), 102655.

Mora, C et al. (2018). Broad threat to humanity from cumulative climate hazards intensified by greenhouse gas emissions. *Nature Climate Change*, 8, 1062–1071.

Peters, GP (2008). From production-based to consumption-based national emission inventories. *Ecological Economics*, 65, 13–23.

Robinson, S and K Thierfelder (2019). Global adjustment to US disengagement from the world trading system. *Journal Policy Modeling*, 41(3), 522–536.

Shao, L et al. (2018). Carbon emission imbalances and the structural paths of Chinese regions. *Applied Energy*, 215, 396–404.

Shigeto, S et al. (2012). An easily traceable scenario for 80% CO_2 emission reduction in Japan through the final consumption-based CO_2 emission approach: A case study of Kyoto-city. *Applied Energy*, 90, 201–215.

Su, B and E Thomson (2016). China's carbon emissions embodied in (normal and processing) exports and their driving forces, 2006–2012. *Energy Economics*, 59, 414–422.

Tang, M, J Hong, G Liu and GQ Shen (2019). Exploring energy flows embodied in China's economy from the regional and sectoral perspectives via combination of multi-regional input-output analysis and a complex network approach. *Energy*, 170, 1191–1201.

Tang, ZP, WD Liu and PP Gong (2014). Measuring of Chinese regional carbon emission spatial effects induced by exports based on Chinese multi-regional input-output table during 1997–2007. *Acta Geographica Sinica*, 69(10), 1403–1413 (in Chinese).

Timmer, MP et al. (2014). Slicing up global value chains. *Journal of Economic Perspectives*, 28(2), 99–118.

Wang, C et al. (2020). Economic impacts of climate change and air pollution in china through health and labor supply perspective: An integrated assessment model analysis. *Climate Change Economics*, 11(3), 2041001.

Wang, LF, LB Cui, SM Weng and CM Liu (2021). Promoting industrial structure advancement through an emission trading scheme: Lessons from China's pilot practice. *Computers & Industrial Engineering*, 157, 107339.

Wang, Z, SJ Wei and KF Zhu (2015). Gross trade accounting method: Official trade statistics and measurement of the global value chain. *Social Sciences in China*, 237(09), 109–128 +206–207 (in Chinese).

Wang, Z, SJ Wei and KF Zhu (2018). Quantifying international production sharing at the bilateral and sector levels. NBER Working Paper No. 19677.

Xia, Y and Z Tang (2017). The impacts of emissions accounting methods on an imperfect competitive carbon trading market. *Energy*, 119, 67–76.

Yan, B, Y Duan and S Wang (2020). China's emissions embodied in exports: How regional and trade heterogeneity matter. *Energy Economics*, 87, 104479.

Zheng, H et al. (2020). Regional determinants of China's consumption-based emissions in the economic transition. *Environmental Research Letters*, 15, 074001.

Zhou, D et al., (2018). Regional embodied carbon emissions and their transfer characteristics in China. *Structural Change and Economic Dynamics*, 46, 180–193.

© 2025 World Scientific Publishing Company
https://doi.org/10.1142/9789819812264_0003

PLANT-LEVEL EVALUATION OF CHINA'S NATIONAL EMISSIONS TRADING SCHEME: BENCHMARK MATTERS[||]

RONG MA[*] and HAOQI QIAN[†,‡,§,¶]

[*]*School of Economics, Fudan University*
Guoquan Road 600#, Shanghai 200433, P. R. China

[†]*Institute for Global Public Policy, Fudan University*
Handan Road 220#, Shanghai 200433, P. R. China

[‡]*LSE-Fudan Research Centre for Global Public Policy, Fudan University*
Handan Road 220#, Shanghai 200433, P. R. China

[§]*Shanghai Institute for Energy and Carbon Neutrality Strategy*
Fudan University, Handan Road 220#, Shanghai 200433, P. R. China
[¶]*qianhaoqi@fudan.edu.cn*

China's national emission trading scheme (ETS) started operating in 2021 after four years of preparation. In the initial stage of national ETS, benchmarking approach is one of the hottest topics that have gained sufficient attention. For the reason that benchmarks will greatly affect the permits allocation results and thus affect the effectiveness of the carbon market. This paper attempts to investigate the impacts of the benchmark designs of China's ETS by using plant-level data. Main results show that the current lax benchmark standards adopted by the national ETS will lead to excess surplus of permits. The whole carbon market will achieve market clearance only when the benchmark standards are set as high as the top 2% efficiency levels. If the carbon price is 200 yuan/ton, the annual trading volume will be 16.4 billion yuan and 13.2 billion yuan in extra will be spent on carbon offsetting for compliance. If the auction mechanism is introduced, the total market size will significantly increase. The auction revenue will exceed 300 billion yuan when 50% of permits are allocated through auction and will exceed 600 billion yuan when all permits are auctioned. These revenues can provide sufficient funds to accelerate China's low-carbon transformation as well as improve social welfare.

Keywords: Emissions trading scheme; permit allocation; benchmarking approach; policy design.

1. Introduction

As the world's largest carbon emitter, China has accelerated the pace of utilizing market-based instruments (MBI) to facilitate peaking its CO_2 emissions before 2030 and achieving carbon neutrality before 2060. MBIs are widely adopted as cost-effective

---

[¶]Corresponding author.
[||]This chapter was originally published in Climate Change Economics, Vol. 13, No. 1 (2022), published by World Scientific Publishing, Singapore. Reprinted with permission.

ways to achieve environmental and climate policy targets through reducing potential resource misallocations in the process of emissions abatement (Qian et al., 2017; Schmalensee and Stavins, 2017; Narassimhan et al., 2018; Xu and Zhang, 2021). The construction of China's ETSs follows a typical marketization reform procedure in China that local pilot markets are established first and then promoted to the national market (Sachs and Woo, 2001; Xu, 2011). China has launched seven pilot and two voluntary emissions trading schemes (ETS) since 2013. In December 2017, China officially announced to launch the national ETS and the market started operating in 2021 after more than three years of preparation. At the initial stage, 2225 power plants are covered by the national ETS and their total CO_2 emissions are estimated to be around 4 billion tons. Zhang et al. (2021) introduce the design of China's national ETS thoroughly. Plants are allowed to use China Certified Emission Reduction (CCER) to offset up to 5% of their emissions for compliance. This offsetting mechanism is expected to promote the development of renewable energies (Lo and Cong, 2017) and will lead to interactions between the national ETS and the green certificate market (Li et al., 2019).

In the existing literature, there has emerged a quite number of studies that investigate China's market-based climate policies from both ex-post and ex-ante perspectives. The ex-ante studies are mainly simulation analyses conducted by using the computable general equilibrium (CGE) models to evaluate the social economic and environmental impacts of climate policies (Yuan et al., 2020; Cao et al., 2021a; Wu et al., 2022a). Several specific topics such as sector coverage (Mu et al., 2018; Qian et al., 2018), permit allocation method (Qi et al., 2020), environmental co-benefit (Chang et al., 2020) and income distribution (Huang et al., 2019; Zhang et al., 2020; Wu et al., 2022b) have been conducted to support the design of national ETS. For the ex-post studies, most of them focus on evaluating policy impacts for China's pilot ETSs based on empirical analyses (Cao et al., 2021b). A comprehensive review of China's pilot ETSs can be found in Zhang et al. (2014). Pilot ETSs have been found effective in reducing CO_2 emissions at the macro level (Gao et al., 2020). From the micro-level perspective, the pilot ETSs were able to provide incentives for firms to develop emissions abatement strategies to reduce total CO_2 emissions (Liu and Wang, 2017; Zhang et al., 2019a; Li et al., 2020; Shen et al., 2020). Zhang et al. (2019b) used propensity score matching and difference-in-difference method to estimate the environmental causal impacts of pilot ETSs. They found that the pilot markets significantly reduced carbon emission in the first stage (2013–2015) while failing to reduce carbon emission intensities. Shen et al. (2020) found the carbon emission reduction effects were more significant among small and nonstate-owned firms, as well as in regions adopting the ex-post permits allocation. But these effects attenuated over time. Deng et al. (2018) conducted survey analyses for firms covered in pilot ETSs. They found that sufficient compulsory force and increased understanding of covered firms were essential to improve the overall compliance rates. Firms that were in shortage of permits were more likely to bear higher pressures and might even buy more permits for banking purposes, and vice versa. Pilot ETSs can also bring significant co-benefits of air pollution reductions and thus improve public health as well as social welfare (Dong *et al.*, 2020; Yan *et al.*, 2020a; Qian *et al.*, 2021). Technological innovations are the most important factor that is induced by the pilot ETSs to realize long-term low carbon transformation not only at the regional level (Dong *et al.*, 2019; Zhang *et al.*, 2020; Lin and Wesseh, 2020; Liu *et al.*, 2020), but also at the firm level (Cui *et al.*, 2018; Zhu *et al.*, 2019; Hu *et al.*, 2020). These results give rise to the possibility for China to realize long-term economic and environmental gains from operating the national ETS.

Despite strong positive findings in the existing literature, as suggested by the experience from mature carbon markets such as the EU Emissions Trading System (EU-ETS), there still exist many challenges for China to establish an effective and efficient national ETS. Typical challenges include quality of monitoring, reporting and verification (MRV), policy interactions, and permit allocation method (Liu *et al.*, 2015; Jiang *et al.*, 2016; Zhao *et al.*, 2016; Jotzo *et al.*, 2018). Misunderstandings of policy design and government's determination were found in firms covered by the ETS. Li *et al.* (2020) found firms' understanding and recognition of the pilot ETSs had improved over time, but there still existed persistent drawbacks in enforcements of MRV. It is the fundamental element for a national ETS to operate successfully to improve MRV quality. Since a reliable real-time CO_2 emissions monitoring system is still in the trial stage, all ETSs are currently relying heavily on joint efforts from firms, third-party verifiers, and regulators to ensure data quality. Firstly, Zhang *et al.* (2019a) find that the MRV qualities in Beijing and Hubei pilot ETSs had improved over time but still need substantial efforts to build those capabilities. Compared to other sectors, China's power sector has relatively better data foundations (Wang *et al.*, 2021), so data quality will cause few concerns in the beginning of the national ETS but will become more severe in the future when more sectors are covered.

Secondly, the policy interactions resulting from the multi-level governance are not seriously considered in the pilot ETSs, but may become a significant issue for the national ETS (Xu, 2021). The first policy interaction issue is related to the green certificate market (green electricity market). both pilot ETSs and national ETS allow firms to offset part of their emissions by using CCERs for compliance. If the relationship between the green certificate and CCER is well defined in the future and renewable energy generation cannot be used twice (i.e., no double counting issue), then the amount of CCER that is allowed to use in the ETS will significantly affect the green certificate market and vice versa. The second policy interaction issue is related to China's ongoing marketization reform of the power sector. After the marketization reform, power firms are expected to gain the ability to pass the carbon permit costs to downstream users, which has theoretically been discussed by Haita (2014), and empirically proven by Fabra and Reguant (2014). Ellerman *et al.* (2016) summarized the pass-through of carbon price to downstream as "windfall profit". Fabra and Reguant (2014) found that pass-through comes from the lack of price elasticity of electricity demand. Hintermann (2016) conducted an empirical test on the cost pass-through between the German electricity market and the EU-ETS, and found that the carbon price is almost completely passed to the electricity price in the average sense. Since the marketization reform procedure is still in progress, this interaction is currently not the main concern for the national ETS, but may become an important issue in the near future.

Thirdly, the permit allocation issue is one of the most pressing issues for the national ETS. According to the "2019–2020 Implementation Plan for National Carbon Emission Trading Total Permits Setting and Allocation (Power Generation Industry)" (hereafter "Allocation Plan"),[1] the national ETS has set relatively lax standards to allocate permits at the beginning, which significantly deviates from academic community's expectations for stricter standards (Deng *et al.*, 2018; Li *et al.*, 2020). This indicates that overall permits may be over-allocated so that the national ETS may take little effect in reducing total CO_2 emissions in the thermal power sector. The resultant low permit prices may not provide enough incentives for firms to enhance their energy efficiencies as well as investments in renewable energies (Mo *et al.*, 2016). Since China's power sector plays a decisive role in achieving China's decarbonization ambitions, it deserves great efforts to make a deep investigation into the design of permit allocation method for China's national ETS (Yan *et al.*, 2020b; Duan *et al.*, 2021; Qian *et al.*, 2021).

Given the gap in the literature that there is rare ex-ante evaluation for China's national ETS at the micro level, this paper attempts to evaluate impacts of different permit allocation designs by using plant-level data. The core conclusion of this paper is that the allocation method adopted in the initial stage of the national ETS will lead to an excess surplus of permits. The whole carbon market will be cleared only when the benchmark standards are set as high as the top 2% efficiency levels. The carbon market can generate large-scale cash flow at both the plant and provincial levels, especially when paid auction of permit and more efficient benchmarks are introduced. If the carbon price reached to 200 yuan/ton and 50% of permits are auctioned, total revenue will be more than 300 billion yuan. When using the top 2% efficiency levels as the benchmark for permit allocation, the cash flow from CCERs can reach 13.2 billion yuan. The contributions of this paper are as twofold. Firstly, this paper evaluates the impacts for China's national ETS from the plant-level perspective. This can provide more accurate estimations that contribute to the existing literature that many studies mainly provide sector-level analyses. Secondly, the paper estimates the potential market sizes of China's national ETS under different permit allocation scenarios. This can provide useful evidence for not only policy makers but also those important market players.

The remainder of this article is organized as follows. In Section 2, we introduce the background of China's ETS and discuss the issues related to permit allocation. Section 3 explains the overall research design including the methodologies as well as the plant-level data. Section 4 presents the main results of different scenarios and

---

[1] 2019–2020 Implementation Plan for National Carbon Emission Trading Total Permits Setting and Allocation (Power Generation Industry), The Ministry of Ecology and Environment, 2020-12-29, https://www.mee.gov.cn/xxgk2018/xxgk/xxgk03/202012/t20201230_815546.html.

provides explanations for the results. Section 5 discusses several additional important issues and gives the concluding remarks.

2. Research Design

2.1. *Calculation of permit allocation*

Although various permit allocation methods are adopted for different sectors in the pilot ETSs, the benchmarking approach is used for the power sector in all pilot ETSs. For the national ETS, the benchmarking approach is also used to allocate permits for covered power plants. According to the Allocation Plan, power generation technologies are divided into four groups and each group uses one specific benchmark to allocate permits. Fig. 1 summarizes the whole framework of benchmarking approach that is used for the national ETS. Conventional coal-fired power plant units are categorized into two groups according to the standard of whether the unit capacity exceeds 400 MW or not. Unconventional coal-fired power plant units including units using circulating fluidized bed boilers (CFB) and gas-fired power plant units use different benchmarks. Thermal power plants combusting other types of fuels are not covered in the initial stage of national ETS. Table 1 explains detailed parameters of the benchmarking approach as shown in Fig. 1. According to the Allocation Plan, 70% of the permits calculated by using 2018 data are pre-allocated to power plants, and the remaining permits will be allocated to power plants after adjustments for their actual production levels. Fig. 1. Framework of benchmarking approach for permit allocation.

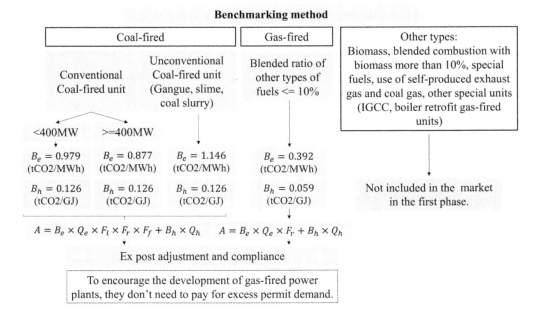

Figure 1. Framework of benchmarking approach for permit allocation.

Table 1. Meanings of parameters.

Notation	Meaning	Unit	Remark
A	Permit allocated	tCO_2	/
B_e	Benchmark for power supplied	tCO_2/MWh	Technology specific
B_h	Benchmark for heat supplied	tCO_2/GJ	Technology specific
Q_e	Quantity of power supplied	MWh	/
Q_h	Quantity of heat supplied	GJ	/
F_l	Cooling mode adjustment factor	/	Cooling mode specific
F_r	Heat supply adjustment factor	/	Technology specific
F_f	Load rate adjustment factor	/	Piecewise function of load ratio.

The national ETS uses relatively lax benchmark standards when compared to those used in pilot ETSs. By using the same categorization rule of nation ETS, Fig. 2 illustrates the comparisons among benchmarks that are used by national ETS and pilot ETSs for two conventional technologies distinguished by the unit capacity. It is clearly shown that benchmarks used in the national ETS are generally higher than those used in pilot ETSs. As a result, power plant units will get more permits in the national ETS than in the pilot ETSs, and national ETS tends to become over-allocated. But this is not the whole picture. In addition to the benchmarks, national ETS also takes different adjustment factors into account when allocating permits. Adjustment factors include units' cooling mode, load rate and heating capacity. Therefore, for many power plant units covered by the national ETS, their final permits will be even higher. Those adjustment factors will be further discussed in Sec. 3.1.

In the pilot ETSs, the benchmark updating approach is also adopted to ensure those benchmarks can continue to take effects on encouraging efficiency improvements among covered power plants. Several pilot ETSs such as Guangdong pilot ETS, Shanghai pilot ETS, Beijing pilot ETS and Fujian pilot ETS had updated the

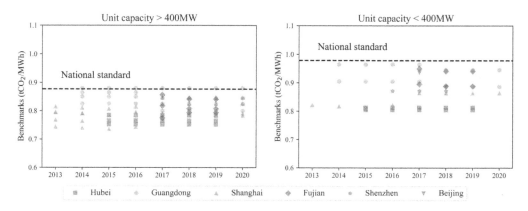

Figure 2. Comparisons among benchmarks used by national ETS and pilot ETSs (tCO_2/MWh).

benchmarks for at least once, this trend can also be seen in Fig. 2. Technological progress and structural change are the key logic behind the benchmark updating approach. On one hand, more advanced technologies will be adopted in the production and existing production technologies will be improved, these will reduce the power plants' coal consumption rates of power supply. On the other hand, with the enhancement of environmental regulation, power plants with low efficiencies will be gradually phased out and be replaced with those with advanced technologies. Fig. 3 shows the evolution of distributions of plant-level emission coefficients from 2010 to 2018. Emission coefficient is defined as CO_2 emissions divided by power supplied. Plant-level data are collected from *Annual Compilation of Power Industry Statistics* and calculated by authors. Coal-fired power plants covered in the calculation are all with total capacity above 100 MW and survive during the sample period. Total amounts of plants increased from 642 in 2010 to 883 in 2018 and the overall distributions of emission factors move toward lower levels, i.e., higher efficiencies. From Fig. 3 we can also see that the current benchmarks used in national ETS will only take effect on a few plants on the right tail of the distribution. If future improvements in emission efficiencies are not taken into consideration, the over-allocation issue will become more severe.

To sum up, the setting of benchmarks is a core issue need to be seriously investigated and evaluated for the construction of national ETS. Based on the aforementioned analyses, we start to conduct the quantitative evaluation of China's national ETS by using plant-level data.

From national ETS's benchmarking framework shown in Fig. 1, the permits allocated is calculated by using the following formula:

$$A_i^u = A_{i,e}^u + A_{i,h}^u. \tag{1}$$

The superscript u stands for unit and subscript I stands for plant. $A_{i,e}^u$ represents permits for electricity supply of unit u of plant i, and $A_{i,h}^u$ represents permits for heat

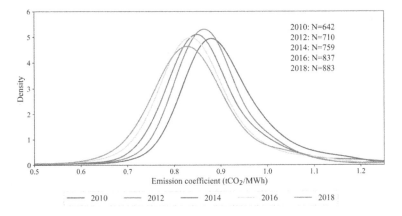

Figure 3. Kernel distributions of plant-level emission coefficients from 2010 to 2018.

supply of unit u of plant i. Permits for electricity supply is determined by three factors: benchmark $B_{i,e}^u$, amount of electricity supplied $Q_{i,e}^u$, and the adjustment factors $F_{i,r}^u$, $F_{i,l}^u$, and $F_{i,f}^u$. The formula is as follows:

$$A_{i,e}^u = \begin{cases} B_{i,e}^u \times Q_{i,e}^u \times F_{i,r}^u \times F_{i,l}^u \times F_{i,f}^u, & \text{for coal,} \\ B_e^u \times Q_{i,e}^u \times F_{i,r}^u, & \text{for gas.} \end{cases} \quad (2)$$

$F_{i,r}^u$ is the heat supply adjustment factor equals $1 - 0.22 \times HR_i^u$ for coal-fired power plant unit and equals $1 - 0.6 \times HR_i^u$ for gas-fired power plant unit, where HR_i^u stands for heating ratio. $F_{i,l}^u$ is the unit cooling mode adjustment factor and it equals 1 for water cooling mode and equals 1.05 for air cooling mode.

For the load rate adjustment factor $F_{i,f}^u$, it is determined by a piecewise function of unit's load rate F_i^u. A unit's load rate equals to its utilization hours divided by its operation hours. The relationship between F_f and load rate is as follows:

$$F_{i,f}^u = \begin{cases} 1.0, & F_i^u \geq 85\%, \\ 1 + 0.0014 \times (85 - 100 F_i^u), & 80\% \leq F_i^u < 85\%, \\ 1.007 + 0.0016 \times (80 - 100 F_i^u), & 75\% \leq F_i^u < 80\%, \\ 1.015^{(16 - 20 F_i^u)}, & F_i^u < 75\%. \end{cases} \quad (3)$$

From a technical perspective, the higher the load rate is, the higher the efficiency is. Therefore, the reason for setting load rate adjustment factor as formula (3) is to compensate for the low load rate that will lead to low combustion efficiency. For example, when one unit's load rate is 30%, $F_{i,f}^u$ will increase to 1.161. This setting also reflects the feature of China's current power dispatching method that power plants have limited influences on deciding their optimal unit load rates. Moreover, due to the rapid development of renewable energies in the past decade, the utilization hours as well as load rates of thermal power plants continued to decline, which brought significant losses in revenue. As a result, all the above reasons contribute to the compensation for low load rate operation when allocating permits.

Permits for heat supply is determined by two factors: benchmark for heat supply $B_{i,h}^u$ and amount of heat supplied $Q_{i,h}^u$, and there is no adjustment factor. The formula is as follows:

$$A_{i,h}^u = B_{i,h}^u \times Q_{i,h}^u. \quad (4)$$

Next, for the actual CO_2 emissions, each unit's total CO_2 emission can be calculated as follows:

$$E_i^u = Q_i^u \times CR_i^u \times ef, \quad (5)$$

where E_i^u stands for actual CO_2 emission of unit u, Q_i^u stands for actual electricity supplied by unit u, CR_i^u stands for coal consumption rate of power supply of unit u. Besides, ef stands for CO_2 emission factor of coal consumptions. It is set as 2.66 tCO_2/tce for coal-fired unit and 1.63 tCO_2/tce for gas-fired unit.

Finally, the net permit of plant i is calculated as the gap between its total permits allocated and its total emission as follows:

$$\text{Net permit}_i = \sum_u A_i^u - \sum_u E_i^u. \tag{6}$$

If the net permit is greater than zero, then it means the power plant has surplus in permit and it can sell the surplus in the market to earn profits and vice versa.

2.2. Scenario settings

In this paper, we construct the scenarios from two dimensions. The first dimension is the choice of benchmarks and the second one is whether permits are free or allocated or auctioned.

For the first dimension, we choose different benchmarks to analyze the impacts on allocations among different power plants. In the baseline (BASE) scenario, benchmarks are set equal to the same values in the current Allocation Plan. Since the overall efficiencies of China's coal-fired power plants had been improving and this trend is expected to continue in the future. We would choose efficiencies of those most efficient power plants as the benchmarks, and this approach is also adopted in the pilot ETSs. In order to choose targeted benchmarks for coal-fired power plants with different technologies, we use kernel density estimation method to estimate the distributions of unit-level efficiencies. In addition to BASE case, we choose top 10% and top 2% efficiency levels as new benchmarks to analyze the impacts of permit allocations, which are shown in Table 2. For the second dimension, since the current Allocation Plan allocates all permits to power plants for free, we would also like to investigate the impacts of switching to auction on cash flows of the ETS. Here the percentages of auctioned permits are chosen as 0%, 50% and 100%. The full auction approach is equivalent to the current "zero free-permits" standards of the power sector in ET-ETS.[2]

Table 3 summarizes the nine scenarios constructed in this paper. Under the ideal equilibrium condition, the auction price should be the same as the average transaction

Table 2. Benchmarks of different standards (tCO$_2$/MWh).

Fuel type	Technology	BASE	Top 10%	Top 2%
Coal	≥ 400 MW	0.877	0.752	0.734
	< 400 MW	0.979	0.790	0.742
	CFB	1.146	0.790	0.750
Gas	—	0.392	0.319	0.293

---

[2]Detailed information can be found on the website of European Commission: https://ec.europa.eu/clima/eu-action/eu-emissions-trading-system-eu-ets/free-allocation/free-allocation-modernisation-energy-sector_en

Table 3. Notations for nine scenarios.

Allocation type	Benchmark standards		
	BASE	Top 10%	Top 2%
Free	S1	S2	S3
50% auction	S4	S5	S6
100% auction	S7	S8	S9

price in the secondary market, so the two prices are assumed to be the same in the remaining analyses and discussions. When there exists excess demand for permits in the permit market, we assume that power plants can still fulfill their compliance obligations through the offset mechanism such as buying CCERs. At present, the limitation of using CCERs to offset is no more than 5% of the total emission. For simplicity, this paper relaxes this limitation to unveil the impact of the national ETS on encouraging renewable energy electricity through offset mechanisms.

2.3. Data

We construct a unique plant-level dataset that contains variables such as unit capacity, fuel type, cooling type, heat type, power generation, coal consumption rate of power supply, utilization hour, and load rate. Most plants with large installed capacity have all the above data at the unit level. Small plants may lack information on variables such as heat supply and load rate, these missing data are interpolated by using the multivariate regression method that can be found in Appendix A.

Data are collected mainly from *Annual Compilation of Power Industry Statistics*, *Manual of National Power Units*, *National Thermal Power Unit Benchmarking and Competition*, etc. The year of sample data used for scenario analyses is 2018. We successfully matched 964 thermal power plants out of 2225 power plants covered in the national ETS. Among these power plants, 871 are coal-fired power plants and 93 are gas-fired power plants. Table 4 shows that our sample has a quite good representativeness. For coal-fired power plants, total installed capacity and power generation of our sample data cover 85.5% and 86.6% of national total values respectively. These two ratios are a little bit lower for gas-fired power plants, total installed capacity

Table 4. Sample representativeness.

Fuel type	Variable	Official statistics ($\geq$ 6 MW)	Sample	Coverage (%)
Coal	Capacity (GW)	1007.94	861.868	85.5
	Power Generation (Billion MWh)	4.4821	3.8805	86.6
Gas	Capacity (GW)	83.13	64.782	77.9
	Power Generation (Billion MWh)	0.2134	0.1748	81.9

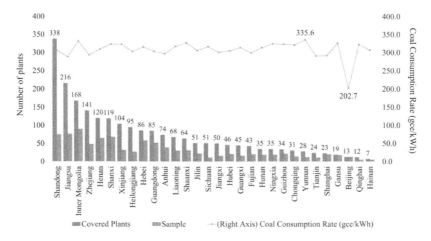

Figure 4. Covered plants in the national ETS.

and power generation of our sample data cover 77.9% and 81.9% of national total values respectively.

Fig. 4 shows basic statistics of the matched sample. The left vertical axis is the number of plants, red bars and blue bars show the number of each province's power plants covered by national ETS and our sample. The right vertical axis is the coal consumption rate of power supply, and each province's average value is calculated by using sample data. Beijing has the lowest average value for the reason that it only uses gas-fired power plants to generate electricity. Among other provinces, Jiangsu, Zhejiang, Tianjin and Shanghai have the highest average efficiency. Yunnan and Inner Mongolia have the lowest average efficiencies. From a regional perspective, eastern coastal areas generally have better energy efficiencies than other regions.

Table 5 shows the descriptive statistics of both coal-fired power plants as well as gas-fired power plants. We can see that these thermal power plants not only are different in their scales, but also have huge heterogeneities in their efficiencies. This technical discrepancy is the foundation of the national ETS. However, the greater the discrepancy, the larger the distributional effect may occur.

Table 5. Descriptive statistics of sample data.

Fuel type	Variables	Unit	Mean	Std.	Max	Min
Coal	Capacity	MW	989.5	794.8	6120.0	6.0
	Generation	GWh	4465.3	3924.1	34290.1	20.7
	Utilization hours	h	4466.8	1272.2	8575.2	134.4
	Coal consumption rate of power supply	gce/kWh	322.1	63.7	1306.0	104.0
Gas	Capacity	MW	696.6	527.3	2766.0	112.0
	Generation	GWh	1910.4	1650.5	8521.4	13.7
	Utilization hours	h	2767.1	1587.5	6526.2	122.3
	Coal consumption rate of power supply	gce/kWh	236.4	31.8	345.0	157.0

3. Results

3.1. *Overall impacts*

Results show that the current Allocation Plan leads to a plenty of net surpluses of permits. As shown in Fig. 5, the total amount of net surplus of permits will reach 658.28 million tons for scenario S1 (also for S4, S7). When we change the benchmark standards, the net surplus of permits in trading will be 50.61 million tons for scenario S2 (also for S5, S8) and net surplus switches to net deficit of permits which will be around −65.89 million tons for scenario S3 (also for S6, S9). The whole national ETS will be balanced when the benchmark standard is chosen between top 2–3% efficiency levels. The significant net surplus of permits will cause an excess supply of permits in the market and it will be highly likely that the resultant carbon prices will converge to a low level.

In Table 6, we estimate the monetary volumes of permit auction, offset and trading among power plants. The monetary volumes of the above markets are highly

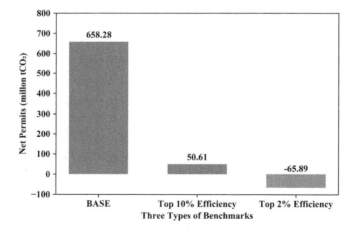

Figure 5. Net surplus of the permits under different benchmarks.

Table 6. Monetary volume of the national ETS in different scenarios.

Type	Benchmark	Scenarios	Auction (billion yuan)	Trading (billion yuan)	Offset (billion yuan)
Free	BASE	S1	0.0	1.8	0
	Top 10%	S2	0.0	17.6	0
	Top 2%	S3	0.0	16.4	13.2
50% auction	BASE	S4	375.8	1.8	0
	Top 10%	S5	315.0	17.6	0
	Top 2 %	S6	303.4	16.4	13.2
100% auction	BASE	S7	751.6	1.8	0
	Top 10%	S8	630.0	17.6	0
	Top 2%	S9	606.7	16.4	13.2

dependent on the carbon price, which should be endogenously determined by demand side and supply side of the ETS. The above market clearance mechanism requires that we need to know the marginal abatement cost curve (MACC) of each power plant. Since the MACCs can be hardly estimated at the micro level, a large amount of the existing studies can only provide sector-level estimations of MACCs. As a result, we use an exogenously determined carbon price that equals 200 yuan/ton to conduct the analyses. This price level is higher than the carbon price in the start period of the national ETS that fluctuates between 40 and 50 yuan/ton, and is also higher than the carbon prices in pilot ETSs that are less than 100 yuan/ton. The national ETS officially made debut on July 16th 2021, with the opening price of the permit at CNY 48 (around 7.4 USD). However, we find that this price of 200 yuan/ton is reasonable for the scenario analyses and can be justified from the following two reasons.[3]

The first reason is that China's carbon price may be significantly affected by the international trade market. The European Commission adopted a proposal for a new Carbon Border Adjustment Mechanism (CBAM) on July 14th 2021 and will officially take effect in 2026.[4] The CBAM is expected to bring significant impacts on the international trade market since it will put a carbon price on the imported goods in European Union (EU). China plays the role as the largest exporter of EU and the trade volume between China and EU reached 586 billion Euros in 2020.[5] The carbon price in EU-ETS has been keeping rising to exceed 60 Euros/ton since November 2021 and is expected to increase to a higher level in the future for the cold wave and soared natural gas prices.[6] The large price gap between China's national ETS and EU-ETS might put great pressure on China. Therefore, there exists a strong possibility that carbon price in China's ETS will increase to a relatively high level.

The second reason is that China is expected to peak its CO_2 emission at a moderate level in order to reduce the barriers to realize carbon neutrality. In the long run, the carbon dioxide capture, utilization and storage (CCUS) will play an important role as the negative emission technology, and will thus become an important determinant of the carbon price. The costs of CO_2 capture are estimated to be 90–390 yuan/ton by 2030 and 20–130 yuan/ton by 2060 (Cai *et al.*, 2021). In addition, a high carbon price can also provide strong incentives for the market players to invest in renewable energies as well as low-carbon technologies.

We can see from Table 6 that China's national ETS is large in market size if all permits are allocated to power plants through auction. Under the assumption that

---

[3] The monetary volumes are essentially calculated based on multiplying carbon price with permits or net permits. As a result, the price level will not change the directions of this paper's results, but will only affect the sizes of the monetary volumes proportionally. So this paper's results are valid whenever the exogenous carbon price is chosen as 50 yuan/ton, 100 yuan/ton, 200 yuan/ton or even higher.
[4] Detailed information can be found on the website of European Commission: https://ec.europa.eu/commission/presscorner/detail/en/qanda_21_3661
[5] Detailed information can be found on the website of European Commision: https://ec.europa.eu/trade/policy/countries-and-regions/countries/china/
[6] Data source: https://www.theice.com/products/18709519/EUA-Daily-Future/data?marketId=400431

carbon price is 200 yuan/ton, total auction revenue will exceed 300 billion yuan if 50% of permits are auctioned and will exceed 600 billion yuan if all permits are auctioned. These auction revenues could provide sufficient funds to accelerate China's low-carbon transformation as well as improve social welfare. Although total auction revenues decrease as benchmarks become stricter, permits trading will become more active which reflects the incentive effects on those power plants with low efficiencies.

Total volumes of trading and offset only depend on the benchmark levels. The total trading volume is only 1.8 billion yuan when using the current national ETS's standards. As benchmark standard becomes stricter, more power plants will switch from surplus in permits to deficit in permits and thus increasing the permit trade volume. Total trading volume is 17.6 billion yuan and 16.4 billion yuan when the benchmarks are used as the top 10% and 2% efficiencies, respectively. The trading volume decreases because the supply of permits from plants with net surplus in the S3 (S6, S9) is less than in the S2 (S5, S8), so the buyers will have to seek for offsetting. For the reason that the whole permit market will only become in shortage of permit when benchmarks are chosen as top 2% efficiency levels, under this situation, the offset volume is 13.2 billion yuan.

3.2. *Plant-level impacts*

Fig. 6 illustrates the relationships among net surplus or deficit of permits and other power plants' characteristics. Red points represent the power plants that need to buy permits from the market, and blue points represent the power plants that have surpluses of permits. We can see from Fig. 6 that more efficient power plants also generally have higher net surpluses of permits, but this relationship is not always the case because permit allocation is affected by many factors. For example, according to formula (2), if one unit's efficiency is lower than another unit's efficiency, it can still receive more permits from compensations such as adjustments for cooling type and heat supply.

Both power generation and CO_2 emissions can measure the production scale of the power plant. Fig. 6 also shows that the larger the production scale, the smaller the variance of the permit surplus ratio. This means that the carbon market will lead to heterogenous incentives to power plants of different sizes. Tightening the standards of permits allocation will have a greater structural adjustment effect on the relatively smaller power plants. The combustion efficiency of small power plants is generally lower than that of large power plants yet the variance is larger. Therefore, the carbon market has more incentive on small-scale power plants whose efficiencies are extremely low. However, since many small-scale power plants take the responsibility to supply heat, some of them may receive high compensations in permits that will lead to higher ratios of net permits. Some of these small-scale power plants may get around twice the permits they actually need. Although these plants have a high rate of net permits, they will not significantly affect the equilibrium condition of the whole permit market.

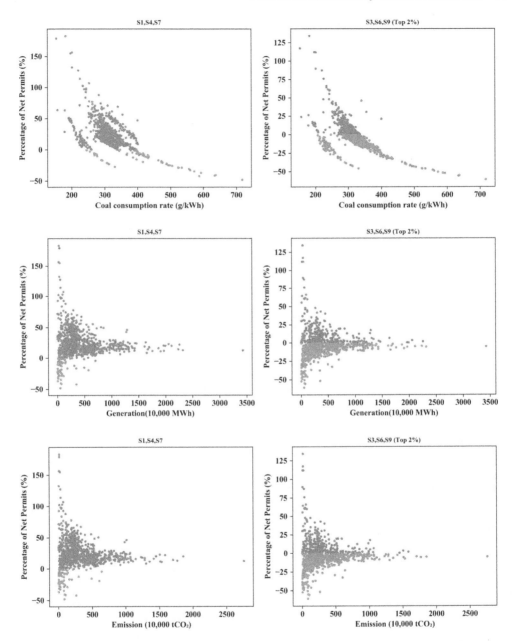

Figure 6. Relationships between net permits and power plants' characteristics.

From the spatial perspective, Fig. 7 shows the geographical distribution of thermal power plants, and each point represents one power plant. We can find that power plants in central regions are relatively less efficient than power plants in other regions. When benchmark standard becomes as top 10% level, most of the power plants in central regions are in shortage of permits while most power plants in eastern and western regions still have surpluses of permits. When the benchmark standard becomes as top

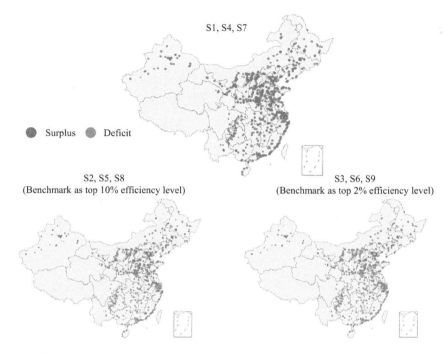

Figure 7. Plant-level net permits of different scenarios (10,000 tCO$_2$).

2% efficiency levels, only a few power plants in northeastern, Xinjiang and Gansu still have surpluses of permits. The reason is that power plants in these regions are typically air-cooled and are responsible to supply heat. Consequently, their permits are more likely to be adjusted upward.

Fig. 8 assesses the permits surplus by four technical types. Overall, coal-fired power plants account for the vast majority of permits and emissions. Coal-fired power units above 400 MW are more likely to have anoverall shortage in permits, which could be counter-intuitive. One explanation is that the current rules may be more "toleran" for units below 400 MW. When the permits are allocated according to top 2% efficiency levels, the overall market can be cleared. Moreover, in fact, there still exists a permits surplus for coal-fired units below 400 MW. The adjustment factors are the main reason to explain the surpluses of permits among these power plants.

3.3. Provincial impacts of different scenarios

When we aggregate net permits of power plants within each province, we can see clear provincial impacts of different benchmarking scenarios. Fig. 9 shows that most central provinces will first face deficits of permits. Inner Mongolia will need to buy a large number of permits from the market when the benchmark standard is set as top 2% efficiency level. Shaanxi, Guizhou and Guangdong will also face a large deficit of permits when the benchmark standard becomes stricter. Similar to the plant-level

Plant-Level Evaluation of China's National ETS 57

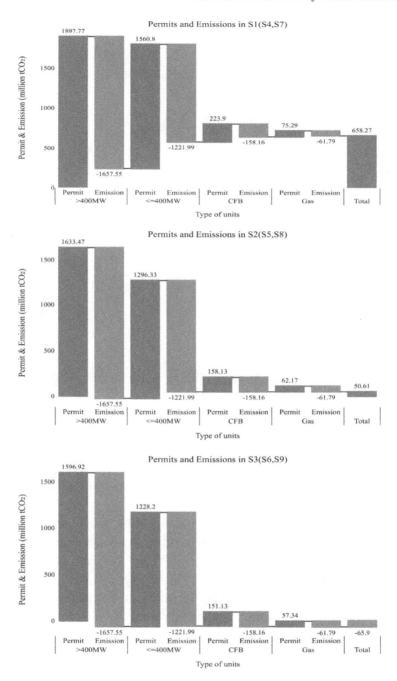

Figure 8. Permits and emission of different types of plants.

results, Xinjiang, Gansu and northeastern provinces together with Hainan will still have surpluses of permits under the strict benchmark standards.

If we divide the aggregated net permits by total emissions to get each province's surplus ratio or deficit ratio, results are similar but discrepancies among provinces are

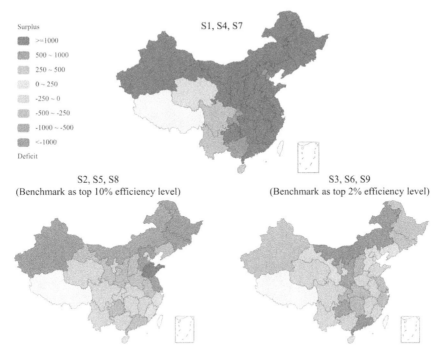

Figure 9. Provincial net permits of different scenarios (unit: 10,000 tCO$_2$).

reduced as shown in Fig. 10. However, northeastern provinces will still have a high surplus ratio when the benchmark standards are set as top 2% efficiency levels. The ratio of deficit ratio is more correlated to actual pressures for buying permits. Results show that Yunnan will have a relatively high pressure, and Inner Mongolia's pressure keeps at a reasonable level. Jilin, Heilongjiang and Beijing will have a relatively high surplus ratio.

Figs. 11–13 show directions of cash flows among provinces in scenario S1, S3, and S6, which are the disaggregated values for results provided in Table 6. The Sankey diagrams illustrate three different types of cash flows that are corresponding to the different money volumes shown in Table 6. The first type of cash flow is the money exchanged among power plants. Since the benchmarks are relatively lax, the permit market is not balanced. Therefore, supplies of permits of all provinces are reduced proportionally to equal the total demand for permits.[7] The second type of cash flow is the money from power plants to suppliers of offset products such as owners of CCERs through the offset mechanism. The destinations of these cash flow are proportionally allocated to provinces according to their amount of electricity generated by wind and solar. The third type of cash flow is the money from power plants to the government through auctions.

---

[7]Although there exists excess supply of permits, permits trading can still occur due to different market designs such price floor, market stability reserve, etc.

Plant-Level Evaluation of China's National ETS 59

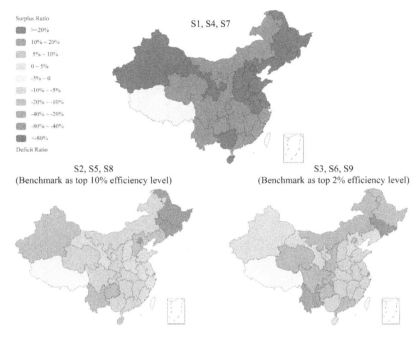

Figure 10. Provincial net permit ratios of different scenarios (unit: %).

Fig. 11 illustrates the cash flow among provinces when there only exists permit trading. When benchmark standards are lax, Inner Mongolia is the biggest buyer for permits and Henan is the second biggest buyer. About 40% of the provinces have no need for the permits. In Fig. 12, when benchmarks become stricter as top 2%

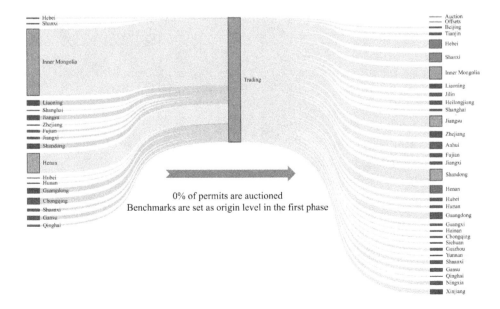

Figure 11. Cash Flows among provinces in S1.

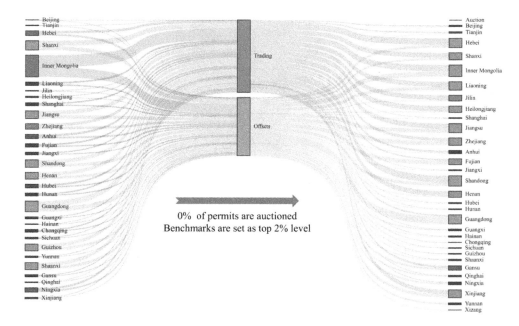

Figure 12. Cash Flows among provinces in S3.

efficiency levels, discrepancies among provinces at the demand side of permits are reduced. Since the permit market is balanced, all provinces' supplies of permits from power plants with high efficiencies are sold out. For example, Inner Mongolia's cost for purchasing the permits can be recycled from the revenue of selling the permits to a

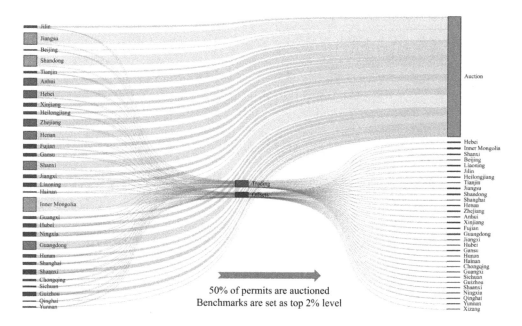

Figure 13. Cash flows among provinces in S6.

large extent. The consequence is that the distributional effect will occur for power plants within Inner Mongolia. Finally, the whole ETS market will be dominated by auction revenues as shown in Fig. 13. The large scale of auction revenue reflects the total costs paid by all provinces. As a result, although in some provinces such as Shandong and Jiangsu, their trading volume is not that big, their total costs will be relatively high when permits are allocated through auction.

4. Discussion and Conclusion

This paper conducts a plant-level evaluation of the impacts of different benchmark designs for China's national ETS. Results demonstrate that the benchmarks used in the initial stage of China's national ETS are relatively lax. This will lead to sufficiently high surpluses of permits. Only when benchmarks are chosen as strict as top 2% efficiency levels can the carbon market be cleared. For the market size, the carbon market can generate large-scale cash flows at both the plant and provincial levels, especially when auction mechanism is introduced. If the carbon price is 200 yuan/ton and 50% of permits are allocated through auction, total revenue can reach more than 300 billion yuan. This number will be doubled if all permits are auctioned to power plants. Total monetary volumes of trading and offset are relatively smaller than that of auction revenue, but they will increase rapidly as benchmark standards become stricter. The policy implication is thus straightforward that permit allocation standards of China's ETS should be tightened gradually in the future in order to have broader socio-economic and technological impacts and emission reduction effects. Meanwhile, the offsetting mechanism should also be carefully designed. On the one hand, it is a complementary instrument that can alleviate power plants' pressures for compliance. On the other hand, it can also be used as an effective instrument to encourage the development of renewable energies.

The plant-level analyses of this paper can also provide some insights into the low carbon development at the provincial level. Firstly, China has an uneven distribution of regional energy consumptions and production opportunities. The eastern part of China is the main contributor of CO_2 emissions (Cheng *et al.*, 2020), while the western part has rich renewable energy endowments (Yan *et al.*, 2019; Wang *et al.*, 2020). Therefore, the national carbon trading market will lead to structural surpluses and shortfalls of carbon permits among different provinces in China. Secondly, heterogeneities of efficiencies will lead to the various status of net permits for power plants within the same province. Risks may occur that power plants within the same province may choose over-the-counter trading to reduce total costs. It may significantly reduce the incentive effects of the carbon market due to the lower prices.

Besides the benchmarking issue, China's national ETS should also learn more from the existing mature carbon markets. Firstly, according to the experience of EU-ETS and other well-operating carbon markets, MRV quality is the fundamental element to ensure the success of the market. It is also a main challenge of the China' national ETS. Zhang *et al.* (2019b) find that the MRV qualities in Beijing and Hubei pilot ETSs had improved over time, but for the national ETS, MRV quality still needs to be substantially improved. Secondly, financial institutions and individuals are not included at the initial stage, and the market only includes spot transactions. In the future, it is necessary to establish the futures market and introduce various types of market players, in order to improve the ability of the market to form stable long-term price signals. The third experience is that the policy mix of carbon tax and carbon market can be considered. At present, the carbon market only includes the power generation sector, yet other energy intensive sectors will also be covered by the market in the future. However, for sectors such as the transportation sector, carbon tax may be the more appropriate policy instrument than ETS. As a result, the realization of full carbon pricing in the whole society needs to be supplemented by other policy instruments such as carbon tax.

Acknowledgements

This work was supported by the National Key Research and Development Program of China (2020YFA0608600), the National Natural Science Foundation of China (71925010, 71703027), Shanghai Talent Development Fund (2021098).

Appendix A. Procedures of Data Preparation

(a) Handling outliers. The abnormal values mainly occurred in coal consumption rate and power generation. Basically, the proportion of abnormal values was less than 10% of the sample. The plant-level data and the unit level data are used to conduct the cross validation according to the physical constraints. The abnormal value is replaced with the average value of the same type of unit or power plant.

(b) Processing missing data. In our sample data, there are two types of missing data. The first type is that we only have power plant data without unit-level information. There are around 35% of the sample power plant data belong to this type and most of these power plants have installed capacities less than 400 MW. For these plants, we directly use plant-level data to calculate the permits. Power generation information for almost all units whose installed capacities are above 400 MW are complete.

The second type is that some units lack heating supply data while the power plants containing the units have the heating supply data. For these units, plant-level data are disaggregated into the unit-level data. A multiple regression model is adopted to fit the heat supplied on units' features by using the sample data with complete information, and then interpolating the missing data. Most of the regression coefficients are significant, which indicates that the interpolated values are valid.

References

Cai, B, Q Li, X Zhang *et al.* (2021). 2021 Annual Report on Carbon Dioxide Capture, Utilization and Storage (CCUS) in China: Study of Roadmap for China's CCUS. Published by Chinese Academy of Environmental Planning, Institute of Rock and Soil Mechanics of Chinese Academy of Sciences, The Administrative Center for China's Agenda 21.

Cao, J, H Dai, S Li, C Guo, M Ho, W Cai, J He, H Huang, J Li, Y Liu, H Qian, C Wang, L Wu and X Zhang (2021a). The general equilibrium impacts of carbon tax policy in China: A multi-model comparison. *Energy Economics*, 99, 105284.

Cao, J, M Ho, R Ma and F Teng (2021b). When carbon emission trading meets a regulated industry: Evidence from the electricity sector of China. *Journal of Public Economics*, 200, 104470.

Chang, S, X Yang, H Zheng, S Wang and X Zhang (2020). Air quality and health co-benefits of China's national emission trading system. *Applied Energy*, 261, 114226.

Chen, Z, XC Yuan, X Zhang and Y Cao (2020). How will the Chinese national carbon emissions trading scheme work? The assessment of regional potential gains. *Energy Policy*, 137, 111095.

Cheng, S, W Fan, F Meng, J Chen, S Liang, M Song, G Liu and M Casazza (2020). Potential role of fiscal decentralization on interprovincial differences in CO_2 emissions in China. *Environmental Science & Technology*, 55, 813–822.

Cui, J, J Zhang and Y Zheng (2018). Carbon pricing induces innovation: Evidence from China's regional carbon market pilots. *AEA Papers and Proceedings*, 108, 453–457.

Deng, Z, D Li, T Pang and M Duan (2018). Effectiveness of pilot carbon emissions trading systems in China. *Climate Policy*, 18, 992–1011.

Dong, F, Y Dai, S Zhang, X Zhang and R Long (2019). Can a carbon emission trading scheme generate the Porter effect? Evidence from pilot areas in China. *Science of the Total Environment*, 653, 565–577.

Dong, Z, H Wang, S Wang and L Wang (2020). The validity of carbon emission trading policies: Evidence from a quasi-natural experiment in China. *Advances in Climate Change Research*, 11, 102–109.

Duan, H, S Zhou, K Jiang, C Bertram, M Harmsen, E Kriegler, D van Vuuren, S Wang, S Fujimori, M Tavoni, X Ming, K Keramidas, G Iyer and J Edmonds (2021). Assessing China's efforts to pursue the 1.5°C warming limit. *Science*, 372(6540), 378–385.

Ellerman, A, F Convery and C De Perthuis (2010). *Pricing Carbon: The European Union Emissions Trading Scheme.* Cambridge: Cambridge University Press.

Fabra, N and M Reguant (2014). Pass-through of emissions costs in electricity markets. *American Economic Review*, 104, 2872–2899.

Gao, Y, M Li, J Xue and Y Liu (2020). Evaluation of effectiveness of China's carbon emissions trading scheme in carbon mitigation. *Energy Economics*, 90, 104872.

Haita, C (2014). Endogenous market power in an emissions trading scheme with auctioning. *Resource & Energy Economics*, 37, 253–278.

Hu, J, X Pan and Q Huang (2020). Quantity or quality? The impacts of environmental regulation on firms' innovation–Quasi-natural experiment based on China's carbon emissions trading pilot. *Technological Forecasting and Social Change*, 158, 120122.

Huang, H, D Roland-Holst, C Springer, J Lin, W Cai and C Wang (2019). Emissions trading systems and social equity: A CGE assessment for China. *Applied Energy*, 235, 1254–1265.

Jiang, J, D Xie, B Ye, B Shen and Z Chen (2016). Research on China's cap-and-trade carbon emission trading scheme: Overview and outlook. *Applied Energy*, 178, 902–917.

Jotzo, F, V Karplus, M Grubb, A Löschel, K Neuhoff, L Wu and F Teng (2018). China's emissions trading takes steps towards big ambitions. *Nature Climate Change*, 8, 265.

Li, L, F Ye, Y Li and C Chang (2019). How will the Chinese Certified Emission Reduction scheme save cost for the national carbon trading system? *Journal of Environmental Management*, 244, 99–109.

Li, D, M Duan, Z Deng and H Zhang (2020). Assessment of the performance of pilot carbon emissions trading systems in China. *Environmental Economics and Policy Studies*, 23, 593–612.

Lin, B and P Wesseh (2020). On the economics of carbon pricing: Insights from econometric modeling with industry-level data. *Energy Economics*, 86, 104678.

Liu, L, C Chen, Y Zhao and E Zhao (2015). China's carbon-emissions trading: Overview, challenges and future. *Renewable and Sustainable Energy Reviews*, 49, 254–266.

Liu, C, C Ma and R Xie (2020). Structural, innovation and efficiency effects of environmental regulation: Evidence from China's carbon emissions trading pilot. *Environmental and Resource Economics*, 75, 741–768.

Liu, W and Z Wang (2017). The effects of climate policy on corporate technological upgrading in energy intensive industries: Evidence from China. *Journal of Cleaner Production*, 142, 3748–3758.

Lo, A and R Cong (2017). After CDM: Domestic carbon offsetting in China. *Journal of Cleaner Production*, 141, 1391–1399.

Mo, J, P Agnolucci, M Jiang and Y Fan (2016). The impact of Chinese carbon emission trading scheme (ETS) on low carbon energy (LCE) investment. *Energy Policy*, 89, 271–283.

Mu, Y, S Evans, C Wang and W Cai (2018). How will sectoral coverage affect the efficiency of an emissions trading system? A CGE-based case study of China. *Applied Energy*, 227, 403–414.

Narassimhan, E, K Gallagher, S Koester and J Alejo (2018). Carbon pricing in practice: A review of existing emissions trading systems. *Climate Policy*, 18(8), 967–991.

Qi, S, A He and J Zhang (2020). The effective benchmark selection model and simulation in the power sector of China'S ETS. *Climate Change Economics*, 11, 2041006.

Qian, H, L Wu and W Tang (2017). Lock-in effect of emission standard and its impact on the choice of market based instruments. *Energy Economics*, 63, 41–50.

Qian, H, Y Zhou and L Wu (2018). Evaluating various choices of sector coverage in China's national emissions trading system (ETS). *Climate Policy*, 18(S1), 7–26.

Qian, H, S Xu, J Cao, F Ren, W Wei, J Meng and L Wu (2021). Air pollution reduction and climate co-benefits in China's industries. *Nature Sustainability*, 4, 417–425.

Sachs, J and W Woo (2001). Understanding China's economic performance. *The Journal of Policy Reform*, 4, 1–50.

Schmalensee, R and R Stavins (2017). The design of environmental markets: What have we learned from experience with cap and trade? *Oxford Review of Economic Policy*, 33(4), 572–588.

Shen, J, P Tang and H Zeng (2020). Does China's carbon emission trading reduce carbon emissions? Evidence from listed firms. *Energy for Sustainable Development*, 59, 120–129.

Wang, C, Y Wang, X Tong, S Ulgiati, S Liang, M Xu, W Wei, X Li, M Jin and J Mao (2020). Mapping potentials and bridging regional gaps of renewable resources in China. *Renewable and Sustainable Energy Reviews*, 134, 110337.

Wang, M, M Yao, S Wang, H Qian, P Zhang, Y Wang, Y Sun and W Wei (2021). Study of the emissions and spatial distributions of various power-generation technologies in China. *Journal of Environmental Management*, 278, 111401.

Wu, L, S Zhang and H Qian (2022a). Distributional effects of China's National Emission Trading Scheme with an emphasis on sectoral coverage and revenue recycling. *Energy Economics*, 105, 105770.

Wu, L, Y Zhou and H Qian (2022b). Global actions under the Paris agreement: Tracing the carbon leakage flow and pursuing countermeasures. *Energy Economics*, 105804.

Xu, J and Y Zhang (2021). Has the international climate regime promoted climate justice? Evidence from Clean Development Mechanism projects in China. *Climate Policy*, doi: 10.1080/14693062.2021.2008294.

Xu, C (2011). The fundamental institutions of China's reforms and development. *Journal of economic literature*, 49(4), 1076–1151.

Xu, J (2021). Conflicts in multi-level governance: An analysis of international climate policy implementation at the sub-national level. *Global Public Policy and Governance*, 1(4), 401–420.

Yan, J, Y Yang, P Campana and J He (2019). City-level analysis of subsidy-free solar photovoltaic electricity price, profits and grid parity in China. *Nature Energy*, 4(8), 709–717.

Yan, K, W Zhang and D Shen (2020a). Stylized facts of the carbon emission market in China. *Physica A: Statistical Mechanics and its Applications*, 555, 124739.

Yan, Y, X Zhang, J Zhang and K Li (2020b). Emissions trading system (ETS) implementation and its collaborative governance effects on air pollution: The China story. *Energy Policy*, 138, 111282.

Yuan, Y, H Duan and T Tsvetanov (2020). Synergizing China's energy and carbon mitigation goals: General equilibrium modeling and policy assessment. *Energy Economics*, 89, 104787.

Zhang, D, V Karplus, C Cassisa and X Zhang (2014). Emissions trading in China: Progress and prospects. *Energy Policy*, 75, 9–16.

Zhang, D, Q Zhang, S Qi, J Huang, V Karplus and X Zhang (2019a). Integrity of firms' emissions reporting in China's early carbon markets. *Nature Climate Change*, 9(2), 164–169.

Zhang, H, M Duan and Z Deng (2019b). Have China's pilot emissions trading schemes promoted carbon emission reductions? The evidence from industrial sub-sectors at the provincial level. *Journal of Cleaner Production*, 234, 912–924.

Zhang, Y, W Shi and J Jiang (2020). Does China's carbon emissions trading policy improve the technology innovation of relevant enterprises? *Business Strategy and the Environment*, 29(3), 872–885.

Zhang, X, D Zhang and R Yu (2021). Theory and Practice of China's National Carbon Emissions Trading System (in Chinese). *Management World*, 37(8), 80–95.

Zhang, G and N Zhang (2020). The effect of China's pilot carbon emissions trading schemes on poverty alleviation: A quasi-natural experiment approach. *Journal of Environmental Management*, 271, 110973.

Zhao, X, G Jiang, D Nie and H Chen (2016). How to improve the market efficiency of carbon trading: A perspective of China. *Renewable and Sustainable Energy Reviews*, 59, 1229–1245.

Zhu, J, Y Fan, X Deng and L Xue (2019). Low-carbon innovation induced by emissions trading in China. *Nature Communications*, 10, 4088.

© 2025 World Scientific Publishing Company
https://doi.org/10.1142/9789819812264_0004

THE DISTRIBUTIONAL EFFECT OF INTER-REGIONAL TRANSMISSION GRID EXPANSION ON CHINA'S POWER INDUSTRY[§]

XU TAN[*], SHENG LIN[*] and BAI-CHEN XIE[*,†,‡]

[*]*College of Management and Economics*
Tianjin University, Tianjin 300072, P. R. China

[†]*Energy Policy Research Group (EPRG)*
Judge Business School
University of Cambridge, Cambridge CB2 1AG, UK
[‡]*xiebaichen@tju.edu.cn, xiebaichen@126.com*

China suffers significant heterogeneities in resource endowments and geological conditions across the regions. Ultra-high voltage (UHV) line construction is a project put forward by the government to boost the inter-regional transmission grid expansion, benefiting economic development by reducing pollutant emissions and absorbing more clean energy. This study investigates the extent to which this giant infrastructure has distributional effects on China's power industry. We estimate the distributional effect of UHV lines from the perspective of power deployment, carbon emissions, and producer surplus by simulating an equilibrium model of the national electricity market through the mixed complementarity problems (MCPs) method. Furthermore, the Lorenz curve is also employed to investigate the distributional effect of UHV introduction. The results indicate that: (1) the distributional effect of introducing UHV lines is regressive considering its limited contributions to the equalization of environmental and economic welfare; (2) the emission reduction effect of the UHV lines has been improved between 2015 and 2018; (3) power plants with a large installation capacity could seek more economic profits while emitting more pollution; (4) the deployment of clean power in the resource-abundant regions is far below its potential. Meanwhile, we propose improving the structure and technology of the power mix, which can accelerate China's market-oriented reform of the power system by equally distributing the benefits.

Keywords: Distributional effect; ultra-high voltage; clean power; inter-regional power transmission; China.

1. Introduction

As the global temperature-increase limit has been reduced to below 1.5°C from 2°C,[1] mitigating greenhouse gas emissions is currently one of the most urgent worldwide issues (Li and Wei, 2021; Zheng *et al.*, 2021). The power industry is the primary

---

[‡]Corresponding author.
[§]This chapter was originally published in Climate Change Economics, Vol. 13, No. 1 (2022), published by World Scientific Publishing, Singapore. Reprinted with permission.
[1]The Paris Agreement, Climate Conference in Paris, April 2016.

source of air pollution and CO_2, which contributed 42% of the world's greenhouse gas emissions in 2019. The corresponding shares are 36%, 31%, and 51% for the US, European Union, and India, respectively (International Energy Agency, 2020). As the second-largest economy in the world, China's electricity-related carbon emissions (CEs) account for more than 45% of the world's total (Wei *et al.*, 2020). In September 2020, President Xi Jinping announced that China aims to peak CEs before 2030 and achieve carbon neutrality before 2060 at the 75th United Nations general assembly and the climate ambition summit. China's emission reduction efficiency significantly impacts the global climate governance process (Qi *et al.*, 2020). However, it seems challenging for China to achieve the goal of "net-zero carbon" or "carbon neutrality" due to the multiple uncertainties embedded in economic growth, energy efficiency enhancement, and low-carbon transition (Duan *et al.*, 2018).

An important policy instrument extensively advocated by many jurisdictions to incentivize renewable power generation and decrease CEs is the inter-regional power transmission (Brinkerink *et al.*, 2019). Many agencies have been established to speed up the inter-regional grid, such as the European Network of Transmission System Operators for Electricity (ENTSO-E, 2014), the Central American Electrical Interconnection System (Inter-American Development Bank, 2013), and the Central and Northern Interconnected System in Chile (Quiroga *et al.*, 2019). Generally, inter-regional transmission can allow high variable renewable energy (VRE) penetration and lower curtailment while transferring pollution around the regions (Bird *et al.*, 2016; Jafari *et al.*, 2020; Qureshi *et al.*, 2016).

By acknowledging the various benefits of inter-regional transmission, China has promoted its inter-regional power transmission construction represented by ultra-high voltage (UHV) lines. The advantages of UHV lines include larger capacity, longer transmission distances, higher efficiency, lower power loss, and less land occupation (Liu, 2013). A UHV transmission line connects two individual provinces in the six regional power grids.[2] The voltage level of a UHV line is above +800 kV direct current (DC) or 1000 kV alternating current (AC). By the end of 2020, China had constructed 14 AC UHV and 16 DC UHV transmission lines 48,000 km long (see Figure A.1 for schematic description), whose accumulative investment has amounted to 500 billion CNY (77.5 billion USD). However, the effects of inter-regional transmission construction are still controversial. There are at least three factors that impact the benefits of the line's construction. First, the environmental performance of the generation sector varied significantly in different regions due to the heterogeneities in resource endowments. Second, China's power supply and demand situation is vulnerable to the uneven distribution between electricity generation and consumption centers (Zhang *et al.*, 2018). Third, the development of the electricity industry, which is the pillar and foundation of society, is seriously affected by the unstable economy around the regions (Moore *et al.*, 2016; Wu *et al.*, 2019).

---

[2]They are the Northeast, North, Central, East, and Northwest China Power Grid and China Southern Power Grid.

This paper focuses on the issue of the extent that the inter-regional transmission expansion has on the distributional effects of the power industry. China's unbundling reform of "separating power plants from grids" in 2002 had dismantled the power industry into the generation sector and the grid sector with transmission, distribution, and retail businesses. The top two grid companies, State Grid Corporation of China and China Southern Power Grid, cover 98% of businesses in China. Currently, China is establishing the national power market by pioneering pilot power markets in several provinces. On the one hand, expanding inter-regional transmission lines can provide strong support for China's market-oriented power system reform. It may increase the power trade among regions, ease power supply and demand, and intensify market competition. On the other hand, both power prices determined by the market equilibrium and strategy of the power plant will change as more power generated is integrated into the grid, a physical channel resulting from the introduction of inter-regional transmission network construction. Therefore, the distribution of the participants' revenue also changes significantly along with the market equilibrium changes. As an important measure for regulating the power system, the expansion of inter-regional transmission networks has gained success to a great extent in energy conservation and emission reduction. However, there is still controversy about its influence on the distribution of economic and environmental benefits.

The impact of environmental change is likely to vary across regions, sectors, and groups stemming from the heterogeneities in the local climate, economic development, and adaptive capacity (DePaula, 2020). Most researchers and policymakers understand that the benefits of environmental regulations are unlikely to be evenly distributed; they are interested in analyzing the distribution of environmental benefits (see, e.g., Baumol and Oates (1988) and USGAO (1983)). Hsiang *et al.* (2018) believe that the underlying sources of heterogeneity in different groups may generate distributional effects of environmental policy benefits. Meanwhile, regional differences in the composition of energy sources could also result in widely varying distributional impacts (Rausch *et al.*, 2011). Moreover, policy implementations are considered to produce winners and losers by imposing differing regulatory costs on those who are regulated (Fullerton, 2017). Therefore, the inter-regional transmission expansions are thought to have a distributional effect on power plants located in different regions, with different installed capacities.

This paper aims to investigate the distributional effect of inter-regional transmission grid expansion and its economic and environmental benefits. To the best of our knowledge, this is the first study to explore the distributional impact of China's UHV line construction based on the simulation of the national electricity market. The remainder of the paper is organized as follows. Section 2 provides the literature review. Section 3 presents the methodology and the data sources. Section 4 states the main results and discusses the distributional effect of inter-regional transmission grid expansion. Section 5 concludes the study.

2. Literature Review

The literature has examined the efficiency and overall cost-effectiveness of inter-regional transmissions, but the distributional effects have not yet received enough attention (Puka and Szulecki, 2014; Wei *et al.*, 2017). Burgholzer and Auer (2016) elaborated on the costs and benefits of expanding the Austrian transmission system. Otsuki *et al.* (2016) quantified the potential economic benefits of connecting power grids and developing renewable energies in Northeast Asia. Chen *et al.* (2020) quantified the economic potential of cross-border transmission to a decarbonized future Northwestern European power system. When it comes to the issue of China, Lin and Wu (2017) evaluated the actual cost of long-distance electricity transmission. Li *et al.* (2019) analyzed the economic impacts of inter-regional transmission on power importing provinces based on a computable general equilibrium model. Xu *et al.* (2020) presented a multi-regional power system optimization model to evaluate the potential economic benefits of infrastructure investments for the national inter-regional electricity network.

Present studies show that inter-regional transmission line construction could cost about 400 billion CNY (62 billion USD). Although existing studies have carried out quantitative analysis on the effect of inter-regional transmission, most of them only regard the power sector as a whole to analyze the evolution of its effect, while lacking details of the effect among different parts within the power sector. Previous studies have shown significant differences in economic and social development and resource endowments among different provinces and regions. There is a prominent imbalance in the development of the power sector among provinces.

In addition, some previous publications have studied the environmental benefits of inter-regional transmission from the regional perspective (see, e.g., Li *et al.* (2015), Davis (2015), and Peker *et al.* (2018)). Conlon *et al.* (2019) evaluated the contribution of transmission expansion to achieving increasing renewable generation targets in New York State's regional grid. Pean *et al.* (2016) measured the role of the France–Great Britain electricity interconnection in integrating variable renewable generation. Yi *et al.* (2019) analyzed the effects of inter-regional transmission on renewable energy deployment in China. Xiao *et al.* (2021) indicated that the cross-regional power transmission should be explicitly considered in the potential and possible decarbonization pathway for China's power sector up to 2030. Li *et al.* (2016) investigated the impact of the inter-regional transmission grid capacity expansion on China's power sector decarbonization. In contrast to previous studies, Quiroga *et al.* (2019) addressed the transmission expansion issue by jointly considering the distributive effects of emission policies in 13 regions of Chile. As far as we know, very few studies have estimated the distributional effect of the environmental benefits from inter-regional transmission.

The study of distributional effects of environmental implementations spans around four decades (Gonzalez, 2012). In the early stages, several studies across the world have been interested in the distributional effects of emissions taxing policy (Dissou and Siddiqui, 2014; Jorgenson *et al.*, 1992; Liang and Wei, 2012), energy subsidies (Giuliano *et al.*, 2020; Jiang *et al.*, 2015), energy tariffs (Krauss, 2016; Pearson and Smith, 1991), and so on. Later studies used different approaches to analyze policies such as carbon allowances, command and control environmental mandates, and CO_2 cap-and-trade (Burtraw *et al.*, 2009; Dinan and Rogers, 2002; Fullerton, 2017). There is still considerable debate on whether the environmental implementations are progressive or regressive. Meanwhile, among the points of contention is that it is unknown whether the construction of inter-regional transmission lines has effectively promoted renewable power generation and reduced CEs embodied in regional generation and consumption (Li *et al.*, 2016; Wang *et al.*, 2020). A topic rarely addressed in the literature, especially in China's power sector, is the distributional impact that the adoption of UHV lines would have on generation enterprises.

To sum up, even though many pieces of literature have measured the environmental and economic benefits of inter-regional transmission, they have all ignored the distributions of these benefits. Nevertheless, the vast majority of the results are achieved for the consumers. Comparatively, China is forwarding reforms on both the supply and demand sides to speed up renewable power development; it is necessary to investigate the possible distributional effects of environmental regulations on the power sector.

3. Methodology

This study employs the electricity market equilibrium model based on Limpaitoon *et al.* (2014) and Tan *et al.* (2020). An independent system operator (ISO), power producers, and consumers constitute the electricity market participants. A price-responsive inverse demand function represents the demand of power consumers.

The electricity supply side is assumed to be freely competitive; the notations involved are shown as follows. We let B denote the set of buses (or plants), $T_{\text{non-UHV}}$ represents the set of non-UHV transmission lines, while T_{UHV} is the set of UHV transmission lines. G represents the set of generation firms, the element of which is g; thus, B_g is the set of buses where power plants belonging to firm $g \in G$ are located. We let i and l be the elements in B and $T_{\text{non-UHV}}/T_{\text{UHV}}$, respectively. Let q_i denote the electricity output of plant i, the fuel cost of which is $C_i(q) = c_i q$, and let c_i be the parameter of unit fuel cost. The CEs produced by the power plant are represented by $E_i(q) = e_i q$, where e_i is the emission rate of plant i. Meanwhile, the power demand at bus i is given by $P_i(q) = a_i - b_i(q)$, where a_i and b_i are the parameters of the price-responsive inverse demand function. The total carbon emitted by the power generation is limited to M.

Subsequently, we develop an equilibrium model that contains all the Karush–Kuhn–Tucker (KKT) conditions of the optimization issues faced by all entities. The necessary conditions for a constrained local optimum are called the KKT conditions, which play a significant role in constrained optimization theory. For general convex problems, the KKT conditions could have been derived entirely from studying optimality via subgradients.

3.1. *The ISO issue*

In China, the State Grid Corporation of China and the Southern Grid are the only two large state-owned enterprises controlling the power transmission. We view these two enterprises as the ISO, intending to maximize social welfare. The optimization of the ISO is presented in the following.

3.1.1. *Optimization*

$$\max_{r_i: \forall i \in B} \sum_{i \in B} a_i(r_i + q_i) - b_i(r_i + q_i)^2/2 - C_i(q_i), \tag{1}$$

$$\text{s.t.} \sum_{i \in B} r_i = 0, \quad (\alpha), \tag{2}$$

$$-K_l^{\text{non-UHV}} \leq \sum_{i \in B} \text{PTDF}_{l,i} r_i \leq K_l^{\text{non-UHV}}, \quad (\lambda_l^-, \lambda_l^+), \; \forall l \in T_{\text{non-UHV}}, \tag{3}$$

$$-K_l^{\text{UHV}} \leq \sum_{i \in B} \text{PTDF}_{l,i} r_i \leq K_l^{\text{UHV}}, \quad (\omega_l^-, \omega_l^+), \; \forall l \in T_{\text{UHV}}, \; r_i + q_i \geq 0, \tag{4}$$

$$r_i + q_i \geq 0, \quad (\psi_i), \; \forall i \in B, \tag{5}$$

$$\sum_{i \in B} E_i(q_i) \leq M, \quad (\mu) \tag{6}$$

The ISO considers the power generation of each firm and then decides on the electricity dispatch of each bus to maximize social welfare (1), which is derived from the producer and consumer surpluses. Meanwhile, the ISO faces the following constraints: the total import/export of electricity in a lossless network is zero (2). The flow measured by the power transfer distribution factors (PTDFs) on each transmission line l is restricted to its thermal limit K_l. To the UHV transmission line, the limiting value is represented by (4), while the non-UHV transmission line is (3). Due to the characteristics of nonstorage, the power load in each node must be nonnegative (5), meaning that the net load in a node is at least 0. The total CEs are capped at M (6).

The KKT method is employed to solve the formulations in 3.1.1. The variables in parentheses next to the constraint are the corresponding Lagrange multipliers, and their economic implications are shown in Table 1.

3.1.2. *KKT conditions*

$$\pi_i = \sum_{l \in T_{\text{non-UHV}}} (\lambda_l^-, \lambda_l^+) \text{PTDF}_{l,i} + \sum_{l \in T_{\text{UHV}}} (\omega_l^+ - \omega_l^-) \text{PTDF}_{l,i} - \Psi_i, \quad \forall i \in B, \tag{7}$$

$$P_i(r_i + q_i) - \alpha - \pi = 0, \quad \forall i \in B, \tag{8}$$

Table 1. Variables explanations.

Variables	Mathematical implication	Economic implication
α	Lagrange multiplier corresponding to the lossless energy-balance constraint	System marginal energy cost or price at the reference market
λ_l^+, λ_l^-	Multiplier corresponding to the upper and lower transmission limits of non-UHV lines	Growth in social welfare induced by an increase in unit non-UHV transmission capacity
ω_l^-, ω_l^+	Multiplier corresponding to the upper and lower transmission limits of UHV lines	Growth in social welfare induced by an increase in unit UHV transmission capacity
ψ_i	Multiplier assigned to the non-negative constraint	The electricity is non-storable
π_i	Sum of difference in λ_l^+ and λ_l^-, ω_l^- and ω_l^+ over all the lines l weighted by the PTDF matrix minus ψ_i	Marginal congestion cost of transmission elements associated with i
μ	Multiplier assigned to the emission cap constraint	Price of carbon trading permits among energy producers
ρ_i^-, ρ_i^+	Multiplier assigned to operating limit	Growth in a firm's profit induced by the increase in unit operating capacity
β_g	Multiplier assigned to the residual demand constraint	Growth in a firm's profit induced by the increase in unit residual demand

$$\sum_{i \in B} r_i = 0, \qquad (9)$$

$$\lambda_l^- \left(\sum_{i \in B} \text{PTDF}_{l,i} r_i + K_l^{\text{non-UHV}} \right) = 0, \quad \lambda_l^- \geq 0, \ \forall l \in T_{\text{non-UHV}},$$

$$\lambda_l^+ \left(K_l^{\text{non-UHV}} - \sum_{i \in B} \text{PTDF}_{l,i} r_i \right) = 0, \quad \lambda_l^+ \geq 0, \ \forall l \in T_{\text{non-UHV}},$$

$$\omega_l^- \left(\sum_{i \in B} \text{PTDF}_{l,i} r_i + K_l^{\text{UHV}} \right) = 0, \quad \omega_l^- \geq 0, \ \forall l \in T_{\text{UHV}}$$

$$\omega_l^+ \left(K_l^{\text{UHV}} - \sum_{i \in B} \text{PTDF}_{l,l} r_i \right) = 0, \quad \omega_l^+ \geq 0, \ \forall l \in T_{\text{UHV}}$$

$$\psi_i (r_i + q_i) = 0, \quad \psi_i \geq 0, \ \forall i \in B,$$

$$\mu \left[M - \sum_{i \in B} E(q_j) \right] = 0, \quad \mu \geq 0.$$

3.2. Objective functions of the generation firms

A generation firm faces an optimization issue of determining the output for each plant to maximize its profit, as expressed in (10). The profit of producing one unit of electricity is $\alpha + \pi_i$, to a generation firm. It should accept the reference-price α and the locational congestion premiums π_i, which are determined by all the firms and the ISO, respectively.

The production cost is composed of two parts: the fuel costs and the emission reduction cost. We mainly simulated the power transaction between the ISO and generation firms, and the power transaction information is recorded in an hourly electricity market. From a short-term perspective, we did not consider the operational and fixed costs. The power generated should exceed the minimum operating limit ($\underline{q_i}$) and be below the maximum operating limit ($\bar{q_i}$) (see Eq. (11)). The firm views the sales from other producers as exogenous. Similarly, the KKT method solves 3.2.1, and the formulation in 3.2.2 is the KKT condition.

3.2.1. Optimization

$$\max_{q_i: i \in B_g, \alpha} \sum_{i \in B_g} (\alpha + \pi_i) q_i - C_i(q_i) - \mu E_i(q_i) \tag{10}$$

$$\text{s.t.} \quad \underline{q_i} \leq q_i \leq \bar{q_i}, \quad (\rho_i^-, \rho_i^+), \quad \forall i \in B_g, \tag{11}$$

$$\sum_{i \in B_g} q_i = \sum_{i \in B} \frac{a_i - (\alpha + \pi_i)}{b_i} - \sum_{i \in B/B_g} q_i, \quad (\beta_g). \tag{12}$$

3.2.2. KKT conditions

$$\alpha + \pi_i - \beta_g + \rho_i^- - \rho_i^+ - c_i - \mu e_i = 0, \quad \forall i \in B_g,$$

$$-\beta_g \sum_{i \in B} \frac{1}{b_i} + \sum_{i \in B_g} q_i = 0, \tag{13}$$

$$\sum_{i \in B} q_i = \sum_{i \in B} \frac{a_i - (\alpha + \pi_i)}{b_i}, \tag{14}$$

$$\rho_i^- (q_i - \underline{q_i}) = 0, \quad \rho_i^- \geq 0, \quad \forall i \in B_g,$$

$$\rho_i^+ (\bar{q_i} - q_i) = 0, \quad \rho_i^+ \geq 0, \quad \forall i \in B_g.$$

By combining the KKT conditions of the ISO and generation firms, we can obtain the equilibrium conditions of the market. Generally, these equilibrium conditions constitute a mixed nonlinear complementarity problem. The inverse demand functions, cost functions, and emissions functions are all assumed to be linear forms. Therefore, the market equilibrium would be a linear complementarity problem.

3.3. Data

This study collects the data of transmission lines with a voltage of 500 kVA and above in all the provincial administrative regions (PARs), excluding Hainan, Tibet, Hong Kong, Macao, and Taiwan for data deficiency. There are 249 lines in the non-UHV

Table 2. Descriptive statistics on the deciles.

Decile	1	2	3	4	5	6	7	8	9	10
Average (MW)	1174.4084	1378.1776	1619.5995	2424.7914	2875.7455	3508.7678	4436.7867	5583.0216	8430.4861	16,946.5604
Median (MW)	1265.0774	1387.8141	1530.6297	2472.3317	2845.4188	3488.1308	4509.1855	5559.9450	8255.4813	13,904.1149
Min (MW)	936.4604	1328.5023	1416.5590	2108.4623	2658.0277	3238.9537	3868.2245	5120.5910	6485.0194	10,741.5614
Max (MW)	1324.6261	1409.1650	2071.8953	2657.0045	3221.1420	3821.9401	5073.9506	6399.6000	10,172.1394	36,353.3634
Number	19	19	20	19	20	19	20	19	20	19
Standard deviation	155.8556	25.3611	216.4501	205.0602	189.8558	162.2325	365.4160	424.8379	1163.2595	6546.3170

framework, while 21 more UHV power transmission lines are considered in the 21-UHV framework, increasing the number of transmission lines to 270. Furthermore, we simulate another transmission framework that considers 26 UHV lines[3] (thus, a 26-UHV framework), and then the total number of transmission lines is 275.

The simulation of the electricity market is carried out within an hourly range. Our datasets include all the physical power plants with an installed capacity of over 100 MW distributed across 29 PARs, which belong to 39 generation groups (see Table A.2 for details). The CO_2 emission coefficient of the thermal power plants[4] refers to the guide for calculating CEs from raw coal edited by the Intergovernmental Panel on Climate Change (IPCC). Meanwhile, we deem that clean power does not produce CO_2. Since most power plants have a similar characteristic, we finally integrated them into 194 power plants (nodes in our equilibrium model). For estimating the distributional effect of UHV lines on the generation side, installed capacity was used to split the 194 power plants into 10 deciles $h, h \in \{1, 2, 3, 4, 5, 6, 7, 8, 9, 10\}$. For example, there are 19 representative power plants in decile 1 (see Table 2 for details).

3.4. *Measurement of the Lorenz curve*

This study used a Lorenz curve of the cumulative CEs or producer surplus (PS) distribution by decile h to reflect the distribution of the environmental or economic benefits induced by UHV lines.

Environmental Lorenz curve (ENLC):

$$\text{ENLC}_h = \frac{\sum_1^h \text{CE}_h}{\sum_1^{10} \text{CE}_h}, \quad h \in \{1, 2, 3, 4, 5, 6, 7, 8, 9, 10\}.$$

Economic Lorenz curve (ECLC):

$$\text{ECLC}_h = \frac{\sum_1^h \text{PS}_h}{\sum_1^{10} \text{PS}_h}, \quad h \in \{1, 2, 3, 4, 5, 6, 7, 8, 9, 10\}.$$

The Lorenz curve of CE or PS is then depicted by linking the dispersive point "ENLC_h" or "ECLC_h" together, as shown in Sec. 4.

4. Results and Discussion

4.1. *Analysis of the changes of regional power deployment*

This paper simulates the impact of UHV transmission line construction on power deployment in different PARs under three different load scenarios. We also compare the impact in 2015 and 2018. The power import/export changes in different PARs

---

[3]Based on the transmission framework with 21 UHV lines, we take five more UHV lines into consideration. They are the Chu-Sui ±800 kV UHV DC line, Pu-Qiao ±800 kV UHV DC line, Xin-Dong ±800 kV UHV DC line, Kun-Liu-Long ±800 kV UHV DC line, and Qinghai-Henan ±800 kV UHV DC line. See more details in Table A.1.

[4]The cost of fuel comes from the annual average price of raw coal (5000 calories) of Qinhuangdao Thermal Coal Market for each province in 2015 when the study was conducted, and the annual average price is obtained by weighted averages of the monthly traded price of raw coal.

The Distributional Effect of Inter-Regional Transmission 77

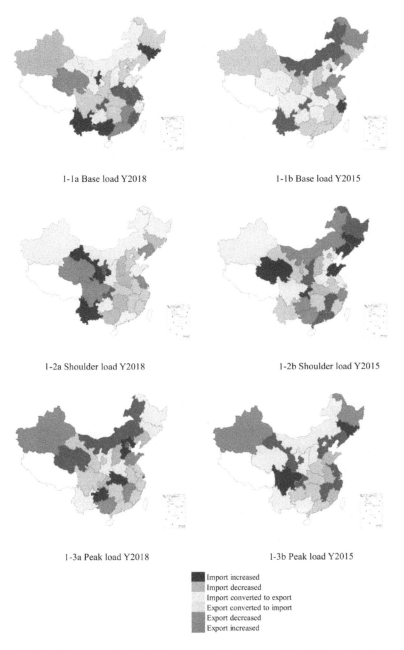

Figure 1. The changes of regional power deployment under different load scenarios.

include six situations after introducing 21 UHV lines, which essentially represent six kinds of effects of the UHV lines on regional power deployment[5] (Fig. 1).

---

[5]Take the "import increased" for example, it means that the corresponding PAR imports more power from other PARs after introducing 21 UHV lines. Similarly, the "import converted to export" means that the PAR imports power in the non-UHV transmission framework, but exports power to other PARs under the 21-UHV transmission framework.

In 2018, under the base load scenario, the introduction of UHV lines meant that the PARs transferred from importing power to exporting power are mainly located in the north of China. On the contrary, those PARs transferred from export to import are mainly located in central China. In addition, east and central China have increased power export, while some southern PARs have decreased power export, such as Guangdong, which even increased its power import. Most PARs, mainly concentrated in the "three North" (Northeast, North, and Northwest), have realized the transformation from importing power to exporting power under the shoulder load scenario. At the same time, PARs in southeastern China all changed from exporting electricity to importing electricity. It is worth noting that the power imported to Gansu and Yunnan both increased, while Ningxia and Chongqing increased their export. In the peak load scenario, the southeast coastal PARs of China have changed from exporting power to importing power.

Central China began to export power in 2015 after introducing UHV lines under the base load scenario, and only Tianjin and Zhejiang increased their power importing. Under the shoulder load scenario, those PARs changing from importing power to exporting power mainly lie in North China, and the power deployment in Inner Mongolia and Southwest China decreased. When it comes to the peak load, the power transmitted from the PARs in northwest and Southwest China to Central and Southern China decreases, and the inter-regional power transmission decreases significantly. Besides, the PARs around the coastal region seem to react consistently to the construction of the UHV lines.

Next, we select several typical situations, "import increased," "import converted to export," "export converted to import," "export increased," to explore the spatial movement under different load levels in 2018 and 2015. In 2018 and 2015, the spatial distribution of "import increased" is quite different under different load levels. On the contrary, the spatial distribution of "import converted to export" is almost unchanged in 2018, and some PARs that change to this situation are only within the same region. While in 2015, the spatial distribution of "import converted to export" suffered a noticeable change. It is impressive to note that the "export converted to import" gradually moves from central to east China in 2018, implying that UHV lines significantly increase the power importing in the eastern region when the power consumption is at the peak load. However, the spatial distribution of "export converted to import" shows a distinct change in 2015, gradually moving toward the center. Simultaneously, the UHV lines significantly increased the power exporting in the north in 2018 and 2015, which can be seen from the movement of the spatial distribution of "export increased."

4.2. *The distribution of carbon emissions from the generation side*

This study has simulated the electricity market equilibrium under three load scenarios. It further employs the Lorenz curve to depict the distribution of CEs generated by the power plants over the 10 deciles, taking the 21-UHV transmission framework as an example. Figure 2 indicates that the CE of all deciles could be divided into high,

The Distributional Effect of Inter-Regional Transmission 79

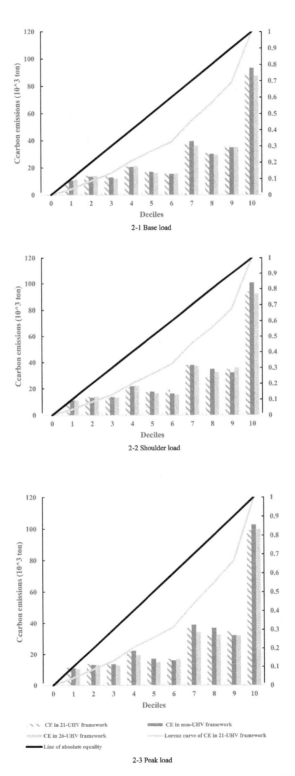

Figure 2. The distribution of carbon emissions over the deciles under different load scenarios.

medium, and low levels under the base, shoulder, and peak load scenarios. Among them, the CE of the power plants in deciles 1–6 is relatively low, the cumulative emissions of these six deciles are about 40%, and the gap between the Lorenz curve and the 45° line shows a growing larger trend. The CE of the power plants in deciles 7–9 increases significantly, and their cumulative emission is equivalent to the first six deciles. The gap between the Lorenz curve and the 45° line is narrowing. The CE of decile 10 accounts for 20% of the total, and the slope of the Lorenz curve increases sharply.

In general, the distribution effect caused by the UHV transmission lines on CEs changes very little as the load fluctuates. The inflection points of the Lorenz curve appear in deciles 6 and 9 under all three scenarios. The uneven distribution of CEs mainly occurs among deciles 1–6. A large installed capacity always leads to more emissions; the CEs almost distribute evenly in the later four deciles, and the Lorenz curve is closer to the 45° line. In addition, we have also compared the total CEs of each decile under the 21-UHV, 26-UHV, and non-UHV transmission frameworks. The results indicate that the UHV transmission line reduces the emissions of power plants with big installed capacities. At the same time, a regressive effect appears for power plants with medium or low installed capacities. Although the power plants in the same decile have similar installed capacities, they may differ significantly in their heterogeneity factors, such as technology, emission level, and geographical location. This results in a thoroughly different effect on reducing emissions caused by UHV transmission line construction. In the following section, the shoulder load scenario is taken as an example to analyze this emission reduction effect distribution within the decile.

After introducing the 21 UHV lines to the transmission framework, we classify the power plants into three groups according to the proportion of CE changes,[6] namely: (1) the plants with emissions decreased; (2) the plants with emissions increased between 0 and 50%; and (3) the plants with emissions increased more than 50%. The latter analysis takes the shoulder load as an example to investigate the proportion of power plants belonging to the above three groups in each decile.

Figure 3 indicates that the power plants witnessing an emission increase between 0 and 0.5 account for almost 50% in each decile. Especially for decile 9, nearly 90% of the power plants lie in the second group. At the same time, we should also note that the power plants with emission increases of more than 50% have the lowest proportion, which is nearly zero for deciles 3, 4, and 8. Besides these, the proportion of power plants with less than 50% emission reduction in low-level deciles is significantly higher than those in high-level deciles.

The shape of the Lorenz curve can also explain the distribution effect to some extent. It is described as "effect neutrality" when the changing rate of the decile's whole emissions is zero. The regressive and progressive effects of UHV lines on

---

[6]Since there are three different transmission frameworks considered in this study, we compare the CE between the non-UHV transmission framework and 21-UHV transmission framework, which is calculated by: $(CE_{21\text{-UHV}} - CE_{non\text{-UHV}})/CE_{non\text{-UHV}}$.

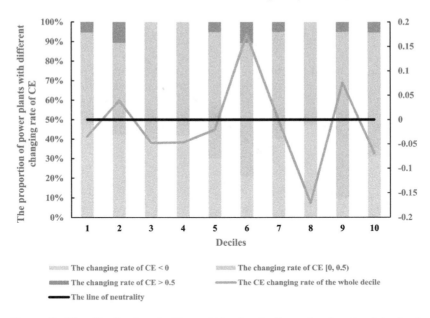

Figure 3. The distributional effect within the decile under the shoulder load.

reducing CEs within the decile are neutralized under this situation. That is to say, the CEs increased by a certain amount of power plants are equivalent to the CEs reduced by others within the decile, resulting in no emission changes. The closer the changing rate of a decile is to the "zero-point line" (neutrality line[7]), the higher the degree of neutrality within the decile, and vice versa.

Figure 3 also shows that the neutrality degree of decile 7 is the highest, and those of deciles 6 and 8 are the lowest. The proportion of emission changes in deciles 1–5 is close to the neutrality line, while most are below. Considering the proportions of emission changes, the neutrality degree of one decile will be significantly higher than the neutrality line if the power plants reduce emissions to less than 20%. The neutrality degree of the decile will be lower than the neutrality line if the power plants reduce emissions by more than 40%. However, it is hard to conclude that the distributional effect of UHV transmission lines on reducing CEs is related to the neutrality for power plants with different installed capacities.

4.3. *The distribution of producer surplus from the generation side*

In addition to environmental benefits, UHV lines will also bring economic benefits to power plants. The following section measures the distribution of PS among groups with different transmission cases: the non-UHV framework, 21-UHV framework, and 26-UHV framework. As shown in Fig. 4, the introduction of the UHV line flattens the

---

[7]In this study, we explain the "neutrality line" by: (1) the effect of the inter-regional transmission lines is regressive to this decile on carbon reduction if the changing rate of emissions in a decile is higher than the neutrality line; (2) the effect is progressive if the changing rate of emissions is lower than the neutrality line.

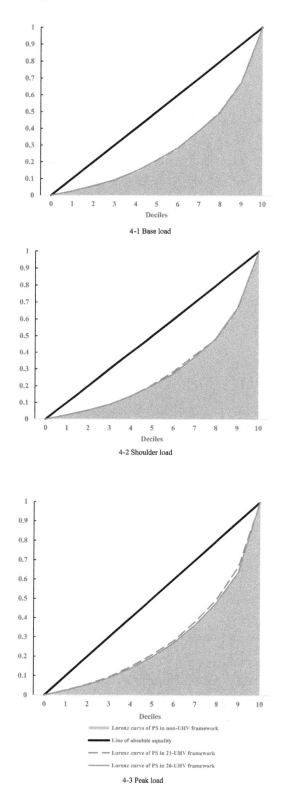

Figure 4. The distribution of producer surplus over the deciles under different load scenarios.

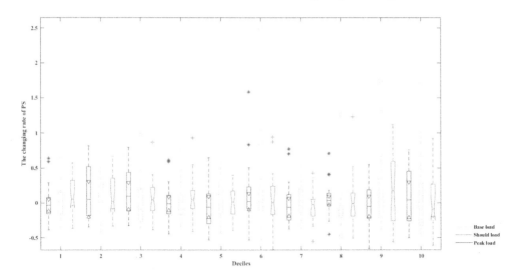

Figure 5. The box-plot of the changing rate of producer surplus.

distribution of PS. Compared with the distribution of PS under the non-UHV framework, the Lorenz curve is closer to the 45° line with the introduction of UHV lines. Especially in the peak load scenario, the Lorenz curve of PS shrinks toward the 45° line after introducing the UHV lines into the transmission framework. However, more UHV lines may not always contribute much to an equal distribution of PS. Under the base and shoulder load, there is no apparent difference between the Lorenz curve of the 21-UHV and 26-UHV frameworks. Even in the peak load, this distributional effect of UHV lines is regressive since the Lorenz curve of the 21-UHV framework is closer to the 45° line than that of the 26-UHV framework.

Nevertheless, the inflection points of the Lorenz curves drawn from these three transmission frameworks are almost the same under different loads. They appear in deciles 6, 8, and 9, respectively. Deciles 1–6 share 30% of the total PS, deciles 8 and 9 possess about 30% of the total PS, and the slope of the Lorenz curve is steeper. The power plants with a high-level installed capacity share 50% of the PS. The progress of the UHV lines on the distribution of PS mainly acts on the power plants with smaller installed capacity.

As mentioned above, the impact of UHV lines on the PS of each power plant within a decile is also distributive. We compare the changing rate[8] of PS of power plants between the non-UHV framework and 21-UHV framework, and draw a box chart of the changing rate, as shown in Fig. 5.

The changes in PS in different deciles are mainly concentrated in -0.2 to $+0.2$ under the base load. In particular, the changes in PS are relatively scattered for deciles 2, 3, and 10. Comparatively, the distribution of the changing rate is concentrated for

---

[8]Similar to the distributional effect on CEs, the changing rate of PS is calculated using $(PS_{21-UHV} - PS_{non-UHV})/PS_{non-UHV}$.

medium and small power plants under the shoulder load, but there is a considerable gap among them. Generally speaking, the power plants located in the middle deciles change very little under the peak load, even though the first and last deciles show different trends.

In general, the proportion of power plants with increased PS under the shoulder load is high, especially for deciles 5, 6, and 7. Meanwhile, the power plants suffering decreased PS of these three deciles account for half under the peak load. On the other hand, the median of most of the deciles is higher than 0, which indicates that UHV lines will lift the PS of at least half of the power plants. It is worth noting that almost all the outliers in the box chart are located in decile 6, which gains the highest PS increase, while the lowest declines appear in decile 8.

4.4. *Discussion*

In terms of the differences among regional power deployments in 2018, the distributional effect caused by UHV lines has almost no differences under the base load and shoulder load, especially in regions such as Northern, Central, and Eastern China. Given the response to the UHV lines, the reversal of power deployment mainly appears in the developed southeast coastal regions in the case of peak load. The expansion of the transmission corridor benefits these areas in meeting the rapidly growing power demand. Comparatively, Qinghai, Inner Mongolia, and Yunnan are rich in clean energy, increasing the power export. The provinces of Northeastern and Northern China that are rich in coal-fired power increase the thermal power export. Xiao *et al.* (2021) stated that it is necessary to build and perfect the UHV transmission lines while the local governments encourage renewable energy development.

This study has also compared the effect of UHV lines in reducing CEs in 2015 and 2018. Our previous research, Tan *et al.* (2020), clearly stated the results of 2015 in detail. Compared to those results, the emission reduction effect caused by the introduction of UHV lines was improved in 2018. The improvement is outstanding under the shoulder load scenario, especially for power plants with low installed capacity. Nevertheless, the UHV lines mainly benefit middle- and high-scale power plants to reduce CEs under the peak load scenario. Those low-level installed plants are instead impeded. It is worth noting that the effect of UHV lines seems to be limited under the base load scenario; carbon pollution emitted by the power plants with different installed capacities tends to be increasing. From the intertemporal perspective, the effect of UHV lines on reducing CEs is progressive. Meanwhile, Zhang and Chen (2020) indicated that the low-carbon transition would increase not only interprovincial electricity transmission but also the transmission distance.

This study measures the CEs of power plants with different installed capacities based on the transmission framework, including UHV lines, and estimates the environmental distributional effect of UHV lines with reference to the Lorenz curve. The CEs are not evenly distributed among power plants under all the scenarios. About 40%

of the power plants generate 60% of the CEs, while those small- and medium-sized power plants emit less. This enlightens us that large power plants are the key to reducing emissions for the generation sector. The heterogeneity of power plants in different deciles would be the significant factor affecting the effect of UHV lines in reducing emissions. In terms of the coordination between the power grid and generation, the power mix adjustment is an appreciated way to take advantage of UHV lines. Also, Kasina and Hobbs (2020) prove that cooperation is important among transmission planners.

The distributional effect of PS change caused by the construction of UHV transmission lines among power plants is not easily affected by load floatation. Compared with the non-UHV transmission framework, the PS is more evenly distributed among power plants after introducing the UHV lines. Although the UHV lines promote the inter-regional flow of electricity and competition in the electricity market, which has little progressive effect on the distribution of benefits, more UHV lines may induce more inequalities. Besides, the aggravation of competition only occurs among the middle- and low-level installed power plants and the high-level installed power plants still hold a high proportion of PS. Thus, the construction of UHV lines has not driven and activated competition among high-level installed power plants.

Therefore, this paper shows that the distributional effect of UHV lines is limited. Even within the decile, the economic benefits caused by UHV lines may be regressive. Among the 10 deciles, there is a significant gap in PS change within the same decile, especially for the peak load scenario. Compared with clean power, the marginal cost of thermal power that is more stable will decrease when the electricity demand increases sharply. Then its outputs increase, inducing a more significant economic benefit.

5. Conclusions

This paper analyzed the distribution effect of inter-regional transmission network expansion from the perspectives of power deployment, CE, and PS. It explored the influence of heterogeneity factors of power plants, such as installed capacity differences, on the distributional effect. This study not only benefits evaluation of the effectiveness of market-oriented reform on China's power sector objectively and scientifically, but also helps to analyze the environmental and economic benefits of China's inter-regional transmission network. The main conclusions are as follows.

First, the distribution effect of the UHV transmission line has decreased to a great extent. On the one hand, the energy resource bases exported less power than expected, especially for the areas with abundant clean energy. On the other hand, the power plant with a large installed capacity can easily gain more PS while producing intensified pollution. China's economic growth model has not been fundamentally changed; it is still at the cost of losing environmental benefits even though the correlation between them has been lessened. Besides, monetization could be an excellent tool to standardize the economic and environmental benefits for the power plants with different types of technology.

Second, the environmental and economic distribution effect of the UHV transmission network was not sensitive to load changes. The introduction of UHV lines led to a more uniform distribution of economic benefits among regions when the power market reached equilibrium. Still, the revenue of thermal power plants increased faster than other kinds of generation forms. Compared to the considerable investment in the construction stage, it is hard to conclude that the UHV line construction has successfully boosted clean power development and produced more social welfare.

Finally, even though the introduction of UHV lines has broadened the chances for inter-regional power transmission, it did not fundamentally intensify the competition in China's power market. Medium and small power plants may face competition, while the generators with a large installed share can easily profit. Therefore, one of the critical works in regulating China's power industry is to optimize the power mix and accelerate the generation technology progress of the big generators sector.

Despite the innovative work in evaluating the distribution effect of inter-regional transmission network expansion represented by UHV lines on environmental and economic benefits from the perspective of regional differences and generation, this paper still has room to improve, such as in the neglect of heterogeneities that existed among regions and generation forms. In addition, the distribution effect analysis is fundamentally based on qualitative analysis; multi-dimensional analysis on economic, social, and environmental analysis may obtain more valuable conclusions when conducting quantitative research on the effectiveness of inter-regional transmission network expansion. Furthermore, besides analyzing different kinds of power plants, more classification methods can be employed to conduct further analysis.

Acknowledgments

We would like to express our sincere gratitude to the editor and reviewers for their positive comments, and insightful and detailed suggestions on the original paper. We appreciate the financial support from the National Natural Science Foundation of China under Grant Nos. 71874121, 71671121, and 71431005, the support from National Key R&D Programme of China under Grant No. 2018YFC0704400, the support from Major Projects of the National Social Science Fund under Grant No. 17ZDA065. We are very grateful for the advice of Professor Yihsu Chen of University of California, Santa Cruz for our earlier draft.

Appendix A

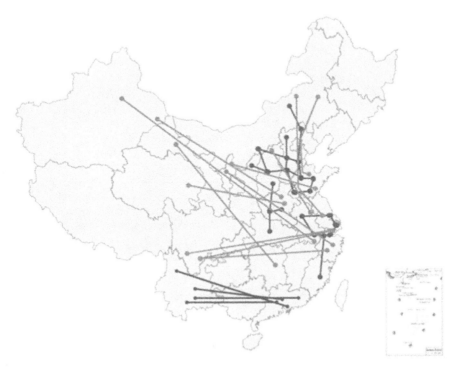

Figure A.1. The UHV power transmission lines in China.

Table A.1. Ultra-high voltage power transmission lines.

Number	UHV lines	AC/DC	Voltage grade (kV)
1	Jinping–Sunan	DC	800
2	Huainan-Zhebei	AC	1000
3	Zhebei-Shanghai	AC	1000
4	Haminan-Zhengzhou	DC	800
5	Zhebei-Fuzhou	AC	1000
6	Huainan-Nanjing	AC	1000
7	Nanjing-Shanghai	AC	1000
8	Ximeng-Shandong	AC	1000
9	Ningdong-Zhejiang	DC	800
10	Mengxi-Tianjinnan	AC	1000
11	Yuheng-Weifang	AC	1000
12	Jiuquan-Hunan	DC	800
13	Jinbei-Jiangsu	DC	800
14	Ximeng-Taizhou	DC	800
15	Shanghaimiao-Shandong	DC	800
16	Zhundong-Wannan	DC	1100
17	Ximeng-Shengli	AC	1000

Table A.1. (*Continued*)

Number	UHV lines	AC/DC	Voltage grade (kV)
18	Zhalute-Qingzhou	DC	800
19	Beijingxi-Shijiazhuang	AC	1000
20	Weifang- Shijiazhuang	AC	1000
21	Mengxi-Jinzhong	AC	1000
22	Qinghai-Henan	DC	800
23	Chuxiong-Guangzhou	DC	800
24	Puer-Jiangmen	DC	800
25	Dali-Shenzhen	DC	800
26	Kunbei-Longmen	DC	800

Notes: Among all the UHV transmission lines listed here, the number 1–21 lines are considered in the "21-UHV framework" and number 1–26 lines are considered in the "26-UHV framework".

Table A.2. The abbreviation of each PAR.

Abbreviation	PARs
AH	Anhui
BJ	Beijing
CQ	Chongqing
FJ	Fujian
GS	Gansu
GD	Guangdong
GX	Guangxi
GZ	Guizhou
HEB	Hebei
HEN	Henan
HLJ	Heilongjiang
HUB	Hubei
HUN	Hunan
JL	Jilin
JS	Jiangsu
JX	Jiangxi
LN	Liaoning
MD	Inner Mongolia East
MX	Inner Mongolia West
MW	Shanxi
NX	Ningxia
QH	Qinghai
SD	Shandong
SX	Shaanxi
SH	Shanghai
SC	Sichuan

Table A.2. (*Continued*)

Abbreviation	PARs
TJ	Tianjin
XJ	Xinjiang
YN	Yunnan
ZJ	Zhejiang

Notes: We assume that each of them has a local power generation group, which constitute 30 of the total 39, and the remaining nine groups are: China Datang Corporation, China Huaneng Corporation, China Huadian Corporation, China Energy Investment Corporation, State Power Investment Corporation Limited, Guohua Group Corporation Ltd., Huarun Group Corporation Ltd., China General Nuclear Power Group, Three Gorges Group.

References

Baumol, WJ and WE Oates (1988). *The Theory of Environmental Policy*. Cambridge, UK: Cambridge University Press. Available at https://doi.org/10.1007/BF01718957.

Bird, L *et al*. (2016). Wind and solar energy curtailment: A review of international experience. *Renewable and Sustainable Energy Reviews*, 65, 577–586. Available at https://doi.org/10.1016/j.rser.2016.06.082.

Brinkerink, M *et al*. (2019). A comprehensive review on the benefits and challenges of global power grids and intercontinental interconnectors. *Renewable and Sustainable Energy Reviews*, 107, 274–287. Available at https://doi.org/10.1016/j.rser.2019.03.003.

Burgholzer, B and H Auer (2016). Cost/benefit analysis of transmission grid expansion to enable further integration of renewable electricity generation in Austria. *Renewable Energy*, 97, 189–196. Available at https://doi.org/10.1016/j.renene.2016.05.073.

Burtraw, D *et al*. (2009). The incidence of U.S. climate policy: Alternative uses of revenues from a cap-and-trade auction. *National Tax Journal*, 62, 1–16. Available at http://doi=10.1.1.168.4787&rep=rep1&type=pdf.

Chen, YK *et al*. (2020). The role of cross-border power transmission in a renewable-rich power system — A model analysis for Northwestern Europe. *Journal of Environmental Management*, 261, 110194. Available at https://doi.org/10.1016/j.jenvman.2020.110194.

Conlon, T *et al*. (2019). Assessing new transmission and energy storage in achieving increasing renewable generation targets in a regional grid. *Applied Energy*, 250, 1085–1098. Available at https://doi.org/10.1016/j.apenergy.2019.05.066.

Davis, S (2015). Renewable electricity generation and transmission expansion: A federal, state or regional approach?. *The Electricity Journal*, 28, 28–35. Available at https://doi.org/10.1016/j.tej.2015.04.005.

DePaula, G (2020). The distributional effect of climate change on agriculture: Evidence from a Ricardian quantile analysis of Brazilian census data. *Journal of Environmental Economics and Management*, 104, 102378. Available at https://doi.org/10.1016/j.jeem.2020.102378.

Dinan, T and DL Rogers (2002). Distributional effects of carbon allowance trading: How government decisions determine winners and losers. *National Tax Journal*, 55, 199–221. Available at https://www.mendeley.com/catalogue/89cfa5eb-83e4-3c30-a1f2-6b96ca0dd46e/.

Dissou, Y and MS Siddiqui (2014). Can carbon taxes be progressive?. *Energy Economics*, 42, 88–100. Available at https://doi.org/10.1016/j.eneco.2013.11.010.

Duan, H *et al.* (2018). Achieving China's energy and climate policy targets in 2030 under multiple uncertainties. *Energy Economics*, 70, 45–60. Available at https://doi.org/10.1016/j.eneco.2017.12.022.

ENTSO-E (2014). 10 Year network development plan 2014. Brussels.

Fullerton, D (2017). *Distributional Effects of Environmental and Energy Policy*. Routledge. Available at https://www.nber.org/papers/w14241.

Giuliano, F *et al.* (2020). Distributional effects of reducing energy subsidies: Evidence from recent policy reform in Argentina. *Energy Economics*, 92, 104980. Available at https://doi.org/10.1016/j.eneco.2020.104980.

Gonzalez, F (2012). Distributional effects of carbon taxes: The case of Mexico. *Energy Economics*, 34, 2102–2115. Available at https://doi.org/10.1016/j.eneco.2012.03.007.

Hsiang, S *et al.* (2018). The distribution of environmental damages. Working Paper, National Bureau of Economic Research. Available at https://www.nber.org/papers/w23882.

Inter-American Development Bank (2013). Energy integration in Central America: Full steam ahead. Available at https://en/news/energy-integration-central-america-full-steam-ahead.

International Energy Agency (2020). CO_2 emissions by sector. Paris. Available at http://www.iea.org/bookshop/757-CO752_Emissions_from_Fuel_Combustion_2017.

Jafari, A *et al.* (2020). Optimal integration of renewable energy sources, diesel generators, and demand response program from pollution, financial, and reliability viewpoints: A multi-objective approach. *Journal of Cleaner Production*, 247. Available at https://doi.org/10.1016/j.jclepro.2019.119100.

Jiang, Z *et al.* (2015). The distributional impacts of removing energy subsidies in China. *China Economic Review*, 33, 111–122. Available at https://doi.org/10.1016/j.chieco.2015.01.012.

Jorgenson, D *et al.* (1992). Carbon taxes and economic welfare. Available at https://ideas.repec.org/r/fth/harver/1589.html.

Kasina, S and BF Hobbs (2020). The value of cooperation in interregional transmission planning: A noncooperative equilibrium model approach. *European Journal of Operational Research*, 285, 740–752. Available at https://doi.org/10.1016/j.ejor.2020.02.018.

Krauss, A (2016). How natural gas tariff increases can influence poverty: Results, measurement constraints and bias. *Energy Economics*, 60, 244–254. Available at https://doi.org/10.1016/j.eneco.2016.09.010.

Li, T *et al.* (2019). Quantify cross provincial power transmission barriers in China. *Energy Procedia*, 158, 465–470. Available at https://doi.org/10.1016/j.egypro.2019.01.136.

Li, X *et al.* (2015). The dynamics of electricity grid operation with increasing renewables and the path toward maximum renewable deployment. *Renewable and Sustainable Energy Reviews*, 47, 1007–1015. Available at https://doi.org/10.1016/j.rser.2015.03.039.

Li, Y *et al.* (2016). The impact of inter-regional transmission grid expansion on China's power sector decarbonization. *Applied Energy*, 183, 853–873. Available at https://doi.org/10.1016/j.apenergy.2016.09.006.

Li, Y and Y Wei (2021). Estimating the potential CO_2 emission reduction in 97 contracting countries of the Paris agreement. *Climate Change Economics*, 12, 2150004.

Liang, QM and YM Wei (2012). Distributional impacts of taxing carbon in China: Results from the CEEPA model. *Applied Energy*, 92, 545–551. Available at https://doi.org/10.1016/j.apenergy.2011.10.036.

Limpaitoon, T *et al.* (2014). The impact of imperfect competition in emission permits trading on oligopolistic electricity markets. *Energy Journal*, 35, 145–168. Available at https://doi.org/10.5547/01956574.35.3.7.

Lin, B and W Wu (2017). Cost of long distance electricity transmission in China. *Energy Policy*, 109, 132–140. Available at https://doi.org/10.1016/j.enpol.2017.06.055.

Liu, Z (2013). *Ultra-High Voltage AC&DC Grid*. Beijing: China Electric Power Press (in Chinese). Available at https://doi.org/10.1016/B978-0-12-802161-3.00005-6.

Moore, JC et al. (2016). Will China be the first to initiate climate engineering?. *Earth's Future*, 4, 588–595. Available at https://doi.org/10.1002/2016EF000402.

Otsuki, T et al. (2016). Electric power grid interconnections in Northeast Asia: A quantitative analysis of opportunities and challenges. *Energy Policy*, 89, 311–329. Available at https://doi.org/10.1016/j.enpol.2015.11.021.

Pean, E et al. (2016). Role of the GB-France electricity interconnectors in integration of variable renewable generation. *Renewable Energy*, 99, 307–314. Available at https://doi.org/10.1016/j.renene.2016.06.057.

Pearson, M and S Smith (1991). The European carbon tax: An assessment of the European commission's proposal. Available at https://core.ac.uk/reader/1686140.

Peker, M et al. (2018). Benefits of transmission switching and energy storage in power systems with high renewable energy penetration. *Applied Energy*, 228, 1182–1197. Available at https://doi.org/10.1016/j.apenergy.2018.07.008.

Puka, L and K Szulecki (2014). The politics and economics of cross-border electricity infrastructure: A framework for analysis. *Energy Research & Social Science*, 4, 124–134. Available at https://doi.org/10.1016/j.erss.2014.10.003.

Qi, S et al. (2020). The effective benchmark selection model and simulation in the power sector of China's ETS. *Climate Change Economics*, 11, 2041006. Available at https://doi.org/10.1142/S2010007820410006672041006-1.

Quiroga, D et al. (2019). Power system expansion planning under global and local emission mitigation policies. *Applied Energy*, 239, 1250–1264. Available at https://doi.org/10.1016/j.apenergy.2019.02.001.

Qureshi, MI et al. (2016). Energy crisis, greenhouse gas emissions and sectoral growth reforms: Repairing the fabricated mosaic. *Journal of Cleaner Production*, 112, 3657–3666. Available at https://doi.org/10.1016/j.jclepro.2015.08.017.

Rausch, S et al. (2011). Distributional impacts of carbon pricing: A general equilibrium approach with micro-data for households. *Energy Economics*, 33, 20–33. Available at https://doi.org/10.1016/j.eneco.2011.07.023.

Tan, X et al. (2020). Has the inter-regional transmission grid promoted clean power development? A quantitative assessment on China's electricity sector. *Journal of Cleaner Production*, 269. Available at https://doi.org/10.1016/j.jclepro.2020.122370.

USGAO (1983). Siting of hazardous waste landfills and their correlation with racial and economic status of surrounding communities. General Accounting Office, GAOfRCED-83-168, Washington, DC, US. Available at https://www.gao.gov/products/rced-83-168.

Wang, Y et al. (2020). Can remotely delivered electricity really alleviate smog? An assessment of China's use of ultra-high voltage transmission for air pollution prevention and control. *Journal of Cleaner Production*, 242. Available at https://doi.org/10.1016/j.jclepro.2019.118430.

Wei, W et al. (2020). Unbalanced economic benefits and the electricity-related carbon emissions embodied in China's interprovincial trade. *Journal of Environmental Management*, 263, 110390. Available at https://doi.org/10.1016/j.jenvman.2020.110390.

Wei, W et al. (2017). Regional study on investment for transmission infrastructure in China based on the state grid data. *Frontiers of Earth Science*, 11, 162–183. Available at https://doi.org/10.1007/s11707-016-0581-4.

Wu, CF *et al.* (2019). The nexus of electricity and economic growth in major economies: The United States-India-China triangle. *Energy*, 188. Available at https://doi.org/10.1016/j.energy.2019.116006.

Xiao, J *et al.* (2021). Decarbonizing China's power sector by 2030 with consideration of technological progress and cross-regional power transmission. *Energy Policy*, 150. Available at https://doi.org/10.1016/j.enpol.2021.112150.

Xu, JH *et al.* (2020). Economic viability and regulation effects of infrastructure investments for inter-regional electricity transmission and trade in China. *Energy Economics*, 91. Available at https://doi.org/10.1016/j.eneco.2020.104890.

Yi, BW *et al.* (2019). The spatial deployment of renewable energy based on China's coal-heavy generation mix and inter-regional transmission grid. *The Energy Journal*, 40. Available at https://doi.org/10.5547/01956574.40.4.bwyi.

Zhang, Q and W Chen (2020). Modeling China's interprovincial electricity transmission under low carbon transition. *Applied Energy*, 279. Available at https://doi.org/10.1016/j.apenergy.2020.115571.

Zhang, Y *et al.* (2018). A multi-regional energy transport and structure model for China's electricity system. *Energy*, 161, 907–919. Available at https://doi.org/10.1016/j.energy.2018.07.133.

Zheng, J *et al.* (2021). Limiting global warming to below 1.5°C from 2°C: An energy-system-based multi-model analysis for China. *Energy Economics*, 100. Available at https://doi.org/10.1016/j.eneco.2021.105355.

© 2025 World Scientific Publishing Company
https://doi.org/10.1142/9789819812264_0005

ASSESSING STRATEGIES FOR REDUCING THE CARBON FOOTPRINT OF TEXTILE PRODUCTS IN CHINA UNDER THE SHARED SOCIOECONOMIC PATHWAYS FRAMEWORK[||]

SI-YU PENG[*], JING-YU LIU[*,†,¶] and YONG GENG[*,†,‡,§]

[*]*School of Environmental Science and Engineering,*
Shanghai Jiaotong University,
800 Dongchuan Road Shanghai 200240, P. R. China

[†]*Shanghai Institute of Pollution Control and Ecological Security,*
Shanghai 200092, P. R. China

[‡]*School of International and Public Affairs,*
Shanghai Jiao Tong University, Shanghai 200030, P. R. China

[§]*School of Business, Shandong University,*
Weihai 264209, P. R. China
[¶]*liu.jingyu@sjtu.edu.cn*

To realize China's target of carbon neutrality by 2060, the country's domestic textile industry faces tremendous pressure to reduce emissions. We assessed the potential of socioeconomic conditions and climate policies for reducing the greenhouse gas (GHG) emissions of textile products in China up to 2050 using a life cycle assessment (LCA) approach and integrated assessment model (IAM) within the Shared Socioeconomic Pathways (SSP) framework. The results showed that a combination of socioeconomic conditions and climate policies can reduce annual carbon emissions by 89.0% and reduce accumulate emissions by 34.3% by 2050. Among the strategies examined in this study, energy decarbonization and power conservation exhibited the highest potential for reducing emissions. We also demonstrated the importance of improving industry interconnectivity, developing textile recycling frameworks, and promoting sustainable consumption.

Keywords: China; mitigation strategies; shared socioeconomic pathways; textile products.

1. Introduction

The carbon neutral target (Xi, 2021) set by China in 2020 has drawn much attention. To meet this target, all industries in China must accelerate carbon dioxide control measures. The textile industry was the first industry in China to promote the industry-level zero-carbon goal. It has a long industrial chain marked by high energy consumption and direct greenhouse gas (GHG) emissions (Scope 1), emissions associated

---

[¶]Corresponding author.
[||]This chapter was originally published in Climate Change Economics, Vol. 13, No. 1 (2022), published by World Scientific Publishing, Singapore. Reprinted with permission.

with electricity use (Scope 2), and emissions associated with intermediate inputs (Scope 3), widely linking various consumers and producers. The development of industry standards and promotion of sustainable consumption behaviors must be accelerated. It is therefore necessary to conduct GHG emission accounting of textile products, explore long-term decarbonization pathways, and establish sustainable textile chains.

China has the world's largest textile industry and thus plays an important role in the global textile chain. China's textile industry accounts for more than a half of global fiber production (Textile Industry Development Plan, 2010–2020). In 2015, Chinese textile enterprises accounted for 6.02% of the carbon emissions of all industrial enterprises (Lin et al., 2018). In 2017, the global textile industry produced about 1.2 billion tons of GHG emissions (Euromonitor International Apparel & Footwear 2016 Edition, 2017). Textiles pose a major climate threat, especially for developing nations in Asia, where manufacturing is concentrated. However, the rush to cut carbon emissions has been overshadowed by pressure to meet basic everyday needs. Consumption drives increases in energy depletion associated with textile production (Wang et al., 2017; Zhang et al., 2018), leading to marked increases in textile waste, inefficient sorting systems (Moorhouse, 2020) and low recycling rates (Ellen Macarthur Foundation, 2017). Carbon emissions associated with end treatment are problematic, and about 26 million tons of used apparel are sent to landfills in China each year (Lee et al., 2018).

Carbon emissions are greatly influenced by socioeconomic conditions, which are in turn related to demographics, human development, economy, technology, natural resources, and policies (O'Neill et al., 2017). Concerns have been raised about the potential impact of socioeconomic changes on the carbon footprint of the textile industry. Previous studies have explored the role of GHG reduction strategies on the textile industry, emphasizing upgraded techniques, clean production, and energy recovery (Lin and Zhao, 2016; O'Neill et al., 2017; Textile Industry Development Plan, 2010–2020). Through scientific production management, enterprises can achieve decarbonization by improving energy efficiency and structure (Lin and Zhao, 2016). Agricultural industries that engage in organic cultivation of natural materials and colors have been shown to reduce upstream textile emissions (Song and Ko, 2017; Mcneill et al., 2020). Emotional connections of consumers with products can extend the service life of textiles, reducing overall demand (Baydar et al., 2015; Song and Ko, 2017; Nature, 2018, Mcneill et al., 2020). Enterprises can also help consumers to make green choices and cultivate preferences for their products, through information transparency (Calamari and Hyllegard, 2017; Moorhouse, 2020) and intuitive design (Zhang et al., 2018; Ener et al., 2019). With the development of end-treatment processes, innovations in waste resource recycling have led to reduced carbon intensity compared with traditional disposal (Zamani et al., 2015).

Previous studies have also shown the importance of industrial ecology to industrial sustainability, suggesting that communication and collaboration within the industries is essential for conserving resources (Oelze, 2017). Upstream of the textile industry, the chemical (Li, 2021) and agricultural industries (Shahid-ul-Islam and Mohammad, 2013) could promote green development through exploiting environmentally friendly raw materials. Enterprises that build photovoltaic power stations for their own use could transfer excess electricity to the grid, thereby sharing energy among industrial systems (Wan, 2021). Moreover, the post-consumer textile processing industry could play an important role in creating a circulating material flow within the textile chain (Fischer and Pascucci, 2017).

Although some studies have assessed carbon footprints based on present socioeconomic conditions, quantitative and comprehensive analyses of the impact of future socioeconomic conditions on textile carbon emissions, particularly in relation to the achievement of net zero emissions, have been lacking. As another research gap, there is a lack of studies on the carbon performance of the textile industry under climate polices. The influence of the carbon price assumed in climate policies has been studied in the steel, construction, and energy industries, but rarely in the textile industry. In addition, long-term GHG reduction strategies should be formulated at the product level before being applied to the industry. A few studies have made good attempts to evaluate long-term product-level decarbonization pathways (Zheng and Suh, 2019; Clark *et al.*, 2020). To our knowledge, the same has not been done for textile products.

Therefore, the objective of this study was to fill these gaps in our knowledge by exploring GHG mitigation strategies for China's textile products that are consistent with the climate goal. To this end, we applied an integrated research framework using a life cycle assessment (LCA) approach and the Asia-Pacific Integrated Model/Computable General Equilibrium (AIM/CGE) model to simulate Shared Socioeconomic Pathway (SSP) scenarios implementing climate policies through 2050. We forecast the future carbon reduction pathway of textile products in China based on current GHG performance and compared a set of mitigation strategies under scenarios characterized by different combinations of socioeconomic conditions and climate policies. The results of this study can be used to assess the effects of socioeconomic conditions on the long-term decarbonization of textile products and to contrast them with the impacts of climate policies.

To demonstrate GHG mitigation performance under integrated socioeconomic development paths, climate change mitigation scenarios were established under certain socioeconomic assumptions based on SSPs (Kr *et al.*, 2017). These SSPs describe five scenarios that can be combined with climate policy assumptions to explore the effects of mitigation paths and to assess the benefits of climate policies under different socioeconomic conditions. O'Neill *et al.* (2017) described the qualitative components of SSPs and identified their key determinants as a basis for devising integrated scenarios.

By integrating the GHG performance of Chinese textile products, the SSP framework can be expanded beyond integrated assessment models (IAMs), and the role of socioeconomic conditions and climate policies in the carbon footprints of industrial products along supply chains can be explored. Forecasting product-level carbon neutral transformation pathways allows stakeholders, such as consumers, producers, and policy makers, to better understand future shifts in socioeconomic conditions in the textile industry, in turn helping them to develop strategies for low-carbon products and decarbonization.

2. Methods

2.1. *Research framework*

Figure 1 shows the research framework. Using the LCA method, a GHG emission dataset for domestic textile products is established to show the current GHG performance of the textile life cycle, considering raw materials, production processing, and end-of-life (EOL) treatment. Based on the LCA results, we selected two objective textile types, cotton yarn and polyethylene terephthalate yarn (PET), as representative products for further study.

The AIM/CGE models provide sector transformation pathways under different SSPs and climate policies. LCA inputs are influenced by the pathways of the sectors. LCA provides the initial life cycle inventory, involving current textile product activity data and emission factors. Activity data under relevant socioeconomic conditions are influenced by the assumptions of SSPs, and the emission factors of the corresponding sectors are adjusted based on carbon prices set under climate policies. Textile industry GHG emission forecasts are dependent on activity data and emission factors for different combinations of SSPs and climate policies. The life cycle of textile products depends on a multi-sector chain that requires multi-sector carbon reduction strategies.

Future GHG emissions' trajectories and the mitigation potential of emission-reduction strategies can be derived from this research framework. The method also enables us to explore and compare mitigation strategies to inform the relevant policy makers and stakeholders under an integrated research framework.

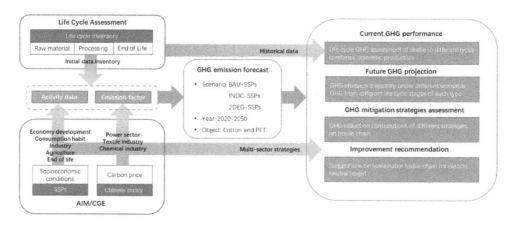

Figure 1. Hybrid LCA–Representative Concentration Pathway (RCP)–SSP framework.

2.2. AIM/CGE model

The AIM/CGE model is a global-scale recursive, dynamic, CGE model. Unlike other early empirical models, the CGE model is an inherently consistent macroeconomic model based on neoclassical micro theory (Lofgren *et al.*, 2001). The CGE model can be used to evaluate the effect of policy implementation comprehensively, and many countries have recently begun to use the model to evaluate the effects of the energy crisis and tax and trade policy reform. The CGE model links all economic sectors and industries within all economic constraints and establishes a quantitative relationship between various components of the economy, enabling us to investigate the effects of disturbances of one part of the economy on other parts (Fujimori *et al.*, 2012, 2014).

Here, we use the AIM/CGE model to provide least-cost energy systems' transformation pathways, including power sector structural change, up to 2050 in different climate policy and SSP scenarios. The climate policy scenarios include a business-as-usual (BAU) scenario, an Intended Nationally Determined Contributions (INDC) scenario, and a global 2°C (2DEG) scenario (see Sec. 2.4). Data on the energy system transformation, emission path, and carbon price have been published elsewhere (Liu *et al.*, 2019).

2.3. Calculation of GHG emissions

LCA allows for quantitative and qualitative analysis of the whole life cycle of a product or service, from raw material acquisition, through product manufacturing and use, to final disposal. The textile life cycle is shown in Fig. S2. LCA includes three stages: (1) the raw material stage, including activities from cradle to gate; (2) yarn processing stage, involving the conversion of raw materials into final products; and (3) EOL stage, which refers to the treatment and disposal processes of textile waste, which are treated as solid waste after screening out waste with use value. Due to the complexity of the textile supply chain, the processing stage is considered to extend from raw materials to finished yarn products, excluding the subsequent stages of reprocessing, use, and transportation. To calculate the total GHG emissions for a given year, the emissions for each type of textile were multiplied by the annual yarn production. GHG emissions for each textile type were calculated as follows:

$$\text{GHG} = \sum Q_{s,i,t} E_{s,i,k,t}, \qquad (1)$$

where $Q_{s,i,t}$ is the annual domestic production of textile of type i in year t under scenario s, and $E_{s,i,k,t}$ is the per-unit weight emissions of GHG by textile type i at life cycle stage k in year t under scenario s.

We used the annual growth rate output from the AIM/CGE textiles and apparel and leather sector model in setting $Q_{s,i,t}$. The future output of the two main textiles examined in this study and industry-level production data in the AIM/CGE model were consistent in changing rate.

The emission coefficient for 2020 was based on data from recent studies. We varied certain parameters according to the SSPs to calculate input activity data, under the assumption that the coefficient would change linearly from 2020 to 2050. Emission factors were modified according to the relevant sectors in the AIM/CGE model. $E_{s,i,k,t}$ was obtained by multiplying the activity data by the emission factors under specific scenarios during 2020 to 2050.

For textiles and their processed products that are exported in part to places where the EOL phase is completed, we assumed that the EOL stage occurs in China and other countries. To enhance the uniformity of the data, we preferentially used data required in the domestic boundary from Chinese sources. The data in the foreign boundary refer to the global average situation from international sources.

2.4. Scenario design

In this study, we developed two-dimensional scenarios, i.e., scenarios with a socioeconomic dimension and climate policy dimension. Climate change mitigation was reflected by a global constraint on emissions in China. A national carbon price was implemented to achieve yearly emission targets. We adopted BAU, INDC, and 2DEG climate policy scenarios. The BAU scenario assumes that social change follows historical trends and that no climate policies are implemented. INDCs are action targets set by nations to address climate change in a domestic context. In this study, the INDC scenario refers to China achieving its national targets by 2030, including reaching the carbon peak in 2030. Both energy and air quality policies follow China's 13th Five-Year Plan, whereas afforestation policies follow China's Land Use Plan. The INDC policy in China was implemented until 2030, and mitigation was delayed compared with the 2DEG scenario. More negative emission technologies were used in the latter half of the century. The 2DEG scenario is consistent with a temperature rise not exceeding 2°C and follows the lowest-cost mitigation scenario, which is often used as the cost-benefit mitigation scenario for the global 2°C target. We assumed that China's emissions in the 2DEG scenario would be consistent with the global trajectory using the equalized emissions per capita principle. The converging year was 2040. From 2020 to 2040, we assumed a linear change. The GHG emission pathways under climate policies in this study refer to Fig. S1.

Regarding socioeconomic conditions, future projections are based on the SSP framework (Fujimori *et al.*, 2017) consistent with the literatures (O'Neill *et al.*, 2017; Vuuren *et al.*, 2017). In SSP1, industrial development is sustainable and there is good awareness of environmental protection. Natural fiber cultivation involves low-carbon agriculture without high yield cost, thereby decreasing the use of chemicals; renewable energy can also be adopted. Textile techniques are highly innovative and have been developed due to the popularity of environmentally friendly products. EOL management makes extensive uses of recycling treatments to promote resource circulation. SSP2 assumes no marked departures from current patterns, where all sectors grow sustainably at a moderate rate. New technologies are presently in their infancy. Moreover, people have a limited sense of the need for environmental protection. SSP3 represents the worst scenario in terms of low carbon development. Due to outdated technology, aging equipment, and poor management, agriculture and industry increase material input and depend on fossil energy, and people tend to pursue material goods while ignoring the need for environmental protection. In SSP4, the development of the entire industrial chain is unbalanced, with rapid development of high-tech and high-efficiency industries (i.e., cotton planting and textile processing) and sluggish development of other industries and EOL management. SSP5 represents advanced technological innovation in textile types and EOL techniques, with heavy reliance on fossil fuels and intensive material management. Other parameter settings of the SSPs are shown in Table S1.

2.5. Calculation of the effects of mitigation strategies

In this study, we used the cumulative carbon emission change data from BAU-SSP2 and INDC-SSP1 in 2050 to analyze the emission reduction strategy. SSP1 is a scenario characterized by sustainable socioeconomic conditions, while INDC considers emission reduction of the whole industrial sector, including the power sector. To analyze the emission reduction potential of climate policies and socioeconomic scenarios, we compared INDC-SSP1 and BAU-SSP2. We varied the socioeconomic conditions according to the elements listed in Table S1. Elements of the same type in different sectors were combined into one strategy, and those that could not be combined were treated separately. Socioeconomic strategies were divided into energy conservation (energy), waste reduction (waste), preference changes (bio-PET and recycled PET preferences), resource circulation (level of renewing and recycling), bio-fuel (bio-fuel preference), and low-carbon agriculture (pesticides, fertilizers, and plastic films). Climate policy strategies include implementing a unified national carbon price and decarbonizing the power system. The effects of these strategies were determined by calculating GHG changes after implementing each strategy. For example, waste reduction requires a change in the amount of discarded materials from medium to low, while leaving all other variables unchanged. The effect of a mitigation strategy is calculated as the difference between the calculated GHG and that of the previous situation.

3. Results

In this study, we selected four natural fibers and five synthetic fibers to establish a dataset covering GHG emissions in various life cycle stages of textiles. On this basis, we simulated GHG emission trajectories for China's textile industry under various socioeconomic conditions and SSP scenarios, with and without the implementation of climate policies, up to 2050. We then compared the emission mitigating effects of strategies under various scenarios differing in terms of climate policies and societal conditions.

3.1. *Current GHG performance of textile products*

First, we established a dataset covering GHG emissions for various textile life cycle stages. GHG emission data for the nine textiles were collected from various reference sources and production data were obtained from the China Textile Industry Development Report 2019–2020. Details are provided in Table S2.

The analysis showed that common fabrics produced in 2019 in the domestic textile market emitted 443.8 megatons of carbon dioxide equivalent (MtCO$_2$e) over their life cycle (Fig. 2). The amount corresponds to 4.6% of the 9729 MtCO$_2$e emitted domestically in 2017 (Shan *et al.*, 2020). The raw material production stage generated the majority of the emissions (60%), followed by the processing stage (35%). The GHG emissions per unit mass for most fabrics show similar magnitudes, such as cotton yarn (6.5 kgCO$_2$e kg^{-1}), flax (3.8 kgCO$_2$e kg^{-1}), PET (5.1 kgCO$_2$e kg^{-1}), nylon (7.3 kgCO$_2$e kg^{-1}), and spandex (5.8 kgCO$_2$e kg^{-1}). Among all textile types, PET and cotton yarn had the highest GHG emissions in the raw material and processing stages.

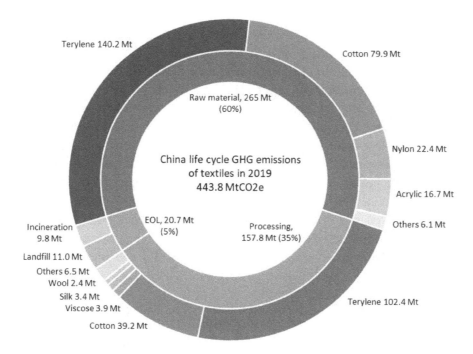

Figure 2. Life cycle GHG emissions of conventional textiles (yarn) in China in 2019 by life cycle stage and textile type. Blue, orange, and green represent raw material production, processing, and EOL management stages, respectively. The emissions from each stage are broken down by textile type or EOL treatment method, as indicated by different shades of the corresponding color.

The production levels of PET and cotton yarn were 47.51 and 18.29 million tons in 2019, accounting for 63% and 24% of China's yarn consumption, respectively, and making significant contributions to GHG emissions. The other textiles showed high emissions per unit mass, such as wool (28.3 kgCO$_2$e kg^{-1}), raw silk (49.1 kgCO$_2$e kg^{-1}), and acrylic (31.0 kgCO$_2$e kg^{-1}); however, their contribution to overall emissions was limited. GHG emissions from bio-based and recycled textiles were not considered in 2019 because the bio-yarns remain on trial and recycled textiles are not included in the statistics by the National Textile Association. The EOL stage accounted for 5% of total life cycle emissions. It is estimated that 35% of textiles are discarded every year (China Waste Textiles Recycling Technology Progress White Paper, 2019) and 54.6% of that are treated as domestic waste (Spuijbroek, 2019). According to the current landfilling and incineration rates in China, 60% of the discarded yarn treated as waste is landfilled and 40% is incinerated. There is no significant difference in GHG emissions between the two methods without energy recovery. However, if displacement of carbon-intensive yarn production by recyclates is considered, the GHG emissions of the EOL stage increase in the recycling input.

3.2. GHG emission projection for 2020–2050

Based on the overall current GHG emissions, we selected PET and cotton yarn as representative textiles to simulate GHG emission trajectories for domestic textile chains under various SSP scenarios, with and without the implementation of climate policies, up to 2050. Figure 3 shows the GHG trajectories of PET and cotton yarn under different SSPs during 2020 to 2050 in the BAU, INDC, and 2DEG scenarios. Details are provided in Tables S3–S5.

As shown in Fig. 3(a), under the BAU scenario, future emissions in 2050 show significant differences according to the five development paths, from 102.3 MtCO$_2$e (SSP1) to 290.7 MtCO$_2$e (SSP5). Socioeconomic conditions have a huge potential influence on future GHG emissions. Comparing 2020 to 2050, the annual GHG emissions are expected to increase by 0.4% in the sustainable development path SSP1. In SSP2, in which social, economic, and technological trends change relative to historical patterns, textile emission is projected to grow from 106.8 MtCO$_2$e in 2020 to 137.2 MtCO$_2$e in 2050, at a growth rate of 28.6%. GHG increases by 10.1% in the inequality development path (SSP4) and by 54.4% in the most challenging path (SSP3). SSP5, with its heavy dependence on fossil fuels, shows higher emissions than other SSPs. Under the INDC scenario, power is decarbonized and GHG emissions from all five SSPs decline rapidly in the future, within a narrow range from 15.1 to 44.5 MtCO$_2$e in 2050. The average emissions' reduction is approximately 71.1%, achieving zero emissions during the textile life cycle in the near future. Even SSP3 and SSP5, which are not sustainable, achieve significant reductions under climate policies. Under 2DEG, emissions from the power sector are further reduced, while overall GHG emissions are significantly reduced after 2020. Compared with INDC, the reduction

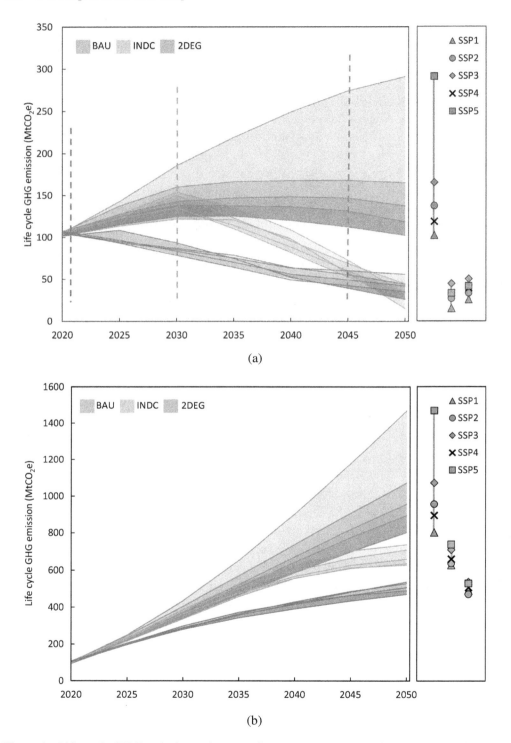

Figure 3. Life cycle GHG emissions of two textiles, cotton yarn and polyethylene terephthalate yarn (PET), in China under three SSP scenarios: BAU, INDC, and 2DEG, for 2020–2050. (a) Annual and (b) cumulative GHG emissions.

trend in 2DEG slows from 2040, resulting in slightly higher GHG emissions than under INDC in 2050, with an average reduction rate of 61.5%.

As shown in Fig. 3(a), the carbon peak occurs at different times and is followed by a downward trend. Under the BAU scenario, textile emission reaches its carbon peak in around 2045, whereas under INDC, the peak is reached in around 2030. Carbon emission abruptly decreases under the 2DEG scenario. The reductions under BAU and INDC did not occur until after the carbon peak, which indicates that 2DEG is the most effective emission reduction pathway, but also the most difficult to implement. If carbon emissions peak by 2030, for carbon neutrality to be achieved by 2060 as planned climate policies will need to be implemented.

As shown in Fig. 3(b), estimated cumulative emissions under the BAU scenario in 2050 range from 802.2 to 1,467.4 MtCO$_2$e. As such, even if GHG emissions were strictly limited between 2020 and 2050 under the BAU scenario, mitigation from socioeconomic conditions alone would likely be insufficient to realize the 2060 targets. In the absence of climate policy, it is difficult to change the trend of cumulative emission growth by improving only socioeconomic conditions. BAU-SSP5 shows the highest growth of emissions among all five SSPs. Even SSP1, which has the best mitigation performance of all pathways, results in rapid and sustained growth of cumulative emissions from the base year without climate policy. Under all climate policies, cumulative emission is gradually mitigated in both future scenarios, and 2DEG stabilizes GHG emissions more rapidly than INDC, with less carbon discharge in 2050. Climate policy greatly accelerates the reduction by 2050, mainly due to the development of zero-carbon technologies for energy systems. However, it will be difficult to achieve carbon neutrality before the specified time through socioeconomic strategies alone. These results demonstrate that the impact of socioeconomic factors is subtle and unclear. A drastic reduction in life cycle GHG emissions of textiles would require implementing both the socioeconomic strategies and climate policies examined at unprecedented scale and pace. Details of Fig. 3(b) are provided in Tables figS6–S8.

Figure 4 shows the breakdown of GHG emissions by life cycle stage for each kilogram of textiles (yarn) derived from different feedstock types in 2050, whose details are provided in Tables S9–S11. For the five SSPs under BAU, the total average life cycle GHG emissions for cotton yarn, fossil fuel-based, bio-based, and recycled PET are 4.3, 1.7, 1.4, and 3.2 kgCO$_2$e per kg textile, respectively. All the fabrics show high mitigation potential in SSP1, but SSP3 is a more problematic development pathway in terms of emissions reduction.

GHG emission per unit mass of cotton yarn is higher under the BAU scenario for all four textile products. The raw material and processing stages contribute 27.3% and 66.3% of the emissions to the life cycle, respectively. Agricultural nitrogen (N) production, N$_2$O from fertilized soil, and power consumption during the industrial processing stage are the main GHG sources, showing that traditional processing techniques eliminate the low-carbon advantage of environmentally friendly natural fibers. The effect of socioeconomic conditions on the cotton yarn emission reduction is

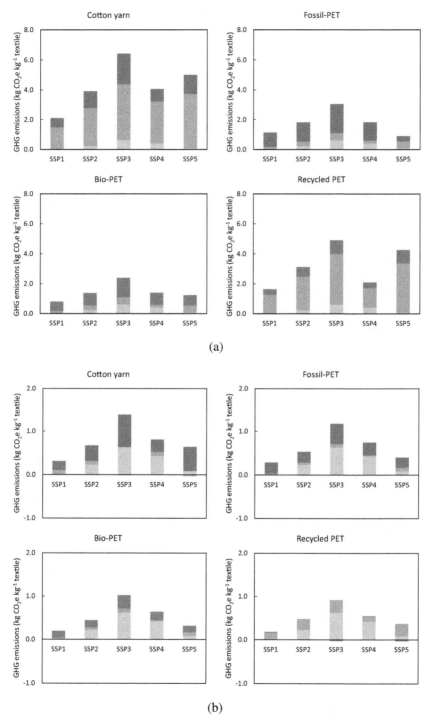

Figure 4. Breakdown of GHG emissions by textile life cycle stage for cotton yarn and PET yarn derived from different feedstock types under SSPs in 2050. GHG emissions in (a) BAU, (b) INDC, and (c) 2DEG scenario.

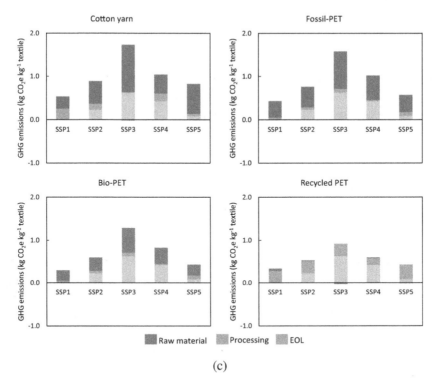

Fig. 4. (*Continued*)

reflected in the life cycle under SSP1, with a 46.3% reduction compared with SSP2. However, if cotton carbon credit is considered, carbon emissions from feedstock are offset and may even reach negative values under SSP1. Previous studies reported a carbon credit amount for cotton growth of $-4.6\,\text{kgCO}_2\text{e}$ and average cotton yarn production emissions of $-0.3\,\text{kgCO}_2\text{e}$ (Yu *et al.*, 2013; Cai, 2017; Wei and Zhang, 2019).

The effect of socioeconomic conditions on PET equates to a 37.6% reduction in fossil-based emissions and a 41.4% reduction in bio-based PET emissions. For fuel fossil-based PET, emissions from the raw material stage account for nearly 66.0% of all emissions in the life cycle, while for bio-based PET, they account for 59.1%. Without climate policies, emissions from raw material do not improve significantly by socioeconomic means alone. Raw materials for fossil fuel-based PET are produced by the chemical industry. The refinement from corn of mono-ethylene glycol (MEG) and purified terephthalic acid (PTA), which are raw materials used in the production of bio-based PET, also occurs within the chemical industry. The raw material production stage is the main contributor to the life cycle emissions of PET due to chemical industry emissions, which masks the mitigating effects of energy-saving spinning during fiber processing. Although substitution of fossil fuel with biomass for feedstock is important, the life cycle GHG emissions of bio-based PET are 16.9% less than those of fossil-based PET.

Discarded polyester bottles are used as the raw materials of recycled PET, which eliminates the need for raw material production and realizes resource circulation, thus the unit emission of raw material is the lowest among all types of textiles. Plastic bottle fragments are processed into polyester particles that must be re-melted and blown to make PET. This process is classified as pellet spinning, consumes considerable energy, and has a larger carbon footprint than directly spun fibers.

The EOL measure in SSP3 and SSP4 is solid waste treatment, with energy recovery and recycling techniques in SSP1, SSP2, and SSP5 producing additional emissions during fiber regeneration. Thus, recycling is more effective than traditional disposal for achieving a smaller carbon footprint. The emissions of each textile product in 2050 under BAU indicate that socioeconomic conditions are effective but limited in their ability to reduce emissions at different stages of the textile life cycle. Differences are due mainly to the type of yarn, which affects feedstock and processing techniques.

When climate policies are implemented, GHG emissions from textiles are reduced by approximately 73.8% in INDC and 65.5% in 2DEG. Climate policies narrow the GHG emission gap between product types. To meet climate policy requirements, the power sector will also adopt carbon-negative technologies such as BECCS in the future, resulting in a negative power emission coefficient. As the power emission coefficient will appear negative in the future, the product production emission in some scenarios will also be negative. A smaller share of emissions from processing stage suggests that upstream and EOL are the main source of GHG in these scenarios, rather than textile industry. At this time, green raw material replacement and waste resource circulation treatment become the focus of emission reduction.

3.3. *Assessment and comparison of GHG mitigation strategies*

We compared the emission-mitigating effects of various strategies under SSPs differing in terms of climate policies and societal conditions. As shown in Fig. 5, the transition from BAU-SSP2 to INDC-SSP1 reduces cumulative GHG emissions by 328.2 MtCO$_2$e. If no mitigation strategies are implemented, GHG will increase significantly in line with production growth and economic development, by 181.6 MtCO$_2$e. Based on the indicator set in each scenario hypothesis, the emission reduction path is decomposed into the superimposed effects of several strategies, involving power decarbonization, energy conservation, carbon price unification, waste circulation, low-carbon agriculture, bio-fuel replacement, renewability improvement, and a preference for green products.

Power decarbonization has the greatest reduction effect (−230.3 MtCO$_2$e), according to the popularization of renewable energy and negative-carbon technology. Saving energy, mainly power, during all stages of production leads to a reduction of 114.0 MtCO$_2$e. These results indicate that reducing the power consumption carbon

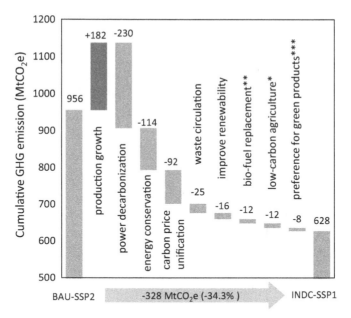

Figure 5. Cumulative GHG emission reduction in the textile life cycle stage for cotton yarn and PET yarn under different strategies and BAU-SSP2 to INDC-SSP1 in 2050.

footprint is critical to the textile emission mitigation pathway, and the production side should always focus on the volume and type of power input. Following industrial improvement, a nationally unified carbon price affects emission upstream of the textile industry, leading to a reduction of 91.6 MtCO$_2$e.

Via the effective strategies described above, EOL management (waste circulation and renewability improvement) reduces carbon by 25.3 MtCO$_2$e and 16.2 MtCO$_2$e, assuming effective garbage sorting and waste recycling systems. Improving waste resource reuse through classification can prevent waste from being discarded. The emissions from recycling technology have strong impact on the supply chain. A reduction of 11.8 MtCO$_2$e is achieved by replacing fossil fuel with bio-based fuel during production. Low agriculture carbonization decreases emissions by 12.4 MtCO$_2$e, through increasing the utilization of agricultural resources and reducing the consumption of fertilizers, pesticides, and plastic films.

Consumption habits directly affect the decisions of producers. Although the effect of consumer behavior on emission reduction is not as significant as that on production, it still requires attention. Consumer-side emission reduction strategies affect both the quantity and type of products. Preference changes contribute an 8.2 MtCO$_2$e GHG reduction. Compared with traditional fossil PET products on the mainstream textile market, people tend to choose bio-PET and recycled PET instead of fossil PET in future scenarios.

Thus, even if production output grows with the domestic economy, actions in all sectors can offset its negative effects. Conversely, no individual strategy is sufficient. If all strategies are implemented simultaneously, the cumulative GHG emissions in 2050 will decrease by 34.3%.

4. Discussion

In this study, we combined SSPs and climate policy scenarios (BAU, INDC, and 2DEG) to explore the ability of various pathways to reduce the carbon footprint of textile products in China. We found that power emission reduction is essential for realizing low-carbon textile products. Power saving and power decarbonization play important roles in the GHG mitigation. All industries related in the textile chain save energy used in SSP1, which makes the largest reduction effect among socio-economic conditions. Under the constraints imposed by climate policies, the power system shows significant decarbonization in which the carbon neutral target is most achievable.

Decarbonization of the power system is fundamental for textile product emission reduction. As an important part of China's INDC, a carbon-neutral goal requires transformation of the power system. The power sector must improve the efficiency of renewable energy technologies, reduce the cost of wind and solar power, and improve the safety of nuclear power. Thermal power generation quotas should be adjusted so that power can be flexibly regulated using carbon capture and storage devices. In this study, the 2050 projections indicated that power decarbonization narrows the emission gap among SSPs and textile types. Achieving a clean power source through electrification has the greatest potential for carbon reduction.

A uniform carbon price in climate policies is important for carbon reduction. Including the textile industry in the regional carbon market can support power conservation efforts. Market-related policies, such as carbon tax and trading, force enterprises to upgrade industrial technology by limiting emission quotas. Energy-efficient equipment, such as electronic yarn-cleaning devices and compressed air supply systems, and processes such as molten direct spinning and waste heat utilization, should be adopted to reduce indirect carbon emissions from the power sector.

Power cycle systems can reduce emissions by reducing power consumption in the textile industry. Renewable power plants can be linked with textile enterprises to ensure sustainable supply via direct power purchase contracts. Textile factories could install solar and rooftop panels to establish photovoltaic power stations for their own use, with surplus power transferred to the grid, to realize complementary energy sources. Waste disposal enterprises could provide heat and electricity for textile mills for EOL management of non-recyclable textile waste, by recovering energy from incineration or landfill gas.

Interconnections among industries maximize the effectiveness of coordinated emission reduction strategies. Decarbonization of the chemical and agricultural industries will improve the performance of these strategies. Pol "Technical Guidelines for Green Agricultural Development (2018-2030)" (2018) and "Opinions on Accelerating the Development of Low-carbon Industrial Clusters and Low-carbon Development of Manufacturing Industry" (2021) promote a low-carbon textile chain, by improving the utilization rate of pesticides and fertilizers, replacing fossil fuels with bio-diesel and biogas, and accelerating electrification by developing electric boilers, electric kilns, and heat pumps.

Consumption plays an important role in reducing the carbon footprint of textile products. Innovation has a positive impact on the carbon footprint by changing consumption habits. As standards of living improve, increased demand for textiles is inevitable. Reducing consumption is a complex issue involving cultural and psychological factors as well as social conformity (Rockstrm et al., 2009; Sandin et al., 2015). However, some strategies have successfully limited the desire for consumption, such as improving durability or fostering emotional connections of consumers with products (Anguelov, 2015; Fletcher, 2017; Ener et al., 2019; Mcneill et al., 2020). Preferences for environmentally friendly products are desirable. Bio-based and recycled PET cost more than conventional textiles, which is a barrier to preference for these sustainable materials. For price-sensitive consumers, buying products in smaller amounts to reduce the environmental load can be the starting point of sustainable consumption habits. Improving garbage sorting behavior by citizens promotes efficient textile waste recycling, which is needed for resource circulation and emission reduction. The changes in attitudes assumed to occur under various socioeconomic conditions act as on-off switches in mitigation strategies. Such strategies depend on consumer awareness and remain in the early stages.

This study had several limitations. Various assumptions were made to simplify the calculation and projection of GHG emissions. For example, the effects of indirect land use change, GHG emissions from agricultural waste (plastic film and straw) treatment, and GHG absorption by natural raw materials (cotton and corn) were excluded from the analysis. Moreover, we combined emissions data from multiple studies and datasets, some of which cannot confirm the consistency of this study. However, there are few related studies on this topic and the data sources are limited. The data used here were the best available after being filtered. In addition, due to its complexity, this study did not cover all aspects of the textile industry. In the future, we plan to extend the boundary to the entire textile chain, involving packaging, use, and other links, and explore emission reduction paths combined with ideal sustainable consumption scenarios. Except for power decarbonization, zero-carbonization of fuel is another important direction of energy transition, and it is also a pathway to be considered in further study.

5. Conclusion

To curb GHG emissions from China's textile industry, it is necessary to implement multi-dimensional emission reduction strategies. Here, we used LCA to calculate the current GHG emissions of textile types and found that cotton yarn and PET were the two textiles with the largest emissions. Under the assumptions of the BAU-SSPs, INDC-SSPs, and 2DEG-SSPs scenarios, the trajectories of GHG emissions from cotton yarn and PET in 2020–2050 were forecasted. The mitigation potentials of strategies related to socioeconomic conditions and climate policies were identified to explore the best emission-reduction path.

The results show that if a textile chain develops at a moderate pace without climate policies, the annual emissions of textiles would increase to 137.2 MtCO_2e by 2050. Combined with rapid sustainable development and climate policy under the INDC scenario, the annual emissions would decrease by 89.0%, and the cumulative emissions would decrease by 34.3% in 2050, comparing with the scenario without any mitigation measures. Among the strategies discussed here, the decarbonization of power systems has the highest GHG mitigation potential, with a reduction rate of 70.2%, followed by power conservation. The key steps to achieving net-zero emissions of textiles involve modifying power generation and consumption.

Overall, feasible and effective strategies to reduce GHG emissions will require a combination of socioeconomic conditions and climate policies, in both the textile industry and other sectors, which can provide high potential for attaining the goal of carbon neutrality. The results of this study will be useful for policymakers, providing a basis for achieving sustainable industry.

Supplementary Material

The supplementary material is available at https://www.worldscientific.com/doi/suppl/10.1142/S2010007822400048.

Acknowledgment

This research was supported by the Natural Science Foundation of China (72004134; 72088101; 71690241; 71810107001) and the Shanghai Pujiang Program.

References

Anguelov, N (2015). *The Dirty Side of the Garment Industry: Fast Fashion and its Negative Impact on Environment and Society*. CRC Press. pp. 345–359.

Baydar, G, N Ciliz and A Mammadov (2015). Life cycle assessment of cotton textile products in Turkey. *Resources Conservation and Recycling*, 104, 213–223.

Cai, S (2017). Low carbon agriculture development in Xinjiang-taking cotton planting as an example. *Taxpaying*, 2017(22), 126.

Calamari, S and KH Hyllegard (2017). An exploration of designers' perspectives on human health and environmental impacts of interior textiles. *Textiles and Clothing Sustainability*, 2(1).

China Waste Textiles Recycling Technology Progress White Paper (2019).

Clark, MA *et al.* (2020). Global food system emissions could preclude achieving the 1.5° and 2°C climate change targets. *Science*, 370(6517), 705–708.

Ellen Macarthur Foundation (2017). A new textiles economy: Redesigning fashion's future. Available at https://www.ellenmacarthurfoundation.org/assets/downloads/publications/A-New-Textiles-Economy_Full-Report.pdf.

Ener, T, F Bikin and N Kln (2019). Sustainable dressing: Consumers' value perceptions towards slow fashion. *Business Strategy and the Environment*, 28(4).

Ener, T, F Bikin and N Kln (2019). Sustainable dressing: Consumers' value perceptions towards slow fashion. *Business Strategy and the Environment*, 28(4), 1548–1557.

Euromonitor International Appareal & Footwear 2016 Edition (volume sales trends 2005–2015) (2017). World Bank, World development indicators-GD.

Fischer, A and S Pascucci (2017). Institutional incentives in circular economy transition. *Journal of Cleaner Production*, 155, 17–32.

Fletcher, K (2017). Exploring demand reduction through design, durability and 'usership' of fashion clothes. *Philosophical Transactions of the Royal Society A: Mathematical, Physical and Engineering Sciences*, 375(2095), 20160366.

Fujimori, S *et al.* (2014). Land use representation in a global CGE model for long-term simulation: CET vs. logit functions. *Food Security*, 6(5), 685–699.

Fujimori, S *et al.* (2017). SSP3: AIM implementation of shared socioeconomic pathways. *Global Environmental Change*, 42, 268–283.

Fujimori, S, T Masui and M Yuzuru (2012). AIM/CGE [basic] manual. Center for Social and Environmental Systems Research.

Kr, A *et al.* (2017). The Shared Socioeconomic Pathways and their energy, land use, and greenhouse gas emissions implications: An overview. *Global Environmental Change*, 42, 153–168.

Lee, SHN, J Ha-Brookshire and PS Chow (2018). The moral responsibility of corporate sustainability as perceived by fashion retail employees: A USA-China cross-cultural comparison study. *Business Strategy and the Environment*, 27(8), 1462–1475.

Li, L (2021). Fine chemical products promote the development of textile industry. *The Light & Textile Industries of Fujian*, 2021(1), 51–53, 56.

Lin, B and H Zhao (2016). Technological progress and energy rebound effect in China's textile industry: Evidence and policy implications. *Renewable and Sustainable Energy Reviews*, 60, 173–181.

Lin, B, Y Chen and G Zhang (2018). Impact of technological progress on China's textile industry and future energy saving potential forecast. *Energy*, 161, 859–869.

Liu, J-Y *et al.* (2019). Identifying trade-offs and co-benefits of climate policies in China to align policies with SDGs and achieve the 2°C goal. *Environmental Research Letters*, 14(12), 124070.

Lofgren, H, RL Harris and S Robinson (2001). A standard computable general equilibrium (CGE) model in GAMS.

Mcneill, LS *et al.* (2020). Fashion sensitive young consumers and Fashion Garment Repair: Emotional Connections to Garments as a Sustainability Strategy. *International Journal of Consumer Studies*, 44(4), 361–368.

Ministry of Agriculture and Rural Affairs: Technical Guidelines for Green Agricultural Development (2018–2030) (2018).

Moorhouse, D (2020). Making fashion sustainable: Waste and collective responsibility. *One Earth*, 3(1), 17–19.

O'Neill, BC et al. (2017). The roads ahead: Narratives for shared socioeconomic pathways describing world futures in the 21st century. *Global Environmental Change*, 42, 169–180.

Oelze, N (2017). Sustainable supply chain management implementation–enablers and barriers in the textile industry. *Sustainability*, 9(8), 1435.

Rockstrm, J et al. (2009). Planetary boundaries: Exploring the safe Operating Space for Humanity. *Ecology and Society*, 14(2), 292–292.

Sandin, G, GM Peters and M Svanstr (2015). Using the planetary boundaries framework for setting impact-reduction targets in LCA contexts. *International Journal of Life Cycle Assessment*, 20(12), 1684–1700.

Shahid-ul-Islam, MS and F Mohammad (2013). Perspectives for natural product based agents derived from industrial plants in textile applications – A review. *Journal of Cleaner Production*, 57(oct.15), 2–18.

Shan, Y et al. (2020). China CO2 emission accounts 2016–2017. *Scientific Data*, 7(1).

Song, S and E Ko (2017). Perceptions, attitudes, and behaviors toward sustainable fashion: Application of Q and Q-R methodologies. *International Journal of Consumer Studies*, 41(3), 264–273.

Spuijbroek, M (2019). Textile Waste in Mainland China. An Analysis of the Circular Practices of Post-Consumer Textile Waste in Mainland China.

Textile Industry Development Plan (2010–2020) (2017). Ministry of Industry and Information Technology of the PRC.

The price of fast fashion. *Nature Climate Change*, 8(1).AQ. Please provide page range.

Vuuren, DPV et al. (2017). Energy, land-use and greenhouse gas emissions trajectories under a green growth paradigm. *Global Environmental Change*, 42, 237–250.

Wan, F (2021). Application of Photovoltaic Power Station in Textile Enterprise. *Cotton Textile Technology*, 2021(5), 66–70.

Wang, L, Y Li and W He (2017). The energy footprint of China's textile industry: Perspectives from decoupling and decomposition analysis. *Energies*, 10(10), 1461.

Wei, X and L Zhang (2019). Research on cotton low carbon production under the constraint of resources and environment in Xinjiang. *Ecological Economy*, 35(7), 129–134, 173.

Xi,J (2021). Strengthen our confidence to tide over the difficulties and To build a better world-the General Debate of the 67th Session of the United Nations General Assembly.

Yu, X, M Chen, amv Z Guo (2013). Analysis of the resistance of cotton cultivation on low carbon development in Xinjiang. *Chinese Journal of Agricultural Resources and Regional Planning*, 34(6), 27–36.

Yueqing Municipal Government: Opinions on Accelerating the Development of Low-carbon Industrial Clusters and Low-carbon Development of Manufacturing Industry 2021.

Zamani, B et al. (2015). A carbon footprint of textile recycling: A case study in Sweden. *Journal of Industrial Ecology*, 19(4), 676–687.

Zhang, Y et al. (2018). Improved design for textile production process based on life cycle assessment. *Clean Technologies and Environmental Policy*, 20(6), 1355–1365.

Zhang, J, Y Liu and L Cheng (2018). Structural changes and growth factors of China's textile industry: 1997-2012. *Fibres and Textiles in Eastern Europe*, 26(2), 20–25.

Zheng, J and S Suh (2019). Strategies to reduce the global carbon footprint of plastics. *Nature Climate Change*, 9(5), 374–378.

© 2025 World Scientific Publishing Company
https://doi.org/10.1142/9789819812264_0006

EXPLORING FAIR AND AMBITIOUS MITIGATION CONTRIBUTIONS OF ASIAN ECONOMIES FOR THE GLOBAL WARMING LIMIT UNDER THE PARIS AGREEMENT[||]

XINRU LI[*], XUEMEI JIANG[*,‡,¶] and YAN XIA[†,§,¶]

[*]School of Economics
Capital University of Economics and Business
Beijing 100070, P. R. China

[†]Institutes of Science and Development
Chinese Academy of Sciences
Beijing 100190, P. R. China
[‡]jiangxuem@amss.ac.cn
[§]xiayan@casipm.ac.cn

Focusing on the mitigation responsibilities and efforts, this paper provides a unified estimation of allowable emission quotas for a number of Asian economies to limit the global temperature rise well below 2°C based on a range of effort-sharing approaches. The study also explores the inconsistency between their planned emission pathways under the Nationally Determined Contributions (NDCs) and the allowable emissions to achieve the 2°C target. The results show that most of the Asian developing economies would be in favor of the Equal-Per-Capita and Grandfather criteria, for which they would obtain more allowable emissions quota. However, even with the most favorable criterion, official mitigation pledges represented by NDCs are far less enough for these developing Asian economies such as China, India, Vietnam, Thailand and Pakistan, as their emission pathways under NDCs significantly exceed the ideal pathways under all effort-sharing approaches. In contrast, most of the Asian developed economies have already planned reductions of annual CO_2 emissions under NDCs, in line with their ideal pathways under the most favorable effort-sharing approach. However, their reductions of emissions require deep strengthening of deployment in low-carbon, zero-carbon and negative-carbon techniques, given the current growing trend of emissions for these economies.

Keywords: Nationally Determined Contributions (NDCs); emission quota; global warming limit; emissions gap; Asia.

1. Introduction

Keeping the global temperature rise well below 2°C or even 1.5°C relative to the pre-industrial levels has been a consensus position of the 196 signatories to the 2015 Paris Agreement. According to the near-linear relationship between global average

---

[¶]Corresponding authors.
[||]This chapter was originally published in Climate Change Economics, Vol. 13, No. 1 (2021), published by World Scientific Publishing, Singapore. Reprinted with permission.

temperature response and cumulative CO$_2$ emissions accepted by the Fifth Assessment Report (AR5) of the Intergovernmental Panel on Climate Change (IPCC), holding temperature increase to below 2°C with a "likely" chance (> 66%) requires cumulative emissions from all anthropogenic sources to be no more than 3670 GtCO$_2$ equivalent since 1870 (IPCC, 2013), implying scarce emission permits remaining and a heavy emissions reduction burden for the whole world (Peters et al., 2015; Millar et al., 2017; Raftery et al., 2017). Given "the common but differentiated responsibilities and respective capabilities", leading economies such as the United States, the European Union, China and India are confronted with huge mitigation challenge under the global rules (Jiang et al., 2019; Deenapanray, 2021). As an urgent response to climate change, the Paris Agreement adopted a bottom–up approach and required each Party to prepare, communicate and maintain successive Nationally Determined Contributions (NDCs) that express national pledges to reduce its emissions to meet the objectives of the United Nations Framework Convention on Climate Change (UNFCCC). Through the Paris Agreement, Parties also agreed to a long-term goal for adaptation — to increase the ability to adapt to the adverse impacts of climate change and foster climate resilience and low greenhouse gas (GHG) emissions development.

However, an enormous gap exists between the estimated emissions pathway under the NDCs and the feasible least-cost pathway limiting warming to below 2°C and 1.5°C above the pre-industrial temperatures of the Paris Agreement goal. According to the United Nations Environment Programme (UNEP) Emissions Gap Report 2020 (UNEP, 2020), if the current unconditional NDCs were fully implemented, the global temperature rise would be limited to 3.2°C (with a 66% probability) by the end of the century, resulting in emission gaps of $\sim$ 15 GtCO$_2$ equivalent (ranging from 12 GtCO$_2$ equivalent to 18 GtCO$_2$ equivalent) annually by 2030 compared with the 2°C scenario. For the 1.5°C scenario, the annual emissions gap would be as high as $\sim$ 32 GtCO$_2$ equivalent (ranging from 29 GtCO$_2$ equivalent to 35 GtCO$_2$ equivalent). The large gaps between NDCs and 2°C-consistent pathways call for a deep strengthening of the ambition of NDCs for all economies (Rogelj et al., 2016; Robiou du Pont et al., 2017; Höhne et al., 2017; Duan et al., 2019; Li and Duan, 2020).

Among all economies, the strengthening of the NDCs of Asian economies is particularly crucial, not only because Asia accounts for 58.9% of world population and 54.5% of the world CO$_2$ emissions (IEA, 2018), but also because Asia is one of the most vulnerable regions to climate change (Kraaijenbrink et al., 2017; Liu et al., 2018; Chevuturi et al., 2018). It is thus not surprising that a lot of literature works have already focused on emission budgets and how much the Asian economies are allowed to emit in the near future, especially the four leading Asian economies, i.e., China, Japan, South Korea and India (Höhne et al., 2014, 2017; Robiou du Pont et al., 2017; Pan et al., 2017). In contrast, very little attention has been paid to the rest of Asia, where $\sim$ 4.7 GtCO$_2$ was emitted in 2017, equivalent to the emissions of the entire USA or one and half times of emissions of the European Union in the same year (IEA,

2018). As these economies often belong to the least developed areas, most of them have established targets of increased emissions by 2030 compared with the 2010 level, to ensure their economic growth and improvement of social welfare.

Moreover, it is noteworthy that in most literature works, the allowable emissions quota for a certain economy in the future was usually calculated by allocating the global remaining emissions budget rather than the total emissions budget. The former is defined as available quota rule and the latter being total quota rule in this paper. The total emissions budget (i.e., total quota) denotes the global allowable emissions since records began until 2100 to make the Paris Agreement goals a reality, while the remaining emissions budget (i.e., available quota) means the global available emissions from now until 2100, which is equal to the difference of total emissions budget and historical emissions (Peters *et al.*, 2015). Available quota rule ignores different historical responsibilities among the economies and allocates remaining emission rights with all economies on an equal footing. Since there is no punishment for historical emissions, economies with high historical emissions may occupy the emission rights of those with very small historical emissions. For most developing economies, it would be more favorable if total quota rule rather than available quota rule is adopted. Due to the relatively small historical emissions, allowable emission quotas of the least developed Asian economies calculated from total quota are presumed to be larger than those calculated from the available quota.

Therefore, in this paper, we will focus on how strengthening of NDCs would allow Asian economies to explore ambitious and fair mitigation contributions to limit the global temperature rise under 2°C. More specifically, climate models have established a robust near-linear relationship between global warming and cumulative CO_2 emissions since industrialization. We will review both the unconditional and conditional NDCs of the major Asian economies, and explore the emissions gap between their NDCs and their cumulative emission budgets for meeting the Paris climate mitigation goals. In the process, the study will employ various allocation approaches corresponding to the widely used criteria including Equal-Per-Capita, Ability-to-Pay, Grandfather and Historical-Responsibility in the allowable quota distribution scheme, in the hope of providing an overall picture of the feasible mitigation pathways for Asian economies consistent with the Paris Agreement goals.

2. Method

2.1. *Estimating allowable emissions quota by economy*

GHG emissions come from three sources — non-CO_2 drivers, fossil-fuel combustion and industrial processes (FFI) and land-use change (LUC) (IPCC, 2013; Friedlingstein *et al.*, 2014; Peters *et al.*, 2015). In this study, we consider CO_2 emissions from FFI only, which play a major role in global warming. Limiting global warming to less than 2°C with a greater than 66% probability requires the global GHG emissions accumulated since 1870 to be no more than 3670 GtCO_2 equivalent, and this amount would be reduced to 2900 GtCO$_2$ when excluding non-CO$_2$ forcing (IPCC, 2013). According to the estimates of emissions from LUC (533 GtCO$_2$ from 1870 to 2014 and 138 GtCO$_2$ from 2014 to 2100) provided by Peters *et al.* (2015), the total CO$_2$ emissions from FFI in the past and future (the "total quota") would be limited to 2230 GtCO$_2$. More explicitly, historical CO$_2$ emissions from FFI from 1870 to 2019 were 1630 Gt[1]; the remaining emissions quota for FFI (the "available quota") would be ~ 600 Gt. Uncertainty arising from engineered sinks (afforestation and engineered carbon dioxide removal) is not within the scope of this paper, although recent research indicated that scalable development in engineered carbon sinks would allow more CO$_2$ to be emitted over time (Rockström *et al.*, 2017; Grassi *et al.*, 2018; Goglio *et al.*, 2020).

In order for integrating historical emissions of different periods and different economies with their current emissions, which makes the calculation simple and feasible, it is assumed that the effect of historical emissions of long-lived gases on global warming remains unchanged (Skeie *et al.*, 2021). Based on whether the historical contribution is taken into account, two methods are adopted to calculate future allowable emissions quota by economy. One starts from the available global quota over the period of 2020–2100, denoted by Q^A, and uses certain allocation approaches directly to obtain the available quota by economy. Another one starts from the total global quota over the period of 1870–2100, denoted by Q^T, and uses certain allocation approaches to get the total quota by economy and then individually subtract cumulative historical CO$_2$ emissions (1870–2019) to obtain the allowable emissions quota from 2020 to 2100. As to the allocation approach for distributing global quota to various economies, we employ three indicators reflecting the principle of "common but differentiated responsibilities and respective capabilities": (1) allocate global quota among economies in proportion to average population during 2010–2019, which corresponds to the Equal-Per-Capita criterion; (2) allocate global quota among economies based on the average GDP during 2010–2019, which corresponds to the Ability-to-Pay criterion; and (3) allocate global quota among economies according to historical CO$_2$ emissions from FFI during 2010–2019, which corresponds to the Grandfather criterion. To align with the Grandfather criterion, the allocation criteria based on historical CO$_2$ emissions are only applied to the available quota. As shown in Table 1, we establish five scenarios to estimate the allowable emissions quota from FFI for Asian economies.[2]

Take economy i as an example, we need to calculate the share of its population in the global population (denoted by p_i^{pop} and population here is quantified by the average population during 2010–2019), the share of its GDP in the global economy (denoted

---

[1]The global CO$_2$ emissions from FFI from 1870 to 2017 are drawn from the Potsdam Institute for Climate Impact Research of Germany (PIK; https://www.pik-potsdam.de), and the data for 2018 and 2019 are estimated based on the growth rate of global emissions released by bp p.l.c. (BP; https://www.bp.com/en/global/corporate/energy-economics/statistical-review-of-world-energy/co2-emissions.html).
[2]Population and GDP by economy are taken from World Bank; historical emissions here are characterized by the average FFI emissions of the past 10 years (2010–2019), using data from PIK and BP mentioned above.

Table 1. List of scenarios to calculate allowable emissions quota.

Scenario	Quota rule	Allocation criteria
S1	Available quota	Equal-Per-Capita/Population
S2		Ability-to-Pay/GDP
S3		Grandfather/CO_2 emissions
S4	Total quota	Equal-Per-Capita/Population
S5		Ability-to-Pay/GDP

by p_i^{GDP} and GDP here is quantified by the average GDP during 2010–2019) as well as the share of its historical emissions in the global historical emissions (denoted by p_i^{hie} and historical emissions here are quantified by the historical CO_2 emissions from FFI during 2010–2019). And then the allowable emissions quota of economy i under the above five scenarios can be calculated by

$$\begin{aligned} \text{quo}_i^{S1} &= Q^A * p_i^{pop}, \\ \text{quo}_i^{S2} &= Q^A * p_i^{GDP}, \\ \text{quo}_i^{S3} &= Q^A * p_i^{hie}, \\ \text{quo}_i^{S4} &= Q^T * p_i^{pop}, \\ \text{quo}_i^{S5} &= Q^T * p_i^{GDP}. \end{aligned} \quad (1)$$

2.2. Assessing ambitions of NDCs by economy

Given the allowable CO_2 emissions quota by economy under the above five scenarios, we followed Raupach *et al.* (2014) and Peters *et al.* (2015), to simulate the emission pathways from 2020 onwards for each economy. Assuming f_0 to represent the emissions in starting year, recent rate of change of emissions (r) to represent the current pathway and decay constant (m) to represent mitigation rate, decaying exponential is introduced to generate a smooth capped-emission trajectory, on which the emissions at time t, $f(t)$, are given by

$$f(t) = f_0[1 + (r+m)t]e^{-mt}. \quad (2)$$

Under the condition that total emissions quota given by the pathway, which is the area under the curve of exponential function (2) in mathematics, is equal to allowable emissions quota denoted by q, which is in accord with the Paris 2015 goals, the decay parameter, m, can be determined by

$$m(q) = \frac{1 + \sqrt{1 + rq/f_0}}{q/f_0}. \quad (3)$$

However, there is no solution for parameter m in the case that emissions are already decreasing at a rate faster than the required mitigation rate, for which a simple decaying exponential is used as an alternative:

$$f(t) = f_0 e^{-mt}. \tag{4}$$

By adjusting the values of variables such as starting year, ending year and committed emissions quota, the above method can also be adopted to simulate the smooth emission pathways under the conditional or unconditional NDCs. Then, the ambition and effectiveness of official commitments are assessed by comparing the ideal pathways consistent with the Paris 2015 goals under various scenarios with the pledged pathways consistent with unconditional or conditional NDCs (Höhne et al., 2017; Robiou du Pont et al., 2017). The NDCs need to be further strengthened if target emission pathways exceed the allowed emission pathways.

In this paper, we mainly focused on East Asia, Southeast Asia and South Asia, for which we have found their NDCs and historical CO_2 emissions from FFI. More specifically, we focused on the ambition of NDCs for 14 Asian economies, including five developed economies (Japan, South Korea, Singapore, Hong Kong of China and Taiwan of China) and nine developing economies (China, India, Indonesia, the Philippines, Pakistan, Thailand, Vietnam, Saudi Arabia and Iran).[3] Other Asian economies are not included in the research because either their NDCs or their historical CO_2 emissions are difficult to capture. In sum, these 14 economies accounted for respectively 84.6% of population, 86.3% of GDP and 88.8% of CO_2 emissions of Asia in 2018.

3. Results

3.1. *Allowable emission quotas from FFI of Asian economies under different scenarios*

Table 2 lists the allowable emission quotas from FFI by economy over the period of 2020–2100 under the five scenarios, with a 2°C (> 66%) of global temperature limit. The allowable emission quotas differ significantly under the five scenarios. By allocation criteria, the Ability-to-Pay criterion increases the allowable emissions quota of developed economies such as Japan, Singapore and Hong Kong of China, as well as the United States and the European Union. This is because developed economies represent a bigger fraction of the global GDP than they do of the total world population and carbon emissions. On the other hand, the Equal-Per-Capita criterion is in favor of economies with large population (such as India, Indonesia, Pakistan and Vietnam), whereas the Grandfather criterion is in favor of economies with high emissions

---

[3]Neither Hong Kong of China nor Taiwan of China is required to submit NDCs and here are replaced with the "Hong Kong's Climate Action Plan 2030+" published by the Environment Bureau and "Greenhouse Gas Emission Reduction and Management Act" passed by Legislative Yuan, respectively. For China and South Korea, we combine their NDCs with carbon-neutral targets by 2060 and 2050, respectively.

Table 2. Allowable emission quotas from FFI by economy over the period of 2020–2100 under the five scenarios, with a 2°C (> 66%) of global temperature limit (in Gt).

Economy	S1 (Available Population)	S2 (Available GDP)	S3 (Available Inertia)	S4 (Total Population)	S5 (Total GDP)
Bangladesh	12.77	1.50	1.47	45.84	3.93
China	112.49	80.96	187.86	186.07	68.87
Hong Kong, China	0.60	2.32	0.85	0.52	6.91
India	107.05	16.84	38.11	343.23	7.96
Indonesia	21.09	7.20	10.47	62.25	10.61
Iran	6.42	3.72	12.13	5.40	−4.67
Iraq	2.86	1.55	3.11	6.18	1.34
Israel	0.68	2.38	1.28	0.09	6.40
Japan	10.46	40.29	22.68	−28.06	82.80
Kuwait	0.30	1.08	1.85	−2.31	0.57
Malaysia	2.47	2.45	4.60	2.97	2.87
Oman	0.34	0.56	1.21	−0.06	0.76
Pakistan	16.25	1.96	3.47	55.16	2.03
The Philippines	8.32	2.28	2.09	27.55	5.12
Qatar	0.20	1.32	2.12	−1.58	2.59
Saudi Arabia	2.56	5.40	9.62	−3.48	7.07
Singapore	0.45	2.43	1.44	−0.13	7.23
South Korea	4.18	11.17	11.89	−2.90	23.09
Taiwan, China	1.93	4.14	5.14	−1.83	6.40
Thailand	5.63	3.28	5.96	12.98	4.24
United Arab Emirates	0.76	2.89	3.51	−1.71	6.21
Vietnam	7.58	1.46	3.71	24.18	1.43
United States	26.25	138.33	100.52	−367.07	49.49
European Union	36.51	115.30	57.09	−150.88	141.97

intensity per capita or per unit of GDP (such as China, Iran, Saudi Arabia, Iraq and Oman).

By quota rule, the total quota rules generally yield lower results than the available quota rules for the economies with large historical emissions. For example, according to the average data in 2010–2019, emissions per capita of Asian developed economies such as Japan, South Korea, Singapore, Hong Kong of China and Taiwan of China as well as the United States and the European Union were high, respectively ranking 10th, 8th, 7th, 16th, 9th, 4th and 14th out of the 24 economies in Table 2. For these economies, available quota rules under the S4 scenario (calculated by the difference between quota allocated from global total quota based on the Equal-Per-Capita criterion and historical emissions) are generally lower than those under the S1 scenario (allocated directly from global remaining quota based on the Equal-Per-Capita criterion). By allocation criteria, the Equal-Per-Capita criterion yields much higher results than the Ability-to-Pay criterion for most developing economies with large population and relatively low GDP per capita, regardless of the quota rule. These economies include Bangladesh, China, India, Indonesia, Pakistan, the Philippines and Vietnam.

In summary, there are three scenarios involving historical emissions in favor of the Asian economies. For economies with lower historical emissions per capita, such as Bangladesh, India, Indonesia, Iraq, Pakistan, the Philippines, Thailand and Vietnam, the S4 scenario considering historical emissions and population is the most favorable. The S5 scenario considering historical emissions and GDP benefits economies with lower historical emissions per unit of GDP, such as Hong Kong of China, Israel, Japan, Qatar, Singapore, South Korea, Taiwan of China and United Arab Emirates. Economies whose historical emissions per capita and historical emissions per unit of GDP were both high, such as China, Iran, Kuwait, Malaysia, Oman and Saudi Arabia, would be benefited from the S3 scenario which neglects historical responsibility but considers emissions inertia.

3.2. *Assessment and comparison of the ambition of Asian economies' NDCs*

Figures 1 and 2 show the emissions trajectory pathways of Asian developed and developing economies under conditional or unconditional NDCs, and compare them with the ideal emission pathways to achieve the global temperature rise below 2°C with a greater than 66% probability under the five scenarios that apply different rules to allocate the global allowable emissions quota. For all scenarios, the historical CO_2 data for FFI from 1990 to 2017 is drawn from PIK, and the data for 2018 and 2019 are estimated based on the growth rate of global emissions released by BP. As aforementioned, from 2020 to 2100, emission pathways of Asian economies are simulated following Raupach *et al.* (2014) and Peters *et al.* (2015) under the constraints of allowable emissions quota calculated based on different effort-sharing approaches (different quota rules and allocation criteria). Conditional or unconditional emissions reduction commitments in the NDCs are shown as the CO_2 trajectories of emissions from 2020 to 2030. In particular, the emission trajectories of China and South Korea under NDCs have also incorporated their recent pledges to become carbon-neutral by 2060 and by 2050, respectively.

As shown in Figs. 1 and 2, gaps exist generally between the emissions under NDCs (conditional or unconditional) and the emissions to achieve Paris Agreement goal for most Asian economies. As a note, the gaps here are not comparable with the total emissions gap published in the UNEP Emissions Gap Report 2020 (UNEP, 2020). A primary reason is that we excluded emissions from LUC when calculating the remaining emissions quota, while the UNEP did not. In addition, emission scenarios established in this paper are less than those in the UNEP Report, which also makes them incomparable.

For the major developing Asian economies, especially China, India, Pakistan, Vietnam and Thailand, the strengths of NDCs are not ambitious enough, regardless of the allocation approaches. There are large gaps between the emission trajectories resulting from their official pledges and from each of the allocating scenarios. More importantly, these five economies are experiencing rapid development and show very high growth rate of annual CO_2 emissions from 1990 to 2019. As a result, their conditional and unconditional NDCs still plan increase of annual emissions until 2030,

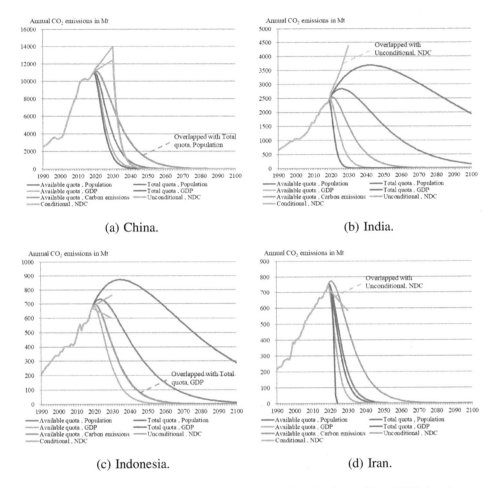

Notes: (1) In panel (a), the emission trajectories of China under conditional and unconditional NDCs have incorporated its recent pledge to become carbon-neutral by 2060. (2) For economies that made no distinction between conditional commitment and unconditional commitment in the NDCs, such as India, Iran, Pakistan and the Philippines, emissions trajectory under conditional NDCs coincided with that under unconditional NDCs. (3) As shown in panels (a), (c), (e) and (h), emission pathways under a certain constraint of allowable emissions quota might be overlapped with other lines due to the nearly equal allowable emission quotas calculated under different scenarios. Take panel (a) as an example; according to Table 2, the allowable emissions quota of China calculated by the available quota rule and Grandfather criterion (the S3 scenario) is 187.86 $GtCO_2$ and that calculated by the total quota rule and Equal-Per-Capita criterion (the S4 scenario) is 186.07 $GtCO_2$. We have inserted a description for those emissions pathway lines that seem to be overlapped under different scenarios.

Figure 1. Emission pathways of Asian developing economies to make Paris Agreement goal a reality under the constraints of different allowable emission quotas versus the CO_2 trajectories of emissions conditionally or unconditionally pledged in their NDCs.

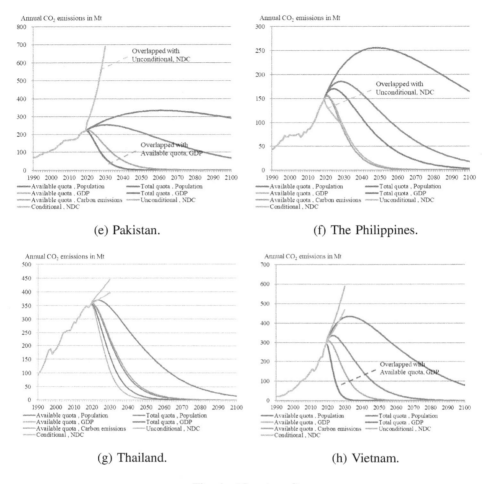

Fig. 1. (*Continued*)

to ensure their further economic and social development. Even with the least stringent allocation rule, i.e., the Scenario 4 that considers the amount of population and small historical emissions, their growing trajectory pathways under NDCs still far exceed their corresponding ideal pathways to achieve global limit of temperature rise below 2°C. It is clear that their ambitions on emissions reduction are in urgent need of strengthening, as overcoming the emissions growth will bear the brunt of it. For the remaining developing Asian economies, including Indonesia, Iran and the Philippines, the trajectory pathways under conditional NDCs show decreases of annual emissions from 2020 to 2030. Therefore, their trajectory pathways under NDCs are within the boundary of their own ideal pathways to achieve global temperature rise limit, showing ambition and effectiveness of their NDCs.

For the major developed Asian economies, including Japan, South Korea, Singapore, Hong Kong of China and Taiwan of China, the strengths of NDCs are to some extent reasonable. In particular, the emission pathways of Hong Kong of China and

Singapore under both unconditional and conditional NDCs are well below their corresponding ideal pathways to achieve global target regardless of the allocation rule, showing ambition and effectiveness of their pledges. For Japan, South Korea, Taiwan of China and Saudi Arabia, the official emission pledges under NDCs are barely satisfactory only when the looser constraint on allowed emissions is applied. For example, the NDCs of Japan, South Korea and Taiwan of China can be considered broadly effective based on the Ability-to-Pay criterion, but fruitless based on the Equal-Per-Capita criterion. However, all the Asian developed economies excluding

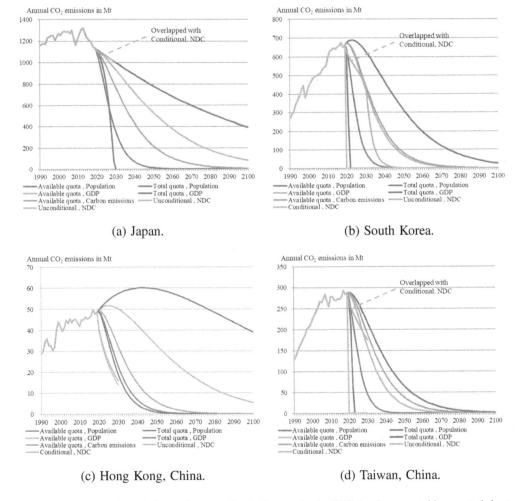

(a) Japan.   (b) South Korea.

(c) Hong Kong, China.   (d) Taiwan, China.

Notes: (1) In panel (b), the emissions trajectory of South Korea under the NDCs has incorporated its recent pledge to become carbon-neutral by 2050. (2) For economies that made no distinction between conditional commitment and unconditional commitment in the NDCs, such as Japan, South Korea, Taiwan of China, Saudi Arabia and Singapore, the emissions trajectory under conditional NDCs coincided with that under the unconditional NDCs.

Figure 2. Emission pathways of Asian developed economies to make the Paris Agreement goal a reality under the constraints of different allowable emission quotas versus the CO_2 trajectories of emissions conditionally or unconditionally pledged in their NDCs.

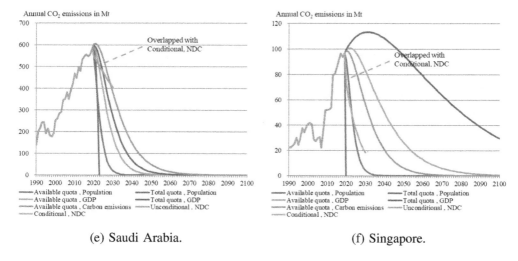

(e) Saudi Arabia. (f) Singapore.

Fig. 2. (*Continued*)

Japan still show an upward trend of annual CO$_2$ emissions until 2019. This implies that they need very stringent policies to achieve their NDCs.

4. Conclusions and Discussion

In this paper, we focused on the Asian economies, and explored their ambitious and fair mitigation contributions to limit the global temperature rise under 2°C. By comparing the CO$_2$ trajectories of emissions that are conditionally or unconditionally pledged in NDCs with the emission pathways of Asian economies to make the Paris Agreement goal a reality under the constraints of different allowable emission quotas, we assessed the ambition and effectiveness of NDCs for the major Asian economies. In the process, various rules addressing historical responsibility, capability, equity and inertia are employed, in the hope to provide an overall picture on the feasible mitigation pathways of Asian economies consistent with the Paris Agreement goals.

Our results show that allowable emission quotas for the major Asian economies are largely determined by the desired effort-sharing approaches. With the exception of a few developed economies in Fig. 2, most Asian economies in Fig. 1 would be benefited from the equity rules based on population and historical emissions with obtaining more allowable emission quotas. Meanwhile, the equity rules based on GDP Ability-to-Pay criterion would bring more pressures and challenges to carbon reduction of the major Asian developing economies with less allowable emission quotas, while most developed economies would obtain higher allowable emission quotas.

Our results also suggest that the official mitigation pledges represented by NDCs until 2030 must be strengthened to close the emissions gap for reaching the 2°C goal for most developing Asian economies. The major developing emitters within Asia, such as China, India, Vietnam, Thailand and Pakistan, are far less ambitious in their NDCs, even compared with the allowable emissions quota under the least stringent scenario based on population and historical emissions. In contrast, most of the developed Asian economies illustrate a reasonable or even ambitious pledges to cut CO_2 emissions that are aligned with the ideal pathways under all scenarios, while the rapid decline in carbon emissions and reaching even zero-carbon by 2050 is still pressing, given their current growing trend of annual CO_2 emissions by 2019. A systemic and comprehensive clarification of Asian efforts is of great significance for consolidating the mitigation effectiveness and international image of Asia, as well as inspiring other regions to make positive contributions.

It should be noted, however, that our analysis only concerns the NDCs until 2030, while some Asian economies have already committed to a much more ambitious net-zero emissions goal by 2050 or 2060. For example, China announced plans to achieve carbon neutrality before 2060, Japan announced a goal of net-zero GHG emissions by 2050 and the Republic of Korea committed to become carbon-neutral by 2050 in a speech to parliament. In fact, 73 UNFCCC parties, 14 regions, 398 cities, 768 businesses and 16 investors have announced net-zero CO_2 emission goals by 2050, according to the release of the 25th session of the Conference of the Parties (COP 25) in 2019. The growing number of economies that are committing to net-zero emission goals by around mid-century is the most significant and encouraging climate policy development. These efforts to realize net-zero carbon dioxide emissions show enormous potential in helping alleviate negative social and ecological effects caused by climate change. To remain feasible and credible, it is imperative that these commitments are urgently translated into strong near-term policies and action, and are reflected in the NDCs, including scalable deployment of low-carbon, zero-carbon and negative-carbon techniques (Jiang *et al.*, 2019; Goglio *et al.*, 2020).

Acknowledgments

This work was supported by the National Natural Science Foundation of China (71873091, 71974183, 5171102058 and 72003133) and the National Fund of Philosophy and Social Science of China (20&ZD055).

References

Chevuturi, A, NP Klingaman, AG Turner and S Hannah (2018). Projected changes in the Asian-Australian monsoon region in 1.5°C and 2.0°C global-warming scenarios. *Earth's Future*, 6(3), 339–358.

Deenapanray, PNK (2021). Increasing the ambition of mitigation action in small emitters: The case of Mauritius. *Climate Policy*, 21(4), 514–528.

Duan, HB, GP Zhang, SY Wang and Y Fan (2019). Robust climate change research: A review on multi-model analysis. *Environmental Research Letters*, 14(3), 033001.

Friedlingstein, P, RM Andrew, J Rogelj, GP Peters, JG Canadell, R Knutti, G Luderer, MR Raupach, M Schaeffer, DP van Vuuren and C Le Quéré (2014). Persistent growth of CO_2 emissions and implications for reaching climate targets. *Nature Geoscience*, 7(10), 709–715.

Goglio, P, AG Williams, N Balta-Ozkan, NRP Harris, P Williamson, D Huisingh, Z Zhang and M Tavoni (2020). Advances and challenges of life cycle assessment (LCA) of greenhouse gas removal technologies to fight climate changes. *Journal of Cleaner Production*, 244, 118896.

Grassi, G, J House, WA Kurz, A Cescatti, RA Houghton, GP Peters, MJ Sanz, RA Vinas, R Alkama, A Arneth, A Bondeau, F Dentener, M Fader, S Federici, P Friedlingstein, AK Jain, E Kato, CD Koven, D Lee, JEMS Nabel, AA Nassikas, L Perugini, S Rossi, S Sitch, N Viovy, A Wiltshire and S Zaehle (2018). Reconciling global-model estimates and country reporting of anthropogenic forest CO_2 sinks. *Nature Climate Change*, 8(10), 914–920.

Höhne, N, M den Elzen and D Escalante (2014). Regional GHG reduction targets based on effort sharing: a comparison of studies. *Climate Policy*, 14(1), 122–147.

Höhne, N, T Kuramochi, C Warnecke, F Röser, H Fekete, M Hagemann, T Day, R Tewari, M Kurdziel, S Sterl and S Gonzales (2017). The Paris Agreement: resolving the inconsistency between global goals and national contributions. *Climate Policy*, 17(1), 16–32.

IEA (2018) CO_2 Emissions from Fuel Combustion, IEA Press, Paris.

Intergovernmental Panel on Climate Change (IPCC) (2013). *AR5 Climate Change 2013: The Physical Science Basis: Contribution of Working Group I to the Fifth Assessment Report of the Intergovernmental Panel on Climate Change*. Cambridge, UK: Cambridge University Press. Available at https://www.ipcc.ch/report/ar5/wg1/. Accessed on 27 Septermber 2013.

Jiang, XM, GP Peters and C Green (2019). Global rules mask the mitigation challenge facing developing countries. *Earth's Future*, 7(4), 428–432.

Kraaijenbrink, PDA, MFP Bierkens, AF Lutz and WW Immerzeel (2017). Impact of a global temperature rise of 1.5 degrees Celsius on Asia's glaciers. *Nature*, 549(7671), 257–260.

Li, MY and MS Duan (2020). Efforts-sharing to achieve the Paris goals: Ratcheting-up of NDCs and taking full advantage of international carbon market. *Applied Energy*, 280, 115864.

Liu, WB, FB Sun, WH Lim, J Zhang, H Wang, H Shiogama and YQ Zhang (2018). Global drought and severe drought-affected populations in 1.5 and 2°C warmer worlds. *Earth System Dynamics*, 9(1), 267–283.

Millar, RJ, JS Fuglestvedt, P Friedlingstein, J Rogelj, MJ Grubb, HD Matthews, RB Skeie, PM Forster, DJ Frame and MR Allen (2017). Emission budgets and pathways consistent with limiting warming to 1.5°C. *Nature Geoscience*, 10, 741–747.

Pan, XZ, M den Elzen, N Hoehne, F Teng and LN Wang (2017). Exploring fair and ambitious mitigation contributions under the Paris Agreement goals. *Environmental Science & Policy*, 74, 49–56.

Peters, GP, RM Andrew, S Solomon and P Friedlingstein (2015). Measuring a fair and ambitious climate agreement using cumulative emissions. *Environmental Research Letters*, 10(10), 105004.

Raftery, AE, A Zimmer, DMW Frierson, R Startz and PR Liu (2017). Less than 2°C warming by 2100 unlikely. *Nature Climate Change*, 7(9), 637–641.

Raupach, M, S Davis, G Peters, R Andrew, J Canadell, P Ciais, P Friedlingstein, F Jotzo, D van Vuuren and CL Quéré (2014). Sharing a quota on cumulative carbon emissions. *Nature Climate Change*, 4(10), 873–879.

Robiou du Pont, Y, ML Jeffery, J Gutschow, J Rogelj, P Christoff and M Meinshausen (2017). Equitable mitigation to achieve the Paris Agreement goals. *Nature Climate Change*, 7(1), 38–43.

Rockström, J, O Gaffney, J Rogelj, M Meinshausen, N Nakicenovic and HJ Schellnhuber (2017). A roadmap for rapid decarbonization. *Science*, 355(6331), 1269–1271.

Rogelj, J, M den Elzen, N Höhne, T Fransen, H Fekete, H Winkler, RS Chaeffer, F Ha, K Riahi and M Meinshausen (2016). Paris Agreement climate proposals need a boost to keep warming well below 2°. *Nature*, 534(7609), 631–639.

Skeie, RB, GP Peters, J Fuglestvedt and R Andrew (2021). A future perspective of historical contributions to climate change. *Climatic Change*, 164(1), 24:1–24:13.

United Nations Environment Programme (UNEP) (2020). Emissions Gap Report 2020. Available at https://www.unep.org/emissions-gap-report-2020#. Accessed on 9 December 2020.

HOW THE SATELLITE CITY IS AFFECTING CO$_2$ EMISSIONS[§§]

DANQI LIAO[*], LISI GUO[*], GENGYUAN LIU[*,†,**,‡‡], FENG WU[‡],
CAOCAO CHEN[§], XIN'AN YIN[*,†], JINGYAN XUE[*], QING YANG[¶],
HUI LI[¶,††,‡‡] and MARCO CASAZZA[‖]

[*]*State Key Joint Laboratory of Environment*
Simulation and Pollution Control
School of Environment, Beijing Normal University
Beijing 100875, China

[†]*Beijing Engineering Research Center for Watershed*
Environmental Restoration & Integrated Ecological Regulation
Beijing 100875, China

[‡]*Center for Chinese Agricultural Policy*
Institute of Geographic Sciences and Natural Resources Research
Chinese Academy of Sciences, Beijing 100101, China

[§]*Beijing Climate Change Research Center, Beijing 100031, China*

[¶]*Key Laboratory for City Cluster Environmental*
Safety and Green Development of the Ministry of Education
Institute of Environmental and Ecological Engineering
Guangdong University of Technology, Guangzhou 510006, China

[‖]*Department of Sciences and Technologies*
University of Napoli 'Parthenope'
Centro Direzionale, Isola C4, Napoli 80143, Italy
[**]*liugengyuan@bnu.edu.cn*
[††]*lihuui0104@gdut.edu.cn*

To achieve the Paris Agreement's goals, many cities are building satellite cities to relieve the population and environment pressure of the central city. However, past experiences showed that long-term effects of such a solution were partially limited, due to limited attention on the effects of energy consumption and carbon emissions, depending on the dynamics of population and industrial development. This paper overcomes the previous limitations, applying a Long-range Energy Alternatives Planning model to the area of Xiong'an New District, an area extending from Hebei province (China) and nearby Beijing, is planned to support the development of Beijing. The proposed model was based on three different population migration, industrial and transposition scenarios to test their impacts on urban greenhouse gas (GHG) emissions. Results show that: (1) Increased population and building area will markedly increase GHG emissions

---

[‡‡]Corresponding authors.
[§§]This chapter was originally published in Climate Change Economics, Vol. 13, No. 1 (2021), published by World Scientific Publishing, Singapore. Reprinted with permission.

from residential consumption in Hebei province, while slightly decrease GHG emissions in Beijing. (2) Green planning, including industrial structure changes, industrial transformation, will markedly decrease the GHG emissions in Hebei provinces and it can take down for the emissions increase due to the population migration. This paper proved the effectiveness of a multi-scalar, multi-dimensional, and multi-actor modeling approach for a satellite city and new town development planning, implying that a similar approach could be applied in planning and managing the development of future satellite cities.

Keywords: Satellite city; GHG emissions; LEAP; Paris Agreement targets.

1. Introduction

1.1. *Background*

Global climate change is an issue of common concern to humankind. The main goal of Paris Agreement is to keep the increase in global average temperature below 2°C in this century and limit its increase to 1.5°C above the pre-industrial level (Rive, 2016). The Emissions Gap Report 2019, released by the United Nations Environment Programme (UNEP), stated that global greenhouse gas (GHG) emissions increased by 1.5% annually over the past decade (UNEP, 2019). To achieve the Paris Agreement's goal of limiting global warming to 2°C before industrialization by 2100, global carbon emissions need to be reduced by 2.7% annually during 2020–2030, while, to achieve the goal of limiting warming to 1.5°C, global carbon emissions need to be reduced by 7.6% annually during 2020–2030 (UNEP, 2019).

Therefore, all countries are exploring ways to reduce their carbon emissions. China proposes to increase its autonomous national contribution and adopt stronger policies and technologies to reach peak CO_2 emissions by 2030 and achieve carbon neutrality by 2060. This is by far the largest climate commitment among countries in the world to reduce global warming expectations, and an important step in the fight against global climate change under the Paris Agreement. China's 13th Five-Year Plan to control GHG emissions points out that, in addition to coordinating the creation of a national low-carbon industrial system and achieving an energy revolution, it is also necessary to analyze the development of cities and towns and adopt different carbon emission control targets for provinces and cities at different stages of development. In particular, some optimization development zones, for example, Beijing, Shanghai, Hebei, etc., should achieve the first peak. Also, the low-carbon development models of some pilot regions will become the reference basis for the future development of other regions. It can be seen that under the Paris Agreement, China's low-carbon development is crucial for the world, and in China, the emission reduction programs of some developed provinces and cities will become an important driving force in the national response to climate change. Since cities cause the vast majority of a country's emissions, low-carbon urban development is important for achieving national carbon neutrality. In the case of Chinese cities, low-carbon development actions are anticipated by planning. Based on economic and social development trends and urban emission features, low-carbon targets are set, while the implementation of low-carbon development actions in cities is prioritized and phased. This process should allow cities to achieve carbon neutrality by improving energy efficiency and renewable energy applications. However, due to the huge population, increasing demanding for transportation and housing solutions, urban emissions remain high, with many industrially developed cities and mega cities emitting over a billion tons of carbon dioxide. Unlike the cities or urban areas that have declared carbon neutrality so far, most of them are post-industrial cities, with a population of 1 million or less and a carbon emissions peak at 10 million tons of CO_2 or less. For some over-populated mega cities with huge carbon emissions, such as Beijing, in addition to low-carbon development planning within the city, there is a need to explore means of emission reduction beyond the city scale. In this context, the development of new cities or satellite cities is considered an important measure for low-carbon transition.

1.2. Literature review

1.2.1. Satellite city construction experiences

The definition of 'satellite city' is still unclear, often being referred to planned new developments around existing (large) cities, meant to solve large city problems or to raise urban competitiveness, targeting specific population groups and/or economic sectors with a specific theme or "brand" (Bontje, 2019). In particular, satellite cities should support the reduction of current population size of central cities and the pressure of urban employment and infrastructure, thereby playing a key role in combating urban diseases caused by the over-expansion of big cities.

Ideally, a new city or a satellite city can achieve the goal of reducing carbon emissions in a quick and effective way by decentralizing its population and industry. However, domestic and foreign experience showed that the construction of new cities or satellite cities may fail or affect other surrounding cities. In fact, the planning and design of a new city, as well as their influence on the life of the central city, were often insufficiently considered (Xie, 2010). For example, in the case of London, the British government established eight new cities in the London area during 1946–1949 to address housing problems and implement rational decentralization of population and industry. However, the adopted decentralization policy resulted in the shrinking of the inner urban areas of London in the mid-to-late 1970s. In 1978, the government passed the Inner Urban Areas Act 1978 and shifted the focus of urban construction onto inner urban areas renewal (Liu, 2018).

Tokyo (Japan) drew on the London model to develop a metropolitan area plan with the core idea of decentralizing the urban functions of central Tokyo and changing the urban form from monocentric to polycentric. The construction of the metropolitan area was able to significantly reduce the pressure of population growth in Tokyo (Sorensen, 2001). However, there was a significant population return problem in the mid-to-late 1990s, due to the separation of jobs and residences, the lack of transportation access between the new city and the old city, and other imperfect infrastructure development (Liu *et al.*, 2018).

Seoul (South Korea) has entered a rapid urbanization phase since the 1960s and urban disease has gradually become serious (Zhang and Dong, 2015). The long-term Seoul population dispersal plan had no obvious effect, even after 1990s, when the Korean government built five new cities around Seoul, focusing on service industry development and supporting transportation construction (Ding, 2007). Finally, the ratio of population and employment opportunities declined in the central city. Then, the new cities experienced rapid economic development and population growth, achieving a significant effect of deconstruction (Zhang and Dong, 2015).

In a comprehensive view, the main purpose of a new city construction is to achieve population and industry diversion from the central city and to promote a coordinated and integrated regional development. The experience of a new city construction in several countries shows that new cities can achieve population decongestion, urban transit development, and regional economic growth. Nonetheless, it also reveals the poor effect of population decongestion in central cities, the return of population from new cities to old cities, the separation of residence and employment and the unsustainability of new cities.

These experiences provide a rich reference and inspiration for solving the problem of "big city disease" and the construction of new cities. In particular, they take the central city as the key object to explore the decongestion effect and the socioeconomic impacts of the new infrastructures. Conversely, the impact of traffic and architectural changes on urban energy demand remain often unexplored.

1.2.2. *Energy consumption and CO_2 emission in new city construction*

In recent years, some studies have attempted to conduct related research, starting from transportation solutions, architecture, and industry sectors. For example, Liu (2010) proposed the development of bus and rail transportation and the design of environment-friendly pavement to improve low-carbon transport solutions in satellite cities. Liu (2018) took Xishan, a new city in Urumqi, as an example and established the "population–economy–land–carbon emission", based on system dynamics, mainly considering population and land use changes, dividing the model internally into five sectors: buildings (including residential buildings and public buildings), commercial services, industry, transportation, and carbon sinks, defining five corresponding sub-models. The author found that industrial carbon emissions account for 50–80% of the total, becoming the key sector for reducing carbon emissions. Building emissions accounted for 10–30% of the total emissions. In parallel, heating was the focus of energy saving, while transportation mode and transport system were coordinated with population density. The author suggested that bus should be the main transportation mode in the early stage of new city construction, while railroad transportation was considered to reduce carbon emissions when the population density is higher. The carbon sequestration capacity of green areas was only one-thousandth of the emissions from building, industry, commercial service and transportation sectors. This is why it would be necessary to build a stronger carbon-capture capacity of green areas.

Earlier experiences of city–regional development strategies were inspiration sources for China, when it started its urban and economic transformation in the late 1970s (Zhang, 2012). Beijing, the capital of China, is striving for the strategic orientation of the capital city in the new era to build a world-class, harmonious, and livable capital. The core strategy fixed by the Central Politburo of the Communist Party of China in 2015 was to decentralize Beijing's noncapital functions in an orderly manner, to adjust its economic structure and spatial structure, to embark on a new path of intensive development, and to explore a model of optimal development in areas with dense population and intensive economy, thus promoting cooperative regional development and forming a new growth pole. However, the development of Beijing and Tianjin is limited by available resources and their environmental conditions. Thus, Research and Development (R&D) achievements are required to produce a sufficient economic performance. Hebei, which surrounds Beijing and Tianjin, can become an important carrier and base for such a purpose. The Xiong'an New Area, composed of Xiong County, Rongcheng County, and Anxin County, together with some surrounding areas in Hebei province, was planned as one of the two new wings of Beijing's development to undertake the historical task of solving Beijing's "urban diseases" and to explore a new model of optimal development in areas with a dense population and an intensive economy.

Many studies focused on overcoming current urban constrains in Beijing. Based on the urban studies on capital regions abroad, Liu (2018) found that the new city and the central city need a reasonable division of labor to prevent the new city from weakening the international influence of the central city. The construction of a new city should be carried out in stages, should emphasize the renewal and transformation of the central city and support the new city, and should build a supporting public transport system and service system. It requires also legally-effective planning and strict law enforcement to guarantee its construction. Zhao (2019), through a system dynamics modeling approach, explored the path of population decentralization in the capital from the perspective of industrial decentralization, proposed to strengthen the top-down design of the government, and optimized a balanced distribution of the capital's population based on its functional orientation, in which there is a favorable effect of the construction of the Xiong'an New Area on the reduction of population pressure and high-quality economic development in Beijing. In the context of Beijing–Tianjin–Hebei cooperative development, Wang *et al.* (2019) proposed improving a top-down design of noncapital functions, establishing a connection mechanism between Beijing's noncapital functional decentralization and the surrounding bearing areas, boosting population decentralization, propelling key new cities in Beijing to carry out the pilot program, comprehensively support reforms, use construction land in a careful and intensive way, and reduce noncapital functional bearing space.

From the perspective of urban planning, most studies considered the aspects that need to be paid attention to in the process of industrial and population transfer. Conversely, there are few studies on the effect of industrial and population migration on the carbon emissions of central and new cities (Tong and Wang, 2016; Tong et al., 2020). This study overcomes such a limitation, proposing the application of a carbon emission research model, in order to examine this issue and to further explore the feasibility and necessity of the development and construction of new cities in the context of global climate change.

The specific research is divided into five sections. Section 1 is the introduction, which summarizes and analyzes the experience of the world satellite city construction, the current situation of urban energy research and the current situation of the study area, etc., and explores the key research objectives of this study. Section 2 is the methodological introduction, which collects data to establish the Long-range Energy Alternatives Planning (LEAP) model for the central city and satellite city. It also analyzes the energy changes in the transportation and building sectors brought by the population and industrial undertaking during the construction of Xiong'an New Area and the area where the New Area is located, and constructs different scenarios. Section 3 is the result analysis, which summarizes the impact of the construction of the Xiong'an New Area (satellite city) on the energy consumption and carbon emissions in Beijing (central city) and Hebei (satellite city location). Section 4 is the discussion, which compares the results with the development goals, and makes policy recommendations. Section 5 is the conclusion, which summarizes the results and the findings of the discussion, and discusses the shortcomings of this study and its importance for future development from a long-term perspective.

2. Methods

2.1. *Energy and CO_2 dynamic prediction model for new city construction*

A variety of dynamic prediction models have been developed for energy resource planning and for the assessment of GHGs emission reduction, including system dynamic models, computable general equilibrium (CGE) models (Fan et al., 2018), improved energy models (Guo, 2011; Khan et al., 2017), and LEAP model (Shin et al., 2005; Cao et al., 2010; Tao et al., 2011; Emodi et al., 2017).

In general, these models can be divided into three categories by modeling approach: top-down models (e.g., CGE); bottom-up models (e.g., LEAP); hybrid models. Top-down models, which take economic models as a starting point, are more often used in regions with more developed market systems and focus on the macroeconomic situation of a region. CGE models are commonly used to study the impact of emission reduction policies on economic development and the environment. Chemingui and Thabet (2014) analyzed the effects of CO_2 emissions on ambient air concentration levels and physical health based on CGE models. Liu and Hu (2015) analyzed the carbon tax on production in the agricultural sector based on the CGE model to explore the extent of the impact of agricultural GHG emission reduction on China's rural economy.

Bottom-up model is an energy technology model, that takes engineering technology as the starting point for a detailed modeling and simulation calculation of energy consumption and production processes, forecasting the long-term energy demand and supply of a certain region or industry and using the results to analyze its impact on the environment. In particular, LEAP can be used as an energy policy simulation tool based on scenario analysis and a database of energy system history. Data requirements are more flexible. Thus, the LEAP model is more suitable for this study. LEAP contains four modules: key assumption, demand, transformation, and resources. The demand and transformation module is the most critical module in the model. This is because energy consumption in the model is the sum of the energy demand for final use and the energy demand in the energy conversion process. In this study, LEAP models were built for the areas of Beijing (LEAP-Beijing) and Hebei (LEAP-Hebei). The model framework is shown in Fig. 1.

The main difference between the LEAP-Beijing and the LEAP-Hebei models design lies in the industrial and service branches of the demand module. According to the Hebei Economic Yearbook, the main energy-consuming sector in Hebei was the industrial sector (The People's Government of Hebei Province, 2020). Therefore, compared to LEAP-Beijing, LEAP-Hebei considered the characteristics of industrial energy consumption in Hebei province and divided industries into key energy-consuming industries and other energy-consuming industries. More detailed divisions were made, such as food, tobacco, and textile and leather under the manufacturing industry. According to the Beijing Statistical Yearbook, the main energy-consuming sector in Beijing was the service industry, which was divided into accommodation and catering, wholesale and retail, education, and real estate (Beijing Municipal Bureau of Statistics, 2019). Such a division was excluded in LEAP-Hebei.

Considering the relocation of some governmental functions and people from Beijing to Xiong'an New Area, the implementation of GHG mitigation measures in Beijing and their influence for Hebei can be analyzed by setting respective parameters in different alternative scenarios. With respect to such alternatives, the Xiong'an New Area undertakes the population and industry of Beijing, alleviating the heavy population and economic burdens of the capital.

Figure 2 visualizes the geographical relationship between Beijing, Hebei, and Xiong'an New Area (three main counties in the Xiong'an New Area: Xiong County, Anxin County, and Rongcheng County). Table A.1 in Appendix A summarizes the changes in industrial characteristics after Xiong'an New Area took over Beijing's industries.

2.2. Scenario building

Three scenarios, S1, S2, and S3, were set both in Beijing and Hebei, based on the size of the population that the Xiong'an New Area would undertake. In these scenarios, the differences involve changes in industrial structure and population. A business as usual (BAU) scenario was defined for Beijing and Hebei based on historical data. The base year was 2015 and the scenario years spanned from 2016 to 2050.

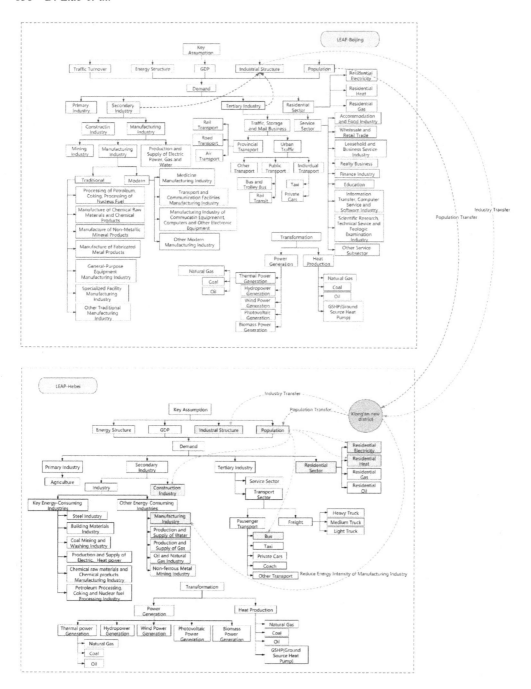

Figure 1. Framework of LEAP-Hebei–Xiong'an–Beijing model.

The baseline scenarios of both areas were established based on historical data. They represent the basic case and no further energy saving measures are considered. On the other hand, three levels of development scenarios were set up at the two areas according to the level of population and industry transfer. In scenario S1, the Xiong'an

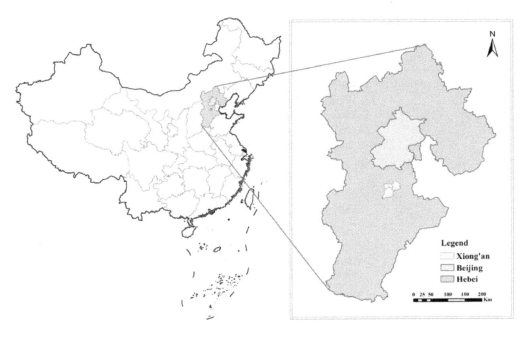

Figure 2. Map of study area.

New Area undertakes a small population and small-scale industries from Beijing, and the economic growth accelerates. Under scenario S2, the population and industry undertaken from Beijing are larger than those in S1 and under scenario S3 the population and industry are larger than those in S2. The list of scenarios is shown in Table 1.

2.3. Parameters setting in model

2.3.1. Population size changes

Based on population size changes, we considered the effects of linkage factors on energy consumption and carbon emissions in Hebei province. The effect of demographic factors on CO_2 emissions can be examined by the overall population size, the population age structure, and the average household population size. The population size can affect production and consumption. Different age structures may affect economic growth. The average household size can affect household consumption (Jin, 2016).

This study examined the effect of these three factors on the division of sector emissions in the model. In particular, changing the population size, the associated variables will change. With respect to other variables, additional scenarios need to be set in the corresponding sectors, that is, transport and construction, to examine their potential changes in energy consumption and CO_2 emissions. Through literature research and expert consultation, we examined the effects of transfer from Beijing to

Table 1. Summary of baseline and alternative scenarios.

Area	Scenario	Details
Beijing	Baseline (BAU)	2016–2050 forecast based on year 2015 data
	S1	Small-scale population transfer
		Decrease in volume of passenger traffic match with population decline:
		By 2025, the initial industrial transfer will be achieved, and by 2035, industrial transfer will be basically completed
	S2	Medium-scale population transfer
		Decrease in volume of passenger traffic match with population decline:
		By 2025, the initial industrial transfer will be achieved, and by 2035, industrial transfer will be basically completed
	S3	Large-scale population transfer
		Decrease in volume of passenger traffic match with population decline:
		By 2025, the initial industrial transfer will be achieved, and by 2035, industrial transfer will be basically completed
Hebei	Baseline (BAU)	2016–2050 forecast based on year 2015 data
	S1	Xiong'an New Area undertaking small population from Beijing
		The increase in the number of buses match with small population
		Increase in floor space match with small population
		Change in economic factors under S1
	S2	Xiong'an New Area undertaking medium-sized population from Beijing
		The increase in the number of buses match with medium-size population
		Increase in floor space match with medium-size population
		Change in economic factors under S2
	S3	Xiong'an New Area undertaking large population from Beijing
		The increase in the number of buses match with large population
		Increase in floor space match with large population
		Change in economic factors under S3

Xiong'an in relation to population size projections of Hebei province. In accordance with the results of the China economic weekly's consultation with experts, to build an ecologically livable city with limited carrying capacity of resources and environment, the long-term population size of Xiong'an should be limited to 2.5 million, with a maximum of 3 million. Approximately, 300,000–500,000 people from Beijing were decentralized to Xiong'an through universities and colleges, scientific research institutes, and enterprises. If the initial population benchmark of Xiong'an was 1 million, a long-term increase of 1.5–2 million people was foreseen, out of which Beijing's population relocation should be of 300,000–500,000 people, accounting for 15–33.3% (Ma and Hou, 2004). Most studies focused on projections of the population size of Xiong'an (Liang *et al.*, 2019; Yang *et al.*, 2019; Research Group on Energy Development and Planning in the Xiong'an New Area Development Research Center of the State Council, 2018). Therefore, no population projections from Beijing to Xiong'an were made. Here, we applied the following formula to project decentralized Beijing's population to Xiong'an:

Decentralized Beijing's population
= Estimated increase in the population of Xiong'an New Area
× Proportion of decentralized Beijing's population. (1)

For the purpose of simplifying the calculation, the average of the maximum and minimum values (24.15%) in the above range is taken as the proportion of decentralized Beijing's population.

The Xiong'an New Area has undergone urban living circle construction in order to take on Beijing's industries and population. This includes a community center, covering 3 km^2 and capable of serving 50,000 people, and an education and health service station covering 1 km^2 and capable of serving 15,000–25,000 people. Based on this, several scenarios were considered with respect to the population projection of the Xiong'an New Area.

Under scenario S1, the planning and construction of the Xiong'an New Area will be developed first with a specific area as the starting area. The starting area is 100 km^2, the medium-term development area is approximately 200 km^2, and the long-term control area is approximately 2000 km^2, with a long-term development intensity of 30% and a total construction land of approximately 530 km^2 (Beijing–Tianjin–Hebei Cooperative Development Leading Group, 2018). The starting area will be completed by 2022, the medium-term development process will reach by 2030, and the long-term development process will reach by 2050. The planning and construction area in the New Area will be kept to a population density of 10,000 people per km^2. Assuming that 1 million people are evenly distributed over 2000 km^2 of land at the beginning, the future population can be projected based on the planned construction area and population density.

Under scenario S2, the total population of the New Area should reach 2 million by 2022, 3.3 million by 2030, and more than 9 million by 2050 (Research Group on Energy Development and Planning in the Xiong'an New Area Development Research Center of the State Council, 2018).

Under the scenario S3, developed using a using a gray projection model (Liang et al., 2019), the population size of the Xiong'an New Area should reach 1.37 million by 2020, 4.047 million by 2030, 7.087 million by 2035, and 12.613 million by 2050.

Tables A.2 and A.3 in Appendix A show the details of Beijing's population undertaken by the Xiong'an New Area, with data for the intervening years and the exact years estimated through regression.

2.3.2. Traffic factors in relation to population size

To achieve the decentralization of Beijing's population and industries to Xiong'an, it is necessary to build an efficient urban transportation network. This study focused on the changes in road traffic in Xiong'an and Beijing. Related research showed that the highway sector is the largest contributor to CO_2 emissions in Beijing's transportation industry, accounting for 71.26% of the total CO_2 emissions in 2015 (Zhang et al., 2019a). Therefore, it is reasonable to focus on the impact on Xiong'an of changes in the transportation sector due to population and industry.

For Beijing, industrial relocation leads to population relocation, which slows down commuting pressure and reduces traffic congestion within the city fundamentally. It is expected that traffic congestion in Beijing is alleviated under the population transfer scenario. According to the scale of population transfer, the growth rate of volume of passenger traffic in Beijing decreases in proportion to the reduction in the resident population compared to the baseline scenario.

For Hebei, according to the planning outline of the New Area, it is essential to build a green intelligent transportation system in Xiong'an, increase the proportions of green transport and public transportation, and build a travel mode of "bus + bicycle + walking". The green transport in the starting area should reach 90%, and the public transport in the starting area should account for 80% of motorized travel.

Based on the above situation, it can be argued that as Xiong'an undertakes Beijing's population, the change in the number of vehicles lies in an increase in the number of public buses, and the change in the structure of vehicles lies in an increase in the proportion of public transportation and a decrease in the proportion of private cars. In this study, these changes were reflected in public transportation vehicles. Changes in the energy structure of vehicles indicated an increase in the proportion of new electric vehicles.

The increase in the number of buses can be calculated based on the number of people moving from Beijing and the bus demand per capita. Table A.4 in Appendix A shows the use of buses in Beijing. According to Table A.4, the number of matched buses per 10,000 people in Beijing has undergone a marginal change in the past decade, holding at approximately 24.5. Therefore, 24.5 standard units were selected for calculation.

Scenario-setting data are presented in Tables A.5 and A.6 in Appendix A. Here, the increase in the number of buses brought about by the population is the only factor taken into consideration, and the transportation sector and energy structure remain unchanged. The change in the proportion of bus energy structure was investigated based on the increase in the number of buses. With reference to the planning of the New Area, the number of electric passenger vehicles will reach 700,000 in 2030 and will rise to more than 2.5 million in 2050. The changes in the future vehicle energy structure can be obtained through a preliminary estimate.

2.3.3. *Building area changes*

The population growth and industrial development in the Xiong'an New Area will certainly require new buildings. The starting area of the Xiong'an New Area is

100 km², the medium-term development area is 200 km², and the planned long-term control area is 2000 km². From the current industrial planning layout of the whole Xiong'an New Area, the overall development is to the east. Rongcheng County, which is 314 km², is the central business district group, which mainly exists as the headquarters of central enterprises and regional administrative office functions. Xiong County, which is 524 km², is the high-tech industrial zone group, mainly to build Xiong'an high-speed railway station, to undertake Beijing universities, hospitals, high-tech industries, etc.

With the infrastructure construction, high-tech high-end industrial layout from the starting area to urban clusters and special villages and towns rapid expansion, a new generation of information technology (IT), high-end manufacturing, biological, green low-carbon, digital creativity, and other industries will become the pillar industries of high-quality development. The total scale of foreseen construction land in the New Area will be about 530 km² and the development intensity is controlled at 30%. An area of 200 km² will be occupied by 2030. Then, 360 km² will be occupied between 2031 and 2050 (Research Group on Energy Development and Planning in the Xiong'an New Area Development Research Center of the State Council, 2018). Three scenarios share the same data.

Since the corresponding infrastructure and building construction, such as greenfield, subway, and housing, are not directly affected by population transfer and industrial transfer, and the energy consumption of Beijing's construction industry accounts for only 1.7% of the city in 2015, changes in Beijing's construction industry are not considered in this study.

2.3.4. Economic indicators

In the case of Beijing, it is assumed in the three scenarios that Beijing continues to promote high-quality economic development and maintains the same economic growth rate after the industrial transfer. As the industrial transfer in Beijing involves various industries in tertiary industries, such as finance, IT, wholesale and retail, etc. The scale of the transfer is still unclear and cannot be considered quantitatively. Moreover, we believe that the transfer of industries in Beijing is to reduce the stock for better development within the industries. Therefore, in the three scenarios of population transfer, we keep the industrial structure in line with the baseline scenario.

By undertaking the labor force population and industries, Hebei's economy should witness some growth (Xinhua News Agency, 2017). According to the historical data from the China Bureau of Statistics, after the establishment of the special economic zone in Guangdong province (Shenzhen) in 1980, the annual gross domestic product (GDP) growth rate of Guangdong province was about 5–10% higher than the result derived from the historical trend in the short term. We make conservative estimates based on this, with parameter settings as shown in Tables A.7 and A.8 in Appendix A.

2.4. Potential green technologies after new city construction

In this study, four types of green technologies are considered from four sectors, including industry, transportation, and buildings in new city. A total of 27 sub-scenarios are created under the S1, S2, and S3 scenarios above, and the sub-scenarios are listed in what follows.

2.4.1. Manufacturing transformation and upgrading

Here, we set three technologies under three sub-scenarios: M1, M2, M3 (see Table 2). Under the M1 sub-scenario, in the three counties in the Xiong'an New Area, traditional industries, such as paper and plastic packaging, calendaring and leather, clothing manufacturing, footwear, and nonferrous metal recycling, were transformed and upgraded. Some relocated low-end industries with high-energy consumption and high

Table 2. Summary of potential green technologies.

Potential green technologies	Codes	Details
Manufacturing transformation and upgrading	Si_M1	The change rate of change of energy intensity in the apparel and textile manufacturing industry is set at −1.5%
	Si_M2	The change rate of change of energy intensity in the apparel and textile manufacturing industry is set at −3%
	Si_M3	The change rate of energy consumption intensity in all sectors of the manufacturing industry is set at −3%
Structural changes in the economic sectors	S1_EG S2_EG S3_EG	The specific changes in GDP growth rate in three scenarios are shown in Table A.9 in Appendix A
Transport electrification	Si_T1	In 2030, public bus trips account for 0.52% of passenger trips, of which public trams account for 19.16% and buses account for 25.1%; cab trips account for 1.75% of passenger trips, of which fuel cabs account for 55.39% and electric cabs account for 19.16%; car trips account for 62.61% of passenger trips, of which fuel cars account for 73.13% and electric cars account for 19.16%
	Si_T2	In 2030, public bus trips account for 0.52% of passenger trips, of which public trams account for 21.9% and buses account for 24.2%; cab trips account for 1.75% of passenger trips, of which fuel cabs account for 52.65% and electric cabs account for 21.9%; car trips account for 62.61% of passenger trips, of which fuel cars account for 70.39% and electric cars account for 21.9%
Construction industry upgrading	Si_C1	The annual rate of change in energy intensity is −1.5%
	Si_C2	The annual rate of change in energy intensity is −3%
	Si_C3	The annual rate of change in energy intensity is −5%

Notes: $i = 1$–3.

pollution were cleaned up. Therefore, the corresponding change rate of energy consumption intensity in the apparel and textile manufacturing industry is −1.5%. Under the M2 sub-scenario, the development of high-end manufacturing industry in the Xiong'an New Area was affected by the apparel and textile manufacturing industry in the surrounding areas, with the change rate of energy consumption intensity in the apparel and textile manufacturing industry being −3%. Under the M3 sub-scenario, the development of high-end manufacturing industry in the Xiong'an New Area benefited the entire Hebei province, with the change rate of energy consumption intensity in all sectors of the manufacturing industry being −3%.

2.4.2. Structural changes in the economic sectors

By undertaking the labor force population and industries, Hebei's economy should witness some growth (Xinhua News Agency, 2017). However, as Xiong'an New Area is committed to building a national model of high-quality development, China's overall economy tends to develop in a more stable manner. Studies have shown that emissions reductions can be achieved by adopting technologies to slow economic growth (Yang, 2019). Therefore, this study uses relevant reference data economic growth rate setting parameters (Yang, 2019). Table A.9 in Appendix A shows the specific changes in GDP growth rate in three scenarios (S1_EG, S2_EG, S3_EG, in Table 2).

2.4.3. Transport electrification

The Beijing–Tianjin–Hebei Clean Air Action Plan 2013–2017 encouraged public transport travel to reach 60% and private car travel to reach 20%. Regarding new electric vehicles in the Beijing–Tianjin–Hebei region, new electric vehicles account for 40% in buses, 40% in taxis, and 5% in private cars. By 2030, new electric vehicles will account for 60% in buses, 20% in taxis, and 10% in private cars (Guo *et al.*, 2017). Based on these ratios, we change the energy structure of buses, taxis, and private cars in Hebei province and set two technologies T1, T2 (see Table 2).

2.4.4. Construction industry upgrading

Considering that the energy intensity of the building sector will be reduced by the introduction of new technologies from the Xiong'an New Area, we set three sub-scenarios, C1, C2, and C3 (see Table 2), and the annual rate of change in energy intensity is −1.5%, 3%, 5%, respectively (Zhang *et al.*, 2019b).

3. Results

3.1. *Energy consumption and CO_2 emission of Beijing and Hebei after new city construction*

3.1.1. *Energy consumption in Beijing*

In 2015, the total energy consumption in Beijing was 69.31 million tons of coal equivalent, and the energy consumption per unit of GDP was 30.2 tons of standard

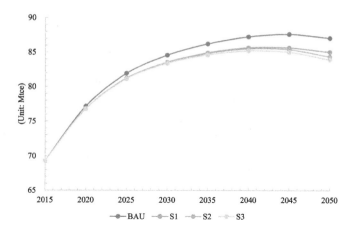

Figure 3. Changing trends in energy consumption in all scenarios in Beijing.

coal per million yuan. The energy consumption in Beijing in all scenarios is shown in Fig. 3. Under each scenario, the future growth of total energy consumption in China would slow down during 2015–2050, with an average growth rate of 1.7% during 2015–2025. After 2025, the volume growth rate of total energy consumption is less than 1%. Under the BAU scenario, there is no downward trend in Beijing's energy consumption, while under the three scenarios of population transfer, Beijing's energy consumption peaks in 2042 under S2 and S3 scenarios, with peaks of 85.60 Mtce and 85.27 Mtce, respectively. Under the S1 scenario, the energy consumption shows a fluctuating trend from 2040–2050. The observed changes (Fig. 4 and Table 3) show that under the S1, S2, and S3 scenarios, energy consumption in Beijing is effectively reduced, with reductions of 3.14 Mtce, 2.70 Mtce, and 2.33 Mtce in 2050, respectively. The S3 scenarios has the largest size of population transfer and the biggest energy savings.

The structure changes in energy consumption by sector for BAU, S1, S2, S3 are shown in Fig. 4. Under the BAU scenario, the proportion of the service sector energy consumption would increase to 45.42% in 2050, and with the development of Beijing's economy, the energy consumption of the service sector would slowly increase year by year, and has not yet reached its peak. Under the BAU, S1, S2, and S3 scenarios, the proportion of transportation energy consumption would account for 15.7%, 13.79%, 13.66%, and 13.51%. The proportion of residential energy consumption increases to

Table 3. Energy consumption reduction ratio by scenario compared to the baseline (unit: %).

Scenario	2015	2020	2030	2040	2050
S1	—	0.47	1.21	1.82	2.65
S2	—	0.49	1.27	1.99	3.06
S3	—	0.51	1.38	2.33	3.57

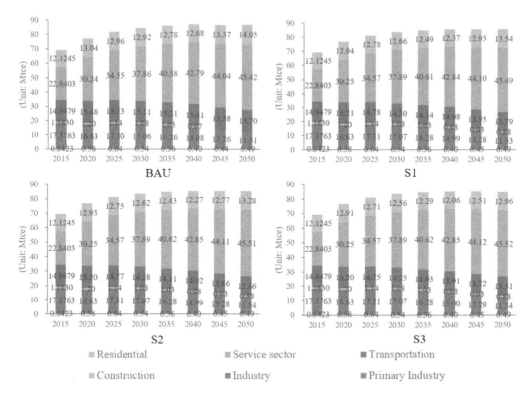

Figure 4. Energy consumption by sector in all scenarios in Beijing.

14.05%, 13.54%, 13.28%, 12.96% under the BAU, S1, S2, and S3 scenarios. This means that the effect of population transfers on the residential sector as well as the transport sector is quite considerable. Overall, under the S1, S2, and S3 scenarios, especially S3, total energy consumption will peak and gradually decline slowly, due to the effective control of the energy consumption of the transport and residential sectors.

3.1.2. CO_2 emissions in Beijing

In all scenarios, the carbon emissions in Beijing peaked in 2020 (see Fig. 5). The peak value was 78.80 million tons under the BAU scenario. Since the initial population transfer, the peak reduction is 0.63, 0.65, and 0.67 million tons of CO_2 under S1, S2, S3 scenario.

Carbon emission reduction ratio by scenarios in Beijing among 2015–2050 compared to the BAU scenario was shown in the table. Emission reductions in 2050 amounted to 4.23, 4.64, and 5.14 million tons of CO_2 under S1, S2, S3 scenario, being equivalent to 5.46%, 5.99%, and 6.63%.

The results of the S1, S2, and S3 scenario analysis indicated that carbon emissions from the transport sector are greatly influenced due to the reduction of travel traffic and the reduction of oil-based energy consumption. Population transfer is indeed conducive to peak carbon emissions, which can lead to a reduction in peak volumes and contribute to the long-term low-carbon development of Beijing, and the achievement

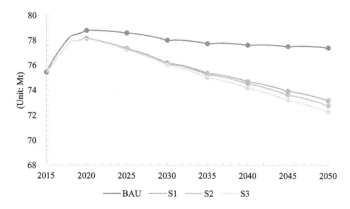

Figure 5. Carbon emissions change of all scenario in Beijing.

of being the first carbon-negative city in China. Under the S3 scenario, although the energy consumption increases by 15.60 million tons of coal equivalent, the total carbon emissions are 3.18 million tons of CO_2 lower in 2050 than in 2015.

Due to the population transfer, it has a favorable impact on Beijing's energy conservation and emission reduction. Hence, the policies of decentralizing the resident population and controlling the population increment are important means of energy saving and emission reduction in Beijing.

3.1.3. Energy consumption in Hebei Province

Energy consumption in the four scenarios mentioned above is shown in Fig. 6.

According to the implementation program for controlling GHG emissions in Hebei province during the 13th Five-Year Plan, the total energy consumption across the province should be kept at 327.85 Mtce by 2020 (The People's Government of Hebei Province, 2017). However, in the BAU, S1, S2, and S3 scenarios, the value of energy consumption in 2020 exceeds 0.68%, 1.17%, 1.05%, and 0.88% of this value, respectively.

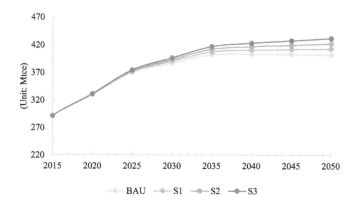

Figure 6. Changing trends in energy consumption in the four scenarios in Hebei.

Figure 6 shows that, under several scenarios, the change trend of energy consumption was the same. The energy consumption in the BAU scenario reached the maximum values of 403.66 Mtce in 2040, whereas other scenarios do not have a peak in energy consumption between 2015 and 2050. In 2050 the energy consumption in the S1, S2, and S3 scenarios increased by 2.83%, 5.11%, and 7.44%, respectively, compared with that in the BAU scenario.

3.1.4. CO_2 emissions in Hebei Province

According to the three scenarios set in this study and the changes in the energy structure in each scenario, the CO_2 emission results obtained by fitting the LEAP model are shown in Fig. 7. CO_2 emissions in the BAU scenario peak at 716.78 Mt in 2035. S1, S2, S3 scenarios also reached peak CO_2 equivalent emissions in 2035, being 1.21%, 2.28%, and 3.38% higher than in the benchmark scenario.

From the perspective of the terminal sector, the industrial sector gave the greatest contribution to CO_2 emissions in all scenarios, and its proportion increased before decreasing in the medium and long term. Moreover, the contribution to CO_2 emissions by the service sector changed remarkably, gradually increasing. However, the changes in other sectors were not significant compared with these two sectors, as detailed in Fig. 8.

By 2050, the CO_2 emissions from the agriculture, industry, transportation, construction, service, and residential sectors were 0.87 Mt, 342.53 Mt, 38.52 Mt, 5.15 Mt, 93.47 Mt, and 72.43 Mt, accounting for 0.16%, 61.92%, 6.97%, 0.93%, 16.90%, and 13.10%, respectively.

3.1.5. Comparing CO_2 emission reductions in Beijing and CO_2 emission increases in Hebei

Among the three scenarios combining population undertaking and industrial decentralization, compared with the baseline scenario, the CO_2 emission in the S1, S2, S3 scenario increased by 16.72 Mt, 29.97 Mt, and 43.53 Mt in Hebei in 2050, respectively, being equivalent to 4.16%, 7.46%, and 10.83%, respectively, and decreased by

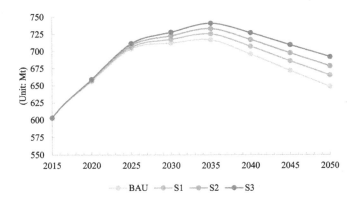

Figure 7. CO_2 equivalent emission scenarios for Hebei province.

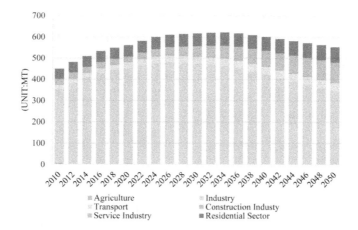

Figure 8. CO_2 equivalent emission change in different sector in the BAU scenarios.

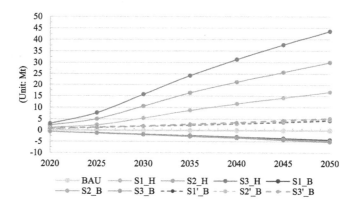

Figure 9. CO_2 emission change in different scenarios in Beijing and Hebei.

4.23 Mt, 4.64 Mt, and 5.14 Mt in Beijing in 2050, respectively, being equivalent to 5.46%, 5.99%, and 6.63%, respectively. The changes can be observed more visually in Figs. 9 and 10.

As can be seen from Fig. 10, without considering the rest of Hebei province, shifting Beijing's population and industries to Xiong'an New Area will result in increased CO_2 emissions for the entire Beijing–Hebei region. It is clear that the more people that are relocated, the more CO_2 emissions will be added. This suggests that a large scale of population transfer may be detrimental to coordinated regional development.

3.2. Changes in CO_2 emissions in Hebei Province after adopting green technologies

3.2.1. CO_2 emissions change under different scenario in Hebei Province

Each sub-scenario under the S1 scenario is synthesized in Fig. 11.

By 2050, compared with the S1 scenario, the CO_2 equivalent emissions in the S1_C1, S1_C2, S1_C3, S1_EG, S1_M1, S1_M2, S1_M3, S1_T1, and S1_T2 scenarios

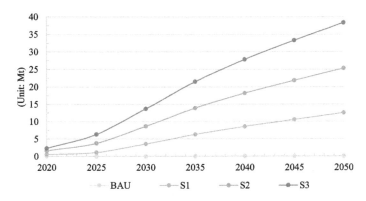

Figure 10. Changes in CO_2 emissions in the Beijing–Hebei region under different scenarios.

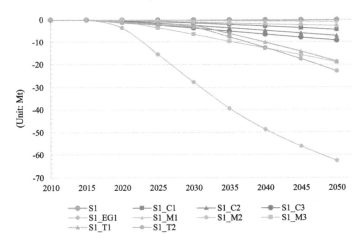

Figure 11. CO_2 emission change in different scenarios in Hebei province under S1 scenario.

decreased by 4.53 Mt, 7.31 Mt, 9.41 Mt, 62.71 Mt, 0.85 Mt, 2.73 Mt, 18.98 Mt, 18.60 Mt, and 22.79 Mt, respectively, with decreases of 1.10%, 1.77%, 2.28%, 15.17%, 0.21%, 0.66%, 4.59%, 4.50%, and 5.51%, respectively. There are three main clusters of curves, with the bottom one being the result of technologies to slow down the economy, the middle one with three curves being the result of increasing the proportion of new electric vehicles and reducing the energy intensity of the manufacturing sector, and the remaining one concentrating on CO_2 emission reductions in the 10 Mt range. Among all technologies, the adoption of technologies to slow economic growth by 5% compared to S1 resulted in the most significant reduction in CO_2 emissions, while only a 1% reduction in the energy intensity of textile-related industries resulted in the least amount of CO_2 emissions reduction, only 0.21%.

Each sub-scenario under the S2 and S3 scenario was synthesized in Figs. 12 and 13, being similar to the results shown in Fig. 11.

150 D. Liao et al.

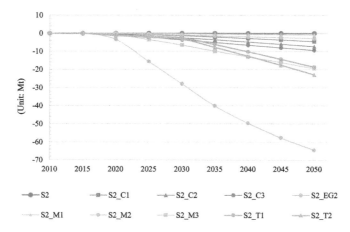

Figure 12. CO$_2$ emission change in different scenarios in Hebei province under S2 scenario.

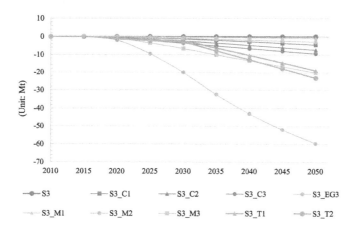

Figure 13. CO$_2$ emission change in different scenarios in Hebei province under S3 scenario.

3.2.2. CO$_2$ emissions in Hebei Province after adopting green technologies

Choose the one with the most emission reductions from the various green technologies and combine them to get the combination of technologies with the most emission reductions. Setting the parameters involved in this combination to the S1, S2, S3 scenarios yields the S1′, S2′, S3′. Then choosing the one with the least emission reductions yields the S1″, S2″, S3″. The result is shown in Fig. 14.

From Fig. 14, it can be seen that for S1, either the strongest or weakest combination of green technologies can bring forward the peak carbon emissions from 2035 to 2025, at 587.43 Mt and 592.65 Mt, respectively. This may suggest that when the Xiong'an New Area hosts a population that complies with the planning requirements, some green technologies will not only offset the incremental emissions from hosting, but also achieve emission reductions. For S2, the adoption of the strongest and weakest combinations of emission reduction technologies advances the peak of CO$_2$ emissions

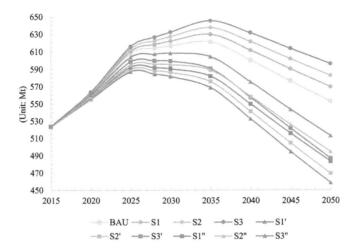

Figure 14. CO_2 emissions in Hebei province after adopting green technologies.

from 2035 to 2025 and 2028, at 590.02 Mt and 596.02 Mt, respectively. This means that an increase in population will increase the resistance to carbon emission reductions. The peak CO_2 emissions are advanced to 2028 and 2030 at 599.95 Mt and 608.65 Mt with two technologies for the S3 scenario, respectively. This result once again confirms the above conclusions.

Since the economic slowdown is not easy to achieve, the CO_2 emission curves S1‴, S2‴, and S3‴ are obtained by removing the effect of this factor, as shown in Fig. 15.

3.3. Sensitivity analysis

The existing population take-up scenario was set to B (S1_B, S2_B, S3_B). The amount of change in the population parameters was considered to be adjusted upward by 10% to form the A scenario (S1_A, S2_A, S3_A) and downward by 10% to form the C

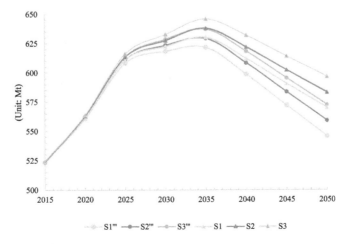

Figure 15. CO_2 emissions in Hebei province after adopting green technologies.

scenario (S1_C, S2_C, S3_C). The results under scenarios A and C were considered as sensitivity analysis of the parameters.

In judging the sensitivity level of the parameter, the proportional change of the result is used. If the change in the final energy consumption increment brought by the 10% upward adjustment and the 10% downward adjustment is greater than 10%, the sensitivity of the parameter is considered higher, and, vice versa, is lower. The proportion of change in the final result with respect to its own parameter adjustment (10%) is defined as the sensitivity index Ω. The sensitivity index is Ω_A for the A-stage scenario and Ω_C for the C-stage scenario,

$$\Omega_A = \frac{\text{Percentage increase in energy consumption in the scenario (A stage} - \text{B stage)}}{(\text{Percentage increase in energy consumption in the B stage scenario})*10\%}$$

$$\Omega_C = \frac{\text{Percentage increase in energy consumption in the scenario (C stage} - \text{B stage)}}{(\text{Percentage increase in energy consumption in the B stage scenario})*10\%}$$

When the sensitivity index Ω_A is less than -1 and Ω_C is greater than 1, the parameter regulated in the scenario is considered to have a high sensitivity.

As shown in Fig. 16, the sensitivity of the model results to the population parameters is low under population take-up scenarios. The variation of the proportional increase in energy consumption of the model results ranges from 0.18% to 0.23% (in 2050) under different grades of population. The sensitivity indices for S1, S2, and S3 scenarios are $\Omega_A = 0.023, 0.019, 0.018$, $\Omega_C = -0.023, -0.019, -0.018$, so there is no significant difference between the results of the Xiong'an New Area population take up scenario in the high- and low-grade scenarios. Results of sensitivity analyses indicate that the increase in domestic energy consumption only due to the increase in population has a little effect on carbon emissions in Hebei province.

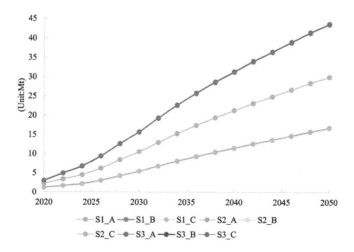

Figure 16. CO_2 emissions in Hebei province after change stage of scenarios.

3.4. Cost analysis

The types of technologies involved in various energy-saving technologies in different industries can be summarized into three categories: technologies for adjusting energy structure, technologies for improving energy efficiency, and technologies for adjusting the internal structure of industries. For China, the cost of carbon abatement for the current structural upgrade of the manufacturing industry is RMB 7789/ton CO_2, the cost of carbon abatement for reduced energy consumption intensity of the manufacturing industry is RMB 1880/ton CO_2; the cost of carbon abatement for the construction industry is RMB 691/Ton CO_2; the carbon emission reduction cost of developing public transportation is RMB 287/ton CO_2, the carbon emission reduction cost of promoting new energy vehicles and biofuels is RMB 7500 yuan/ton CO_2, and the carbon emission reduction cost of reducing the energy intensity of the transportation industry is RMB 442/ton CO_2; the cost of carbon emission reduction for service industry energy intensity reduction is RMB 600/ton CO_2 (Liu et al., 2019). In addition, the cost of carbon emission reduction shows an upward trend with the decrease of carbon emission intensity, and the rate of increase increases with the decrease of carbon emission intensity (Liu and Gao, 2016). Therefore, we can set the above data as the carbon emission reduction cost of various technologies in 2020, and observe the carbon emission intensity changes in the following years, then analyze the carbon emission reduction cost quantitatively and qualitatively. Since the green technologies taken for Hebei under S1, S2, and S3 scenarios are the same, this section takes the S1 scenario as an example for discussion. The changes in carbon emission reduction costs in 2020 and long-term carbon emission intensity change under various technologies are shown in Table 4.

It can be seen that the highest cost is currently required to achieve a slowdown in economic growth, accounting for about 0.76% of Hebei's GDP in that year, followed by a change in the energy mix of the transportation sector. The cost of carbon reduction

Table 4. The changes in carbon emission reduction costs in 2020 and long-term carbon emission intensity change under various technologies.

Scenarios	Carbon reduction cost in 2020 (billion yuan)	Change in carbon emission intensity in 2035 (t/yuan)	Change in carbon emission intensity in 2050 (t/yuan)
S1_C1	1.74	-6.94×10^{-9}	-5.56×10^{-8}
S1_C2	3.42	-1.37×10^{-8}	-9.85×10^{-8}
S1_C3	5.59	-2.23×10^{-8}	-1.41×10^{-7}
S1_EG	276.64	-9.81×10^{-8}	-1.09×10^{-6}
S1_M1	0.58	-8.52×10^{-10}	-1.09×10^{-8}
S1_M2	2.30	-3.38×10^{-9}	-3.88×10^{-8}
S1_M3	16.00	-2.35×10^{-8}	-2.70×10^{-7}
S1_T1	71.59	-2.64×10^{-8}	-1.71×10^{-7}
S1_T2	93.57	-3.45×10^{-8}	-2.14×10^{-7}

in the manufacturing and construction sectors increases as the intensity of energy consumption decreases. The transition difficulty weight of each type of energy efficiency technology is determined by the abatement cost of the technology, and the difficulty of implementing three types of technologies, namely, technologies to adjust the energy structure, technologies to improve energy efficiency, and adjusting the internal structure of industries, increases in that order. In the medium term and long term, as time goes by, the intensity of carbon emission reduction increases, so the cost of carbon emission reduction needed to be paid will also increase, but the specific data changes need to be further explored in the future by integrating factors such as technological progress. The above-mentioned green technologies are set from the planning outline of Xiong'an New Area. The Xiong'an New Area covers about 0.94% of Hebei and 1.58% of the population, but the cost of the costliest technology required, carbon emission reduction, is only 0.76% of GDP. Therefore, from the perspective of carbon emission reduction, the current construction of Xiong'an New Area has no significant impact on the green development of Hebei province.

4. Discussion

First, from the above results, it can be seen that when Beijing transfers people to the Xiong'an New Area, the increase in CO_2 emissions in Hebei is greater than the decrease in CO_2 emissions in Beijing, being about three to nine times the reduction in emissions. This increases the CO_2 emissions of the entire Beijing–Hebei region. As the number of people taken over increases, the incremental increase in CO_2 emissions is also greater. Second, the results of carbon emission peak and time to peak of Hebei in the baseline scenario of this study compared with other studies are shown in Table 5.

Table 5 demonstrates that the peak carbon emissions obtained from this study using LEAP model calculations are 10.38% ($< 20\%$) larger than the value obtained by Wang (2019) using STIRPAT model. This is due to the different models used and the difference in the parameters involved. However, the predicted time to peak is the same, in 2035. This means that Hebei is likely to reach its carbon peak by 2035, if it continues to develop at its current level without any changes. This is inconsistent with China's commitment to reach peak carbon emissions by 2030, as required by the Paris Agreement. So, whether or not Xiong'an New Area takes over Beijing's population

Table 5. Comparison of peak time and CO_2 emission peak to other studies and target.

Peak time	CO_2 emission peak (Mt)	Reference
2035	716.78	—
2035	650	Wang, 2019
2030	—	Target

and industries, it must adopt green to control the trend of future carbon emission growth.

Second, S1 scenario is based on the planning outline of Xiong'an New Area. The planning and construction of Xiong'an New Area will be developed with a specific area as the starting area, the starting area is 100 km², the medium-term development area is about 200 km², the long-term control area is about 2000 km². The development intensity is controlled at 30% in the long term and the total scale of construction land is about 530 km². S2 scenario is based on the "Xiong'an New Area Energy Development Planning Study" project team's estimation that the total population of the New Area will reach 2 million in 2022 and 2 million in 2030. The population size is set according to the projection of 2 million in 2022, 3.3 million in 2030, and more than 9 million in 2050, while the population size is set according to the literature of S3 scenario. For the economic growth rate and industrial structure, the GDP growth rate of Guangdong province is increased by 5–10% after the establishment of Shenzhen Special Economic Zone and the GDP growth rate of Hebei province is increased after the construction of Xiong'an New Area. At the same time, the new construction area proposed by the "Xiong'an New Area Energy Development Planning Study" is nearly 200 km² by 2030, and 360 km² from 2031 to 2050. Based on the above data and the carbon emission value after taking green technologies in Hebei, we set the urban development threshold in the model, predicted the carbon emission threshold in Hebei province and considered the energy use issues that need attention in the development of Xiong'an New Area. The results are shown in Table 6.

In the table, the peak carbon emissions in the three take-up scenarios (725.45 Mt, 733.15 Mt, 741.02 Mt) increase by 1.21%, 2.28%, and 3.38% compared to the peak carbon emissions in the baseline scenario (716.78 Mt) in this study.

In addition, the minimum values of peak carbon emissions in Table 6 for S1, S2, and S3 scenarios increase by 12.24%, 12.81%, and 12.81% respectively, the maximum values increase by 38.6%, 40.15%, and 41.68%, respectively, compared to the carbon emission values of Hebei in 2020.

Table 6. Carbon emission thresholds in Hebei after Xiong'an takes over population.

Scenario	Number of people to be taken over by Beijing in Xiong'an New Area (10,000)	New construction area in Xiong'an New Area	Peak CO_2 emission threshold (Mt)
S1	27.5(2020) → 70.0(2030) → 88.9(2040) → 145.7(2050)	Nearly 200 km² will be added in 2030, and a total of 360 km² from 2031 to 2050	587.43–725.45
S2	30.2(2020) → 79.7(2030) → 115.9(2040) → 217.4(2050)		590.02–733.15
S3	33.1(2020) → 97.8(2030) → 171.2(2040) → 304.3(2050)		599.95–741.02

As we can see, some green technologies can be taken in Hebei to save itself. Among some types of technologies: reducing the intensity of energy consumption in the construction and manufacturing industries, increasing the proportion of new energy transportation and slowing down the economic growth, slowing down the economic growth of emission reduction is the most effective. But in the process of social development, economic growth slowdown may also bring about problems such as economic recession. Therefore, it is not easy to achieve this technology.

Combining the strongest and weakest of the various types of technologies get two combinations of technologies. For S1, S2, S3, both combinations can make the peak time of CO_2 emissions earlier. However, as the population increases, the resistance to reducing carbon emissions also increases. Removing the effect of the S_EG type technologies, which are difficult to achieve, it can be found that the carbon emission peaks do not change in any of the three scenarios, though they can offset the incremental CO_2 emissions brought by population transfer to the Beijing–Hebei region.

Technologies, such as external transfer of green power, increasing the proportion of green buildings and developing new energy sources, need to be included in future studies. Moreover, the study did not investigate the effect of industrial decentralization and population undertaking on Beijing's economic development. The effect of large-scale population undertaking on economic growth needs to be further studied using appropriate models.

5. Conclusion

This paper presented an explorative analysis on the extent and which ways Xiong'an, as a satellite of Beijing, as well as parts of Hebei province, could impact on CO_2 emission. Results were obtained applying different scenarios, based on the existing policy indications. The results showed that the "Enclave Model" of satellite city could temporarily lower emissions of Beijing, but increased Hebei's emission might offset that. Green technologies can enable Hebei to save itself, however, a larger decentralized population would take longer to strike the balance.

This paper aimed to prove the effectiveness of a multi-scalar, multi-dimensional, and multi-actor perspective for a satellite city and new town development planning, implying a change of its energy strategy on a large scale. The study confirms the effectiveness of technologies such as slowing economic growth, reducing the energy intensity of construction and manufacturing, and increasing the proportion of new electric vehicles in Hebei province in reducing CO_2 emissions. However, due to the lack of data, some technologies, such as forest carbon neutrality, external transfer of green power, and development of green buildings, cannot be analyzed. Moreover, the target of achieving carbon neutrality in China by 2060 is not taken into account. This is why these topics which will be further explored in the future.

Acknowledgments

This work is supported by the Beijing Municipal Science & Technology Commission (No. Z181100009618030), National Natural Science Foundation of China (No. 52070021), and the 111 Project (No. B17005).

Appendix A

Table A.1. Industrial characteristics of Xiong'an New Area.

Area		Before	After	Difference
Xiong'an New Area	Rongcheng County	The garment industry in Rongcheng County has a history of more than 30 years of development, with a total of nearly 1000 garment enterprises	The positioning of Xiong'an New Area is to undertake the noncapital functions of Beijing and develop high-tech industries. The focus of the undertaking is on the administrative institutions, headquarters enterprises, financial institutions, universities, research institutes, etc. that Beijing has evacuated	Promote the expansion and extension of traditional enterprises in research and design and marketing services. Develop high-tech industries
	Xiong County	The main characteristic industries of Xiong County are pipes and plastic packaging products. Four pillar industries have been formed: plastic packaging, electrical cables, calendaring, and latex products		
	Anxin County	Anxin County industry has three leading industries, nonferrous metal recycling, footwear industry, and down industry		

Table A.2. Beijing's population undertaken by the Xiong'an New Area (unit: 10,000 people).

Scenario	2020	2030	2035	2050
S1	27.5	70.0	88.9	145.7
S2	30.2	79.7	115.9	217.4
S3	33.1	97.8	171.2	304.3

Table A.3. Projection of the total resident population in Beijing and Hebei (unit: 10,000 people).

Area	Scenario	2020	2030	2035	2050
Beijing	BAU	2144.6	2059.4	1918.3	2188.6
	S1	2117.1	1989.4	1829.4	2042.9
	S2	2114.4	1979.7	1802.4	1971.2
	S3	2111.5	1961.6	1747.1	1884.3
Hebei	BAU	7700.0	8150.0	7910.0	7550.0
	S1	7727.5	8220	7998.9	7695.7
	S2	7730.2	8229.7	8025.9	7767.4
	S3	7733.1	8247.8	8081.2	7854.3

Table A.4. Development of bus use in Beijing.

Year	Number of buses (vehicle)	Population (10,000 people)	Buses per 10,000 people (vehicle)
2015	23,287	2171	24.58
2016	22,688	2173	24.31
2017	25,624	2171	26.55

Source: National Bureau of Statistics of the People's Republic of China; China National Health and Family Planning Commission.

Table A.5. Number of new buses in Xiong'an New Area (unit: vehicle).

Scenario	2020	2030	2035	2050
S1	302.5	770	977.9	1602.7
S2	739.9	1952.65	2839.55	5326.3
S3	810.95	2396.1	4194.4	7455.35

Table A.6. Number of buses in Hebei province (unit: vehicle).

Scenario	2020	2030	2035	2050
BAU	28,600	36,400	39,000	42,640
S1	28,903	37,170	39,978	44,243
S2	29,340	38,353	41,840	47,966
S3	29,411	38,796	43,194	50,095

Table A.7. Hebei GDP annual growth forecasting (2016–2050).

Scenario	2016–2020 (%)	2021–2025 (%)	2026–2030 (%)	2031–2035 (%)	2036–2040 (%)	2041–2045 (%)	2046–2050 (%)
BAU	6.8	5.8	4.8	4.0	3.5	3.0	2.5
S1	6.9	5.9	4.9	4.1	3.6	3.1	2.6
S2	7.0	6.0	5.0	4.2	3.7	3.2	2.7
S3	7.1	6.1	5.1	4.3	3.8	3.3	2.8

Table A.8. Changes in industrial structure in Hebei province.

Scenario	Year	Primary industry (%)	Secondary industry (%)	Tertiary industry (%)
BAU	2020	8.90	43.00	48.10
	2030	5.90	31.00	63.10
	2040	3.40	23.00	73.60
	2050	2.00	18.00	80.00
S1	2020	8.70	42.80	48.50
	2030	5.70	30.80	63.50
	2040	3.20	22.80	74.00
	2050	1.80	17.80	80.40
S2	2020	8.55	42.75	48.70
	2030	5.55	30.75	63.70
	2040	3.05	22.75	74.20
	2050	1.65	17.75	80.60
S3	2020	8.40	42.70	48.90
	2030	5.40	30.70	63.90
	2040	2.90	22.70	74.40
	2050	1.50	17.70	80.80

Source: Ding (2019); Hebei Economic Yearbook; International Monetary Fund.

Table A.9. GDP annual growth forecasts in Hebei province (2016–2050).

Scenario	2016–2020 (%)	2021–2025 (%)	2026–2030 (%)	2031–2035 (%)	2036–2040 (%)	2041–2045 (%)	2046–2050 (%)
S1_EG	6.8	5.6	4.6	3.8	3.3	2.8	2.3
S2_EG	6.5	5.5	4.5	3.7	3.2	2.7	2.2
S3_EG	6.4	5.4	4.4	3.6	3.1	2.6	2.1

References

Bontje, M (2019). Shenzhen: Satellite city or city of satellites? *International Planning Studies*, 24(3–4), 255–271.

Beijing–Tianjin–Hebei Cooperative Development Leading Group (2018). Planning outline of Xiong'an new area in Hebei province.

Beijing Municipal Bureau of Statistics (2019). Beijing Statistical Yearbook. Beijing: China Statistics Press.

Cao, B, JY Lin, SH Cui and LN Tang (2010). Scenario analysis of reduction potentials of energy demand and GHG emissions based on LEAP model in Xiamen city. *Acta Ecologica Sinica*, 30(12), 3358–3367.

Chemingui, MA and C Thabet (2014). Taxing CO_2 emissions and its ancillary health benefits: A computable general equilibrium analysis for Tunisia. *Middle East Development Journal*, 6(1), 108–145.

Ding, C (2007). Evaluation of international satellite city development strategies. *Urban Development Research*, 14(002), 121–126.

Ding, Y (2019). Study on the influence of energy structure adjustment on carbon emission in Hebei province based on LEAP model, PhD thesis, North China Electric Power University.

Emodi, NV, CC Emodi and ASA Emodi (2017). Energy policy for low carbon development in Nigeria: A LEAP model application. *Renewable & Sustainable Energy Reviews*, 68(1), 247–261.

Fan, J, L Kong and X Zhang (2018). Synergetic effects of water and climate policy on energy-water nexus in China: A computable general equilibrium analysis. *Energy Policy*, 123, 308–317.

Guo, F (2011). Research and application of Beijing energy demand and environment integration model, PhD thesis, North China Electric Power University.

Guo, X, F Liu, P Guo, J Lang and Y Jia (2017). Scenarios prediction of energy saving and emission reduction in the road transport sector of Beijing-Tianjin-Hebei region. *Journal of Beijing Polytechnic University*, 43(11), 1743–1749.

Jin, Y (2016). The impact of Shanghai population variable factors on carbon emission, Master thesis, Shanghai Normal University.

Khan, Z, P Linares and J García-González (2017). Integrating water and energy models for policy driven applications. A review of contemporary work and recommendations for future developments. *Renewable & Sustainable Energy Reviews*, 67, 1123–1138.

Liang, L, J Zeng and B Liu (2019). Future population trend prediction and policy suggestions in Xiong'an new area. *Contemporary Economic Management*, 41(07), 59–67.

Liu, GY, JM Hu and ZF Yang (2019). Analysis of medium- and long-term coupling effect of energy- and water-saving policies in urban and rural areas in Beijing. *Strategic Study of Chinese Academy of Engineering*, 21(5), 120–129.

Liu, C and Y Gao (2016). Research on the cost of carbon abatement among my country's industrial sectors under carbon trading. *Soft Science*, 30(03), 85–88.

Liu, LY, BH Zheng and KB Bedra (2018). Quantitative analysis of carbon emissions for new town planning based on the system dynamics approach. *Sustainable Cities and Society*, 42, 538–546.

Liu, X (2010). Low-carbon perspective of satellite city transportation planning and construction. *China Market*, 19, 15–16.

Liu, Y and Z Hu (2015). Study on the impact of agricultural greenhouse gas emission reduction on China's rural economy — An analysis of carbon taxation in the agricultural sector production based on CGE model. *China Soft Science*, 09, 41–54.

Liu, J (2018). Reference and enlightenment of planning and construction of foreign typical Stolichna Oblast new town to Xiong'an new area (China). *Economic Review*, 386(01), 114–122.

Liu, Z (2016). Research on carbon emission reduction potential from the perspective of industrial structure, PhD thesis, Capital University of Economics and Business.

Ma, X and Y Hou (2004). A study on Beijing's population variation trend in the future 50 years. *Market & Demographic Analysis*, 02, 46–49.

Research Group on Energy Development and Planning in the Xiong'an New Area, Development Research Center of the State Council (2018). The realization path of zero carbon smart green energy system in Xiong'an new area. *Development Research*, 09, 16–19.

Rive, VJC (2016). Reflections on the Paris Agreement. *SSRN Electronic Journal*, 13, 115–124.

Shin, HC, JW Park, HS Kim and ES Shin (2005). Environmental and economic assessment of landfill gas electricity generation in Korea using LEAP model. *Energy Policy*, 33(10), 1261–1270.

Sorensen, A (2001). Subcentres and satellite cities: Tokyo's 20th century experiences of planned polycentrism. *International Planning Studies*, 6(1), 9–32.

Tao, Z, L Zhao and Z Changxin (2011). Research on the prospects of low-carbon economic development in China based on LEAP model. *Energy Procedia*, 5(5), 695–699.

The People's Government of Hebei Province (2020). Hebei Economic Yearbook. China Statistics Press.

The People's Government of Hebei Province (2017). The implementation program for controlling greenhouse gas emissions in Hebei province during the 13th five-year plan.

Tong, Y, S Shan and J Gong (2020). Estimating the population retention scale in Beijing in the context of industrial decongestion. *Population & Economics*, 2, 1–11.

Tong, Y and Y Wang (2016). Dynamic simulation and policy analysis of Beijing population. *China Population, Resources and Environment*, 26(02), 170–176.

United Nations Environment Programme (UNEP) (2019). Emissions gap report. Retrieved from https://www.unenvironment.org/resources/emissions-gap-report-2019.

Wang, D, J Xu and X Gao (2019). Non-functional ease Beijing capital ideas and countermeasures under the joint development of Beijing, Tianjin and Hebei background. *Economic Research Guide*, 09, 53–54.

Wang, Q (2019). Research on peak carbon emission prediction in Hebei province based on STIRPAT model, PhD thesis, North China Electric Power University.

Xie, P (2010). Experience and lessons of London's new town planning and its revelation to Beijing. *Economic Geography*, 030(001), 47–52.

Xinhua News Agency (2017). Cultivating a new engine for China's economic growth. Retrieved from http://news.sina.com.cn/c/nd/2017-04-03/doc-ifycwunr8648275.shtml.

Yang, F (2019). Carbon emission scenario prediction study in Hebei province based on IGWO-SVM model, Master thesis, North China Electric Power University.

Yang, Z, Y Rong, L Tian, Z Zhang, HE Ding and MA Quanbao (2019). Analysis on the coordinated development of Beijing-Tianjin-Hebei urban network and study on the population scale of Xiong'an new area. *Journal of Arid Land Resources and Environment*, 12, 8–15.

Zhang, D, G Liu, C Chen, Y Zhang, Y Hao and M Casazza (2019a). Medium-to-long-term coupled strategies for energy efficiency and greenhouse gas emissions reduction in Beijing (China). *Energy Policy*, 127, 350–360.

Zhang, K, X Liu, P Guo, J Fang and J Yao (2019b). Spatial-temporal differences of CO_2 emissions of transport sector in Beijing-Tianjin-Hebei region. *Systems Engineering*, 37(05), 12–20.

Zhang, K and J Dong (2015). Seoul case and its implication to Beijing in relieving non-capital function. *China Business and Market*, 29(11), 64–71.

Zhang, J (2012). From Hong Kong's capitalist fundamentals to Singapore's authoritarian governance: The policy mobility of neo-liberalising Shenzhen, China. *Urban Studies*, 49(13), 2853–2871.

Zhao, C (2019). Study on the influence path and effect of population deconstruction in Beijing from the perspective of regional cooperative development, Master thesis, Beijing University of Posts and Telecommunications.

© 2025 World Scientific Publishing Company
https://doi.org/10.1142/9789819812264_0008

ANALYSIS OF THE SYNERGISTIC EFFECT OF CARBON TAXES AND CLEAN ENERGY SUBSIDIES: AN ENTERPRISE-HETEROGENEITY E-DSGE MODEL APPROACH[†]

QIANYANG TU and YING WANG[*]

College of Finance and Statistics
Hunan University, Changsha 410006, P. R. China
*wy311066@hnu.edu.cn

The application of clean energy is one effective way to alleviate the economy's dependence on fossil energy while reducing greenhouse gas (GHG) emissions. However, the complementary and synergistic effects of environmental policy in clean energy promotion remain controversial. This paper aims to investigate the role of structural carbon taxes and clean energy subsidies in low carbon transition. Heterogeneous environmental dynamic stochastic general equilibrium (E-DSGE) approach with firm heterogeneity is applied to describe the impact path of structural environmental policy on China's environmental-economic system. The results show that the structural carbon emission reduction policy has synergistic effects and can balance the relationship between energy demand and economic growth. Furthermore, distinguishing production technology and green innovation technology can promote energy-saving enterprises and improve the industrial structure. This paper might be the first attempt to discuss the synergistic effects of climate policy based on heterogeneous E-DSGE model.

Keywords: DSGE model; carbon taxes; clean energy subsidies; China; economic fluctuation.

1. Introduction

At present, climate change and global warming caused by greenhouse gas (GHG) emissions have become the focus of the international community and environmental economists. The continuous growth of fossil fuel consumption is one of the most urgent policy challenges (Acemoglu *et al.*, 2012). As the largest exporter and energy consumer in the world, China plays a pivotal role in the global low-carbon transition. In 2020, the Chinese government proposed to "peaking carbon emissions by 2030 and achieving carbon neutrality by 2060". Renewable energy could be a viable alternative to fossil fuels in low-carbon transition and sustainable development (Panwar *et al.*, 2011). The promotion of clean energy by the governments helps their countries reduce GHG emissions and meet energy needs simultaneously (Argentiero *et al.*, 2017).

---

[*]Corresponding author.

[†]This chapter was originally published in Climate Change Economics, Vol. 13, No. 1 (2022), published by World Scientific Publishing, Singapore. Reprinted with permission.

To achieve the carbon reduction target, China has implemented carbon trading in pilot areas since 2013 and officially launched a national carbon trading market in 2021. However, compared with market behavior, government intervention has a greater impact on carbon reduction. For example, the introduction of environmental tax has addressed the difficulty in collecting sewage charges (Yu, 2013; Xiong et al., 2016; Zhu and Lu, 2017). Thus, this paper aims to investigate the impact of carbon taxes and clean energy subsidies (price-oriented climate-related government interventions) on China's environmental economic system.

Clean energy subsidies and carbon taxes have proved to be feasible carbon emission reduction tools. They are also necessary means to correct the two market failures of R&D spillover and pollution. Carbon taxes can internalize the externalities of environmental pollution and transform social costs into production costs of enterprises. Clean energy subsidies can increase the flexibility of substitution between clean energy and fossil energy and stimulate green innovation in enterprises. At present, a single policy has disadvantages such as weak pertinence and distortion of government expenditures, so it is particularly important for the government to give full play to the synergy between policies. "Synergy" was first proposed by Haken and Graham in 1971, with the synergy theory systematically discussed (Haken and Graham, 1971). "Synergistic effect", also known as the "1 + 1 > 2" effect, refers to adding or mixing two or more components together, with the effect greater than the sum of the effects of various components applied alone.

This paper establishes a small closed-economy heterogeneous environmental dynamic stochastic general equilibrium (E-DSGE) model with firm heterogeneity to investigate the synergistic effects of carbon taxes and clean energy subsidies. It is found that the structural carbon emission reduction policies have synergistic effects and can well balance the relationship between energy demand and economic growth. This paper might be the first attempt to discuss the synergistic effects of climate policy under the framework of heterogeneous E-DSGE model. We attempt to introduce heterogeneity and structural characteristics on the basis of dynamic simulation theory to promote the application of simulation theory and method concerning climate change policy effects.

2. Literature Review

In recent decades, the climate-economic integrated assessment model (IAM) and computable general equilibrium (CGE) model have been widely applied to study carbon emission reduction and environmental policies (Li et al., 2019). These two models, however, cannot handle the uncertainty in the economic system well (Pindyck, 2013). Dynamic stochastic general equilibrium (DSGE) has outstanding advantages in simulating the randomness of the economy by setting exogenous shocks (Xiao et al., 2018). Generally, DSGE models can be divided into new Keynes (NK) framework and real business cycle (RBC) structure according to whether nominal price rigidity is adopted or not. Since Angelopoulos first introduced environmental pollution into the RBC model, increasing studies have applied the E-DSGE model to study the dynamic effects of environmental policies on the macroeconomics (Angelopoulos et al., 2010). Specifically, these studies can be roughly divided into the following three categories.

The first is to study the optimal dynamic environmental policy. The research of Angelopoulos (Angelopoulos et al., 2010), as a pioneering paper under the RBC framework, took the lead in regarding pollution as a by-product of output and environmental quality as a public product and analyzed the welfare changes caused by optimal and sub-optimal environmental policies under economic uncertainty. Subsequently, Fischer and Springborn (2011) compared the dynamic effects of three different carbon emission reduction policies and found that the impact of emission intensity targets on economic growth is greater than the emission ceiling or carbon tax. Angelopoulos et al. (2013) introduced exogenous shocks into the model of Angelopoulos et al. (2010) and studied the impact of uncertainty on macroeconomic results, environmental quality, and ultimately social welfare. By comparing optimal and sub-optimal environmental policies, they found that higher environmental uncertainty can increase welfare under optimal policies. Fischer and Heutel (2013), after reviewing the application research of macroeconomic methods in environmental policy evaluation, proposed that the New keynesian- dynamic stochastic general equilibrium (NK-DSGE) model framework will be the best tool for environmental policy analysis. Later, Annicchiarico and Dio (2015) improved the model of environmental policy analysis under the framework of new Keynesian DSGE and analyzed the performance of different environmental policy rules under real and nominal uncertainty and finally obtained the optimal environmental policy to deal with inflation.

The second is to analyze the periodic problems of carbon emissions and carbon emission reduction policies. Heutel (2012) modeled pollution into pollution stock and pollution flow and analyzed how carbon tax and quota policies adapt to periodic changes in economy. Lintunen and Vilmi (2013) studied the periodicity of optimal emission tax and emissions based on an RBC model containing pollution stock and proved the optimality of emission tax under typical procyclical conditions by deducing the procyclical conditions of optimal emission tax. Later, Xiao et al. (2018) established an E-DSGE model under the framework of new Keynesianism and found that environmental policies are countercyclical, and emission intensity policies have the best effect on controlling fluctuations.

The third is to measure the macro-economic effect of carbon emission reduction policies. Annicchiarico et al. (2018), by analyzing the impact of emission reduction process on economic activities and competition in a NK-DSGE model including endogenous enterprise entry and environmental policies, found that appropriate environmental policies played a positive role in alleviating tax distortions and promoting decarbonization. Based on the two-dimensional model of Heutel (2012), Hashmat et al. (2019) constructed an E-DSGE model containing four exogenous shocks to study the relationship between structural technological shocks and emissions. They also verified the positive correlation between technological impact and emissions and output. With China's economic data, Zhang and Zhang (2020) established an energy-emission DSGE model to test the impact of China's carbon tax and carbon intensity target on economy and environment. They found that both of the two policy targets have negative effects on China's economy and environment and that of carbon tax is greater. Pan *et al.* (2020) constructed a multi-region DSGE model to study the dynamic effects and spillover effects of environmental expenditure shocks in the Beijing–Tianjin–Hebei region of China. They found that environmental expenditure has a significant crowding-out effect on local consumption and investment, but a certain positive impact on the economy of external regions. Chan (2020) compared the inhibition effect of standard macroeconomic tools (fiscal and monetary policies) and carbon taxes on air pollution. They found that although the two can stabilize carbon emissions, their internal mechanisms differ. Fiscal policy is the only policy that can maintain emission levels while increasing household consumption and welfare of workers.

The mentioned research above has yielded fruitful results in studying policy periodicity, optimal policy rules and welfare. With the acceleration of global low-carbon transition, the application of clean energy and the construction of heterogeneous models have become one of the frontiers of climate policy issues. The pollution reduction effect of clean energy has been extensively verified (Fouqueta and Pearson, 2012; Shmelev and Speck, 2018) and some believe that the development of renewable energy contributes to economic growth (Alper and Oguz, 2016; Cherni and Jouini, 2017).

The characterization of enterprise heterogeneity is currently in the exploratory stage in the construction of the DSGE model of climate issues and environmental policies. The heterogeneity DSGE model has a certain research foundation in studying the economic effects of taxation policies, which is specifically reflected in the economic effects of tax cuts in consumption tax, capital income tax and labor income tax (Domeij and Heathcote, 2004), but few studies have adopted it to study the economic effects of environmental policies. In recent years, a few scholars have introduced corporate heterogeneity into environmental RBC and open economy DSGE models to analyze the role of environmental policies in promoting the development of renewable energy. Acemoglu *et al.* (2012) considered the heterogeneity of pollution emission sources and divided production inputs into "polluting" and "clean" types. They pointed out that carbon tax can reduce carbon emissions by restraining the output of enterprises, but it can also lead to excessive distortion. Instead, encouraging clean technology development is a more effective policy measure. Argentiero (2017) divided the energy part into fossil energy and clean energy and constructed a three-country RBC model to investigate the role of the energy policies of 15 EU countries, the United States and China in promoting the development of clean energy and their macroeconomic impact. Argentiero *et al.* (2018) tried to determine the effectiveness of incentive mechanisms that include carbon taxes and public capital stocks and found that technology-based environmental policies have better dynamic effects than equivalent subsidy policies. Xiao et al. (2020) took China and the European Union as examples to explore the effectiveness of bilateral climate policies in an open economy DSGE model that includes heterogeneous production sectors.

The heterogeneity of enterprises corresponds to policy structure. The existing research mainly focuses on the type of policy, implementation method and volatility in policy design, but lacks attention to the structure of policy. Doda (2016) pointed out that incorporating responsiveness to the design of carbon pricing tools can distribute the regulatory burden more flexibly over time, thereby reducing the regulatory burden. Chan (2020) formulated the Taylor rule for carbon dependence policy, that is, when the current emission level is higher (lower) than the target, the carbon tax rate and nominal interest rate will increase (decrease), government expenditures will decrease (increase), and the cost equivalence method will be adopted for welfare analysis. Examples related to the synergistic effects of environmental polices include: Li and Yao (2020) and Wang et al. (2017), who studied the synergistic effects of environmental policies in CGE models. In detail, Li and Yao (2020) studied the single and synergistic policy effect of carbon tax and coal capacity reduction from the energy demand side and energy supply side and evaluated their synergy in energy conservation, emission reduction and economic growth. Wang et al. (2017) studied whether sulfur tax and carbon tax have synergistic effects. The results show that the two policies do not bring double dividends, but that multiple taxes will cause double burden on the economy. In addition, Chen et al. (2018) established a bottom-up model to estimate the synergistic impacts of China's subsidy policy and battery electric vehicles (BEVs) credit regulation. The results show that the two policies will complement each other during the transition period.

In summary, existing research focuses on exploring the optimal environmental policies, analyzing the periodicity of pollution and policies, and measuring the macroeconomic effects of carbon emission reduction policies. In terms of model framework, a few scholars have introduced corporate heterogeneity into the multi-country model to explore the effectiveness of multilateral climate policies, while few studies have discussed China's climate policies under the heterogeneous NK-DSGE framework. In terms of policy choices, although most studies have proved that carbon taxes, licensing systems, carbon emission intensity caps, carbon quotas and other systems have significant effects on curbing the production of polluting enterprises and reducing carbon emissions. Nevertheless, there is little research that focuses on the synergistic effects of structural environmental policies. As for policy setting, most scholars are more concerned about the policy dependency rules, while they lack consideration on setting structural environmental policies for heterogeneous manufacturers in the context of low-carbon transition.

Based on the existing research, this article attempts to further advance and supplement the NK-EDSGE model in two aspects. The first is to take the low carbon transition process into consideration. Heterogeneous firms are introduced into the small closed economy NK-DSGE model, and labor, capital and wages are allocated according to the progress of energy transition. The second is to formulate a structural environmental policy so that the corresponding carbon tax and clean energy subsidy system can be implemented simultaneously according to the performance of the two types of manufacturers in environmental pollution. Also, since there are few studies on structural environmental policies from dynamic perspective, this paper expands the application of heterogeneous DSGE model in environmental economics by studying the impact of carbon taxes and clean energy subsidies on China's environment and economy.

3. Modeling

Due to its outstanding advantages in simulating future uncertainty and fluctuations, DSGE model has been widely applied in government macro policy research and is a primary tool for policy decisions in the long term (Linde, 2018). The structural and microscopic DSGE model can well simulate the dynamic behavior and fluctuation response under random shocks in short-term and long-term equilibrium (Xiao, 2018).

Based on the NK-EDSGE model of Annicchiarico and Dio (2015), this paper makes some improvements in manufacturer heterogeneity and structural environmental policies. These changes can simulate the long-term and short-term effects of the two environmental policies in energy transition. In terms of firm heterogeneity, this paper divides intermediate product manufacturers into polluting and clean ones. As for structural environmental policy, this paper adopts different environmental policies according to the performance of two kinds of intermediaries in environmental pollution. In addition to providing financial subsidies for clean energy enterprises to promote clean technology R&D, the government imposes carbon taxes on polluting enterprises to increase their pollution costs and internalize external pollution problems.

The proposed model includes four parts: final goods producers, heterogeneous intermediate goods producers, household sector and government sector under closed economic rules. The framework of this model is shown in Fig. 1.

3.1. *Intermediate goods producers*

It is assumed that there are two types of intermediate goods producers (polluting and clean) in the economy, and the homogeneous intermediate products produced by them are regarded as intermediate inputs of the final product producers. Only the polluting intermediate goods producer will cause environmental pollution. Clean producers use clean energy for production, so they have no pollution emissions. Both types of enterprises are faced with the optimal choice of profit maximization.

3.1.1. *Polluting intermediate goods producers*

Under the A_t total factor productivity (TFP) level, polluting producers produce intermediate products by purchasing capital $K_{P,t}$ and labor force $L_{P,t}$ in each period.

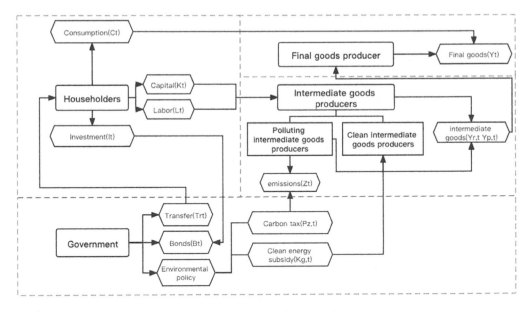

Figure 1. Model framework.

Assuming that environmental pollution and environmental regulation will reduce the production efficiency of enterprises (Heutel, 2012), then the production function should include pollution inventory reduction

$$Y_{P,t} = \left(1 - d_0 - d_1 M_t - d_2 M_t^2\right) A_t K_{P,t}^{\alpha} L_{P,t}^{1-\alpha} V_t^{-1}, \qquad (1)$$

where α is the capital elasticity and d_0, d_1, d_2 are the secondary impairment function coefficients. V_t is the degree of price dispersion under Calvo pricing:

$$V_t = (1 - \omega_P)\frac{P_t^{*-\theta_T}}{P_t} + \omega_P \Pi_t^{\theta_T} V_{t-1}, \qquad (2)$$

where P_t is the price level at time t, P_t^* is the optimal price, Π_t is the inflation rate, ω_P is the nominal rigidity and θ_T is the price stickiness.

The pollution stock of the current period M_t is affected by four factors: the pollution stock of the previous period M_{t-1}, the pollution of current period Z_t, the self-purification capacity of environment $(1 - \delta_Z)$ and foreign carbon emissions $\bar{Z}$:

$$M_t = Z_t + (1 - \delta_Z)M_{t-1} + \bar{Z}. \qquad (3)$$

The TFP follows the AR (1) distribution:

$$\log(A_t) = \rho_A \log(A_{t-1}) + \varepsilon_{A,t} \quad \varepsilon_{A,t} \sim i.i.d.N(0, \sigma_A^2). \qquad (4)$$

Under the constraints of carbon tax, polluters bear the additional cost $P_{Z,P,t}$ brought about by environmental regulation and will strive to reduce pollution emissions (Annicchiarico and Dio, 2015; Heutel, 2012):

$$Z_t = (1 - e_t)\phi_3 Y_{P,t} V_t, \qquad (5)$$

where e_t is the degree of pollution reduction efforts of the enterprise and ϕ_3 is the pollution output ratio.

According to the polluter pays principle, polluting manufactures need to bear the cost of their own emission reduction $\phi_1 e_t^{\phi_2} Y_{P,t}$ and pay a carbon tax $\frac{P_{Z,P,t}}{P_t} Y_{P,t}$ based on their output. Their optimal decision can be expressed as a profit maximization problem

$$\max E_0 \sum_{t=0}^{\infty} Q_{P,t} \left[\frac{P_t^*}{P_t} Y_{P,t} - \frac{W_{P,t} L_{P,t}}{P_t} - \frac{R_{K,t} K_{P,t}}{P_t} - \phi_1 e_t^{\phi_2} Y_{P,t} - \phi_3 (1-e_t) \frac{P_{Z,P,t}}{P_t} Y_{P,t} \right.$$
$$\left. + \pi_{P,t} \left((1 - d_0 - d_1 M_t - d_2 M_t^2) A_t K_{P,t}^\alpha L_{P,t}^{1-\alpha} V_t^{-1} - Y_{P,t} \right) \right], \tag{6}$$

where $Q_{P,t}$ is the stochastic discount factor, $\pi_{P,t}$ is the Lagrangian multiplier, $W_{P,t}$ is the nominal wage, $R_{K,t}$ is the capital interest rate, and ϕ_1 and ϕ_2 are the emission reduction cost coefficients.

The capital demand equation, labor demand equation, expression of unit emission reduction cost, and marginal cost expression can be obtained by solving the first-order condition

$$\frac{R_{K,t}}{P_t} = \alpha \pi_{P,t} \frac{Y_{P,t}}{K_{P,t}}, \tag{7}$$

$$\frac{W_{P,t}}{P_t} = (1-\alpha) \pi_{P,t} \frac{Y_{P,t}}{L_{P,t}}, \tag{8}$$

$$P_{Z,P,t} = \frac{\phi_1 \phi_2}{\phi_3} e_t^{\phi_2 - 1}, \tag{9}$$

$$\pi_{P,t} = -\left(\frac{1}{(1-d_0-d_1 M - d_2 M^2) A_t \alpha^\alpha (1-\alpha)^{1-\alpha}} \left(\frac{R_{K,t}}{P_t} \right)^\alpha \left(\frac{W_{P,t}}{P_t} \right)^{1-\alpha} \right.$$
$$\left. + \phi_1 e_t^{\phi_2} + \frac{P_{Z,P,t}}{P_t} \frac{Z_t}{Y_{P,t}} \right). \tag{10}$$

3.1.2. Clean intermediate goods producers

It is assumed that the production efficiency of clean manufacturers is not affected by the reduction of pollution inventory and they will not produce environmental pollution during the production. Clean manufacturers produce intermediate products by purchasing capital $K_{R,t}$ and labor force $L_{R,t}$ in each period. At the same time, it is also assumed that the government levies environmental taxes on polluting enterprises to subsidize clean manufacturers to promote their R&D of clean technology. Then there is

$$Y_{R,t} = A_t \text{CT}_t K_{R,t}^\alpha L_{R,t}^{1-\alpha} V_t^{-1}. \tag{11}$$

Clean energy subsidies can promote the progress of clean energy technology CT_t (Blackburn and Cipriani, 2002)

$$\text{CT}_t = \frac{1 + a_1 \gamma_1 K_{G,t}^{\gamma_2}}{1 + \gamma_1 K_{G,t}^{\gamma_2}}. \tag{12}$$

Under structural environmental policy, all the carbon tax levied by the government from polluting enterprises is used as clean energy subsidy to clean manufacturers for the development of clean energy technology and the R&D of storage technology, so as to promote the transition of polluting enterprises to clean energy enterprises.

$$P_{Z,P,t} = K_{G,t}. \tag{13}$$

Clean enterprises maximize their profits by solving the optimal selection problems of labor and capital

$$\max E_0 \sum_{t=0}^{\infty} Q_{R,t} \left[\frac{P_{R,t}^*}{P_t} Y_{R,t} - \frac{W_{R,t}L_{R,t}}{P_t} - \frac{R_{K,t}K_{R,t}}{P_t} + \pi_{R,t}(A_t CT_t K_{R,t}^\alpha L_{R,t}^{1-\alpha} V_t^{-1} - Y_{R,t}) \right]. \tag{14}$$

From the above formula, the first-order partial derivatives of the two input factors $L_{R,t}$ and $K_{R,t}$ are obtained, respectively. Then the first-order conditions and marginal cost expression for maximizing the profits of clean manufacturers can be obtained

$$\frac{R_{K,t}}{P_t} = \alpha \pi_{R,t} \frac{Y_{R,t}}{K_{R,t}}, \tag{15}$$

$$\frac{W_{R,t}}{P_t} = (1-\alpha) \pi_{R,t} \frac{Y_{R,t}}{L_{R,t}}, \tag{16}$$

$$\pi_{R,t} = -\frac{1}{\alpha^\alpha(1-\alpha)^{1-\alpha}A_t CT_t} \left(\frac{R_{K,R,t}}{P_t}\right)^\alpha \left(\frac{W_{R,t}}{P_t}\right)^{1-\alpha}. \tag{17}$$

3.2. Final goods producer

Assuming that the final goods producer is symmetric and the final product market is perfectly competitive, and it buys intermediate products produced by both polluting and clean intermediate manufacturers to produce final products, then its production function is in the form of constant elasticity of substitution (CES):

$$Y_t = \int_0^1 \left(Y_{P,t,j}^{\frac{\varpi_Y-1}{\varpi_Y}} + Y_{R,t,j}^{\frac{\varpi_Y-1}{\varpi_Y}} \right) dj^{\frac{\varpi_Y}{\varpi_Y-1}}, \tag{18}$$

where Y_t is the total output of final products, $Y_{P,t}$ and $Y_{R,t}$ are the outputs of polluting and clean intermediate products, respectively, and ϖ_Y is the elasticity of substitution between polluting intermediate products and clean intermediate products.

As the profit of the manufacturer in the final product market with perfect competition is zero, the Dixit-Stiglitz price level index can be obtained

$$P_t = \int_0^1 \left(P_{P,t,j}^{1-\varpi_Y} + Y_{R,t,j}^{1-\varpi_Y} \right) dj^{\frac{1}{1-\varpi_Y}}. \tag{19}$$

The optimal price is set by the method of Calvo (1983). The producer of intermediate goods with a proportion of $1 - \omega_P$ can adjust its optimal price at time t to maximize profit

$$\max_{P_{j,t}} E_t \sum_{s=0}^{\infty} \omega_P^s \Lambda_{t,t+s} \left[\frac{P_{j,t}^*}{P_{t+s}} \left(\frac{P_{j,t}}{P_{t+s}} \right)^{-\theta_T} Y_{t+s} - \frac{MC_{t+s}}{P_{t+s}} \left(\frac{P_{j,t}}{P_{t+s}} \right)^{-\theta_T} Y_{t+s} \right], \quad (20)$$

where MC_{t+s} is the marginal cost of final goods producer and $\Lambda_{t,t+s}$ is the stochastic discount factor for nominal payoffs.

The optimal price level can be obtained by solving the above profit maximization problem

$$\frac{P_{j,t}^*}{P_t} = \frac{\theta_T}{\theta_T - 1} \frac{E_t \sum_{s=0}^{\infty} (\beta \omega_P)^s \Lambda_{t,t+s} MC_{t+s} \left(\frac{P_{t+s}}{P_t} \right)^{\theta_T} Y_{t+s}}{E_t \sum_{s=0}^{\infty} (\beta \omega_P)^s \Lambda_{t,t+s} \left(\frac{P_{t+s}}{P_t} \right)^{\theta_T - 1} Y_{t+s}}. \quad (21)$$

3.3. Household sector

It is assumed that the household sector is homogeneous and sustainable, and owns capital and labor, and gains positive utility through consumption and negative utility through labor. The goal of a representative household is to maximize it utility over a life time

$$\max E_0 \sum_{t=0}^{\infty} \beta^t \left[\log(C_t) - \delta_L \frac{L_t^{1+\phi_L}}{1 + \phi_L} \right], \quad (22)$$

where C_t is the consumption of the final product by a household in period t, L_t is the labor provided by the household in period t, β is the discount factor, δ_L is the coefficient of labor's negative utility, and ϕ_L is the reciprocal of labor's substitution elasticity for real wages.

The intertemporal budget constraint of the household sector is

$$C_t P_t + I_t P_t + B_{t+1} \leq W_t L_t + R_{K,t} K_t + D_t P_t + B_t R_{B,t} - \text{Tr}_t, \quad (23)$$

where $I_t P_t$ is the nominal investment of the household at period t, B_{t+1} is the amount of nominal risk-free bond purchases in the current period of t, $W_t L_t$ is the household's nominal labor income, and $R_{K,t} K_t$ is the nominal income from capital rent. $D_t P_t$ is the nominal profit of the intermediate product manufacturer, and Tr_t is the government transfer payment. At time t, the family holds capital K_t and uses I_t as the current investment. The capital accumulation equation is as follows:

$$K_{t+1} = (1 - \delta_K) K_t + \left[1 - \frac{\vartheta}{2} \left(\frac{I_t}{I_{t-1}} - 1 \right)^2 \right] I_t, \quad (24)$$

where δ_K is the capital depreciation rate, $\left[1 - \frac{\vartheta}{2} \left(\frac{I_t}{I_{t-1}} - 1 \right)^2 \right] I_t$ is the capital adjustment cost, and ϑ is the corresponding capital adjustment cost coefficient.

The representative household maximizes its utility under budget constraints by determining its labor, consumption, investment, and bond holdings. Furthermore, the first-order conditions of household related consumption and investment and labor supply are solved as follows:

The household's Euler equation

$$\frac{1}{C_t} = \beta E_t \frac{R_{B,t}}{\Pi_{t+1} C_{t+1}}. \tag{25}$$

The household's labor supply equation

$$W_t = \delta_L \frac{L_t^{\phi_L}}{\lambda_{1,t}}. \tag{26}$$

Lagrange multiplier

$$\lambda_{1,t} = \frac{1}{C_t}. \tag{27}$$

Optimal investment equation

$$-q_t \lambda_{1,t} + \beta q_{t+1}(1-\delta_K) + \beta \lambda_{1,t} \frac{R_{K,t+1}}{P_{t+1}} = 0, \tag{28}$$

$$-\lambda_{1,t} + q_t \lambda_{1,t} \left[1 - \frac{\vartheta}{2}\left(\frac{I_t}{I_{t-1}} - 1\right)\right]^2 + \vartheta q_t \lambda_{1,t} I_t \left(\frac{I_t}{I_{t-1}^2} - \frac{1}{I_{t-1}}\right),$$

$$+ \beta \vartheta q_{t+1} \lambda_{1,t+1} \frac{I_{t+1}^2}{I_t^2}\left(\frac{I_{t+1}}{I_t} - 1\right) = 0, \tag{29}$$

where q_t is an approximate measure of asset price fluctuations.

3.4. *Government sector*

The government sector is divided into environmental protection departments and monetary authorities. The former formulates environmental policies to correct negative environmental externalities, while the latter formulates monetary policies. In order to reflect the effects of structural environmental policies, the following four policy scenarios are compared in this paper:

(1) No policy

In the absence of environmental protection policies, companies have no pollution costs ($P_{z,t} = 0$), so they will not implement low-carbon emission reduction measures ($e_t = 0$) initiatively. Thus, the government's budget constraint is $G_t P_t = T_t$, where T_t is the tax revenue.

(2) A single clean energy subsidy

Clean energy subsidies are provided by the government for R&D investment in hydrogen fuel cells, biomass energy, solar energy, and nuclear energy. The government provides clean energy technology capital support to clean manufacturers through public capital stock and imposes no regulations on polluting enterprises.

In this case, the government's budget constraint is $G_t P_t = T_t + K_{G,t} P_t$.

(3) A single carbon tax

The government imposes a carbon tax on the pollutants produced by polluting intermediate manufacturers in the percentage of $P_{Z,P,t}$ and provides no incentives to clean enterprises. The carbon tax is levied at a rate equal to the unit pollution cost of enterprises.

Because polluting intermediate companies will bear the additional costs for environmental control, they will take carbon emission reduction measures to maintain their economic level. The emission reduction cost of polluting companies is $\phi_1 e_t^{\phi_2} Y_{P,t}$. The government's budget constraint is $G_t P_t = T_t$.

(4) Structural carbon reduction policy

Structural carbon emission reduction policy combines different policies and implements different rewards and punishments according to the pollution emission of manufacturers.

In order to promote the transition of enterprises from polluting type to clean one, the government will use all the carbon taxes levied on polluting enterprises to subsidize the development of new clean energy technologies, so $P_{Z,P,t} = K_{G,t}$. Then the government's budget constraint is $G_t P_t = T_t + K_{G,t} P_t$.

The setting of monetary rules conforms to the general practice, in the simple form of Taylor rule:

$$\frac{R_t}{R} = \left(\frac{\Pi_t}{\Pi}\right)^\ell \eta_{R,t}, \tag{30}$$

$$\log(\eta_{R,t}) = \rho_R \log(\eta_{R,t-1}) + \varepsilon_{R,t} \quad \varepsilon_{R,t} \sim i.i.d.N(0, \sigma_R^2). \tag{31}$$

3.5. Market clearing and equilibrium conditions

This paper assumes that the three elements of capital, labor, and wages in the factor market are divided into two parts according to the degree of energy transition ϖ, that is, clean manufacturers and polluting manufacturers, respectively, use ϖ and $1 - \varpi$ of capital, labor, and wages. A larger ϖ indicates a higher degree of transition from a polluting enterprise to a clean one.

$$L_t = (1 - \varpi) L_{P,t} + \varpi L_{R,t}, \tag{32}$$

$$K_t = (1 - \varpi) K_{P,t} + \varpi K_{R,t}, \tag{33}$$

$$W_t = (1 - \varpi) W_{P,t} + \varpi W_{R,t}. \tag{34}$$

The equilibrium condition of the model can be obtained by combining the budget constraints of households, enterprises, and government with the first-order conditions:

$$Y_t = C_t + I_t + G_t + \phi_1 e_t^{\phi_2} Y_{P,t}. \tag{35}$$

4. Parameter Calibration and Estimation

The parameters in this paper are divided into static parameters and dynamic parameters. The parameters are assigned by referring to relevant studies and Markov chain Monte Carlo (MCMC) method-Bayesian estimation.

4.1. *Static parameter calibration*

The static parameters are assigned based on the basic characteristics of China's economic situation, some of which are obtained through literature reference, and the rest are calculated and calibrated from the actual economic data. The static parameter assignment is showed in Table 1.

4.1.1. *Parameters of environment variables*

The degree of energy transition introduced in this paper is calculated by the ratio of China's clean energy consumption to its total energy consumption in 2019. The clean

Table 1. Static parameter assignment.

Parameter	Value	Definition	Source
α	0.33	Capital elasticity	Fischer and Springborn (2011)
β	0.99	Discount rate	Çebi (2012)
ϑ	5.74	Investment adjustment factor	Del Negro et al. (2007)
δ_K	0.025	Capital depreciation rate	Heutel (2012) and Xiao (2018)
δ_Z	0.0021	Depreciation rate of pollution stock	Heutel (2012) and Annicchiarico and Dio (2015)
θ_T	6	Price stickiness	Annicchiarico and Dio (2015)
ω_P	0.75	Nominal rigidities	Annicchiarico and Dio (2015)
δ_L	19.8413	Labor disutility coefficient	Annicchiarico and Dio (2015)
ϕ_L	2	The inverse of labor supply elasticity	Lintunen and Vilmi (2013) and Pop (2017)
ϕ_1	0.18	Emission reduction cost coefficient 1	Pizer and Kopp (2005)
ϕ_2	2.8	Emission reduction cost coefficient 2	Wilbanks (2008)
ϕ_3	0.4	Pollution output ratio	Xiao et al. (2018)
d_0	0.001395	Secondary impairment function coefficient	Heutel (2012)
d_1	−6.7E−06	Secondary impairment function coefficient	Heutel (2012)
d_2	1.5E−08	Secondary impairment function coefficient	Heutel (2012)
ϖ	0.153	Degree of energy transition	The proportion of clean energy consumption to total energy consumption

energy consumption is an equivalent of 74,358 tons of standard coal and the total energy consumption is an equivalent of 486,000 tons of standard coal, so the calibrated degree of energy transition is 0.153.

The depreciation rate of pollution stock and the secondary impairment function coefficient of production function of polluting enterprises refer to the setting of classical research on environmental policy (Heutel, 2012; Xiao, 2018; Annicchiarico and Dio, 2015) and are calibrated to 0.0021, 1.395E–03, –6.7E–06, and 1.5E–08, respectively. The pollution output ratio is set to 0.4 through the calculation method of Xiao et al. (2018) based on China's carbon emissions. With reference to the method of Pizer and Kopp (2005), the emission reduction cost coefficient 1 is calibrated to 0.18 making the ratio of emission reduction cost to output 0.15%. The emission reduction cost coefficient 2 is calibrated to 2.8 after referring to approaches of Wilbanks (2008) and Annicchiarico and Dio (2015).

4.1.2. Basic parameters of economic variables

The price stickiness and nominal rigidity in the model were first introduced to the new Keynesian DSGE model that includes the environmental sector (Annicchiarico and Dio, 2015). This paper refers to the practice of the two authors and calibrates the two parameters to 6 and 0.75 under the benchmark model. The investment adjustment cost coefficient is calibrated to 5.74 by referring to Del Negro et al.'s (2007) study. Labor disutility coefficient is set to 19.8413 through the calculation method of Annicchiarico and Dio (2015). The discount rate, capital elasticity, and labor supply elasticity are recognized as basic parameters in relevant empirical studies. In this paper, they are set to 0.33, 0.99, and 2, respectively, with reference to Fischer and Springborn (2011), Del Negro et al. (2007), and Pop (2017).

4.2. Dynamic parameter estimation

The external observation data adopted in this paper are China's GDP, household consumption levels and social fixed asset investment, from the first quarter of 2000 to the fourth quarter of 2019. The X-13-ARIMA method is used to adjust the observable variables seasonally, and the data are de-trended by the unilateral HP filtering method.

TFP, clean energy technology, government expenditure, and monetary rules obey the AR(1) distribution, so the prior distribution of the model is set by referring to the method of Del Negro et al. (2007). This paper assumes that the prior distribution of the random shock duration coefficient obeys the Beta distribution. The Bayesian estimation results of dynamic parameters are showed in Table 2.

MCMC univariate and multivariate diagnostics are used to test the astringency and reliability of Bayesian parameter estimation. The results of estimation diagnostics are showed in Figs. 2 and 3. MCMC diagnostic graph measures the first-, second- and third-order moments of variables to judge the stationarity and convergence of Markov

Table 2. Bayesian estimation of dynamic parameters.

Policy scenario	Parameter	Priori mean	Posterior mean	Lower limit of confidence interval (90%)	Upper limit of confidence interval (90%)
No policy	ρ_A	0.85	0.8368	0.7918	0.888
	ρ_{AR}	0.85	0.9979	0.9959	0.9998
	ρ_G	0.97	0.8497	0.7206	1
A single subsidy	ρ_A	0.85	0.2052	0.1976	0.2129
	ρ_{AR}	0.85	0.8405	0.8402	0.8409
	ρ_G	0.97	0.9996	0.9996	0.9997
A single carbon tax	ρ_A	0.85	0.998	0.9962	0.9999
	ρ_{AR}	0.85	0.8396	0.7936	0.8867
	ρ_G	0.97	0.843	0.7025	0.9999
Structural policy	ρ_A	0.85	0.9978	0.9958	0.9998
	ρ_{AR}	0.85	0.8384	0.7917	0.8878
	ρ_G	0.97	0.8495	0.7185	1

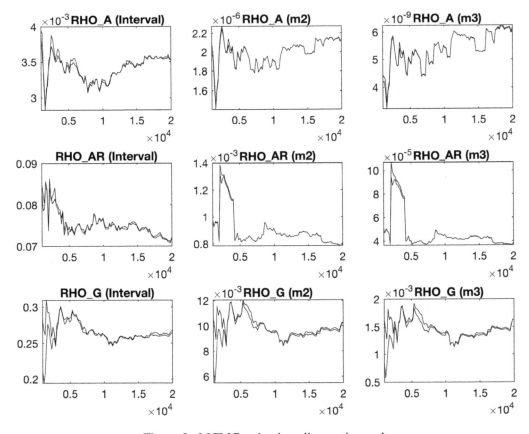

Figure 2. MCMC univariate diagnostic result.

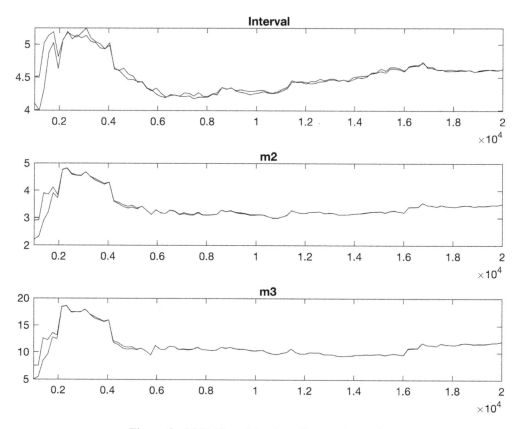

Figure 3. MCMC multivariate diagnostic result.

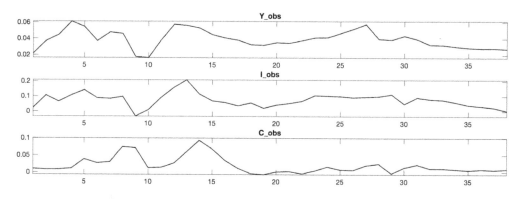

Figure 4. Historical and smoothed variables simulation results.

chains. Both univariate and multivariate diagnostic results show that all the estimated variables satisfy the convergence condition. Two chains gradually approach and become stable, which implies that the Markov chains of the three estimated parameters converge to be stable. The method and technical details of estimation and sampling are referred to An and Schorfheide (2007).

4.3. System robustness test

Referring to the method of Nimark (2009), this paper compares the observed data after detrending with the fluctuation value of simulated data. Figure 4 shows that the model simulation results are consistent with the fluctuation of the observed data. This implies that the empirical model can describe the actual fluctuation of observation data. It is hoped that this model can be used as a data simulation platform for the effect of environmental policy.

5. Dynamic Simulation and Policy Effect Analysis

5.1. Impact on the environment and economy

The main ways of economic low-carbon transition include expanding the scale of clean energy use, reducing the total consumption of fossil energy, and promoting a green energy structure. This section will analyze the impact of the introduction of clean energy on the environmental economic system.

Table 3 shows the changes in steady-state values before and after the introduction of clean energy. Two conclusions can be drawn from the table: First, the development of clean energy is one of the important ways to limit climate change caused by the increasing consumption of fossil fuels. Second, the market access of clean intermediaries can partly promote economic growth.

Specifically, regardless of the additional technology development and storage costs of clean energy, that is, under the premise of great flexibility in energy substitution, the introduction of clean energy can greatly promote environmental pollution control, with the current carbon dioxide emissions reduced by 49.59% and the carbon dioxide stocks by 5.68%. Since the production efficiency of clean intermediate product manufacturers is not reduced by environmental pollution, under the new steady state, the total output will increase by 0.33%, and the total consumption by 1.19%. The other major economic indicators (capital, investment, and wages) rise slightly, while labor drops gently.

Table 3. Steady-state values before and after the introduction of clean energy.

Index	Before the introduction of clean energy	After the introduction of clean energy	Change ratio (%)
C	0.1170	0.1183	1.19
I	0.0130	0.0131	0.34
K	3.4026	3.4140	0.33
L	1.9323	1.9268	−0.28
M	715.1770	674.5680	−5.68
W	4.3667	4.3938	0.62
Y	0.4300	0.4314	0.33
Z	0.1720	0.0867	−49.59

5.2. Effects of structural carbon emission reduction policy

Grimaud *et al.* (2011) pointed out in his research report that R&D subsidies and carbon taxes are necessary means to correct market failures. In order to compare the synergistic and complementary effects of carbon tax and clean energy subsidy, this paper sets up four scenarios: no policy, single clean energy subsidy, single carbon tax, and structural policy. Table 4 shows the changes in steady-state values in the four cases.

In general, on the assumption that government expenditures are unlimited, clean energy subsidies to clean companies will directly boost their output, and labor and wages will increase accordingly. But this will lead to increased fiscal pressure, further distortions in government taxation and fiscal spending, and most importantly, the continued deterioration in environment because the production of polluting companies is not directly inhibited. In contrast, a single carbon tax can significantly improve the environmental quality, but it will also greatly inhibit the economic development, similar to the results of Heutel (2012) and Annicchiarico and Dio (2015). The main economic variables all decline to a certain extent and are subjected to the cost effect. The structural carbon emission reduction policy takes into account both environmental protection and sustainable growth. It not only has the advantages of carbon tax in improving environment, but also boosts the overall economy by subsidies for clean energy. Although economic growth has not been achieved under the current energy transition level, the decline in output is smaller than that in the case of a single carbon tax, which has a certain buffer effect.

Table 4. Comparison of steady-state values under four environmental policy scenarios.

Index	No policy (1)		Single clean energy subsidy (2)		Single carbon tax (3)		Structural policy (4)	
C	0.118		0.111	−6.32%	0.113	−4.85%	0.115	−2.95%
I	0.300		0.300	0.00%	0.300	0.00%	0.300	0.00%
K	0.013		0.014	3.54%	0.013	−4.06%	0.013	−2.74%
L	3.414		3.535	3.54%	3.275	−4.06%	3.321	−2.74%
M	1.927		1.994	3.48%	1.957	1.55%	1.948	1.10%
Πp	674.568		675.758	0.18%	665.321	−1.37%	666.852	−1.14%
Πr	0.300		0.322	7.43%	0.296	−1.46%	0.333	10.89%
W	4.394		4.408	0.32%	4.311	−1.88%	4.359	−0.79%
Y	0.431		0.447	3.54%	0.426	−1.37%	0.428	−0.84%
Z	0.087		0.089	2.88%	0.067	−22.40%	0.071	−18.69%
YP	0.217		0.223	2.88%	0.208	−3.88%	0.209	−3.71%
YR	0.357		0.370	3.81%	0.355	−0.36%	0.358	0.31%
KP	0.522		0.541	3.54%	0.501	−4.06%	0.508	−2.74%
KR	0.522		0.541	3.54%	0.501	−4.06%	0.508	−2.74%
LP	0.180		0.185	2.56%	0.179	−0.69%	0.176	−2.02%
LR	0.295		0.305	3.48%	0.299	1.55%	0.298	1.10%
WP	0.669		0.671	0.32%	0.630	−5.86%	0.645	−3.61%
WR	0.672		0.674	0.32%	0.660	−1.88%	0.667	−0.79%

The results of model (2) show that public expenditure subsidies have a direct effect on the production of enterprises. It increases the total output by 3.54% and the total output of clean manufacturers by 3.81%, yet decreases the consumption level by 6.32%. The environmental pollution increases because polluting enterprises are not subject to environmental controls. The fifth column of Table 4 shows the macro effect of the carbon tax. As polluting companies bear the additional cost of environmental control, the level of economic activity is reduced, but the improvement in environmental quality is obvious. Specifically, the total output sees a decline of 1.37%, mostly contributed by polluting enterprises. The consumption level falls by 4.85%, and the levels of capital, labor and welfare all decline to a certain extent. The seventh column in Table 4 presents the new steady-state values under the structural policy. All the carbon tax collected from polluting companies is used to support clean energy development, alleviating the economic contraction resulted from the carbon tax. The output of clean enterprises increases by 0.31%, the total output of enterprises drops by 0.84%, and the consumption decreases by 2.95%. Moreover, the levels of investment, capital, and labor all decline slightly. These changes under structural policy are between those of scenarios of single policies. At the same time, under the dual effects of carbon taxes and financial subsidies, the current environmental pollution has been greatly reduced.

5.3. *Impose response results of exogenous shocks*

Under different environmental policies, the dynamic response and short-term fluctuation of the economy to uncertain exogenous shocks may differ. Economic fluctuation is an important criterion to evaluate the effect of environmental policies in the presence of random disturbance. Therefore, three sources of uncertainty are adopted to further evaluate the dynamic characteristics of structural carbon reduction policies under the influence of short-term exogenous shocks. In the simulation, the shocks are temporary and occur in period 1.

5.3.1. *Shock of production technology progress*

Technology shock is one of the most critical factors causing economic fluctuation (Smets and Wouters, 2003). It is necessary to study the policy effect of carbon emission reduction policy under the technology shock. Figure 5 shows the response results of 1% positive TFP shock in the five scenarios: before the introduction of clean energy, after the introduction of clean energy, clean energy subsidy, carbon tax, and structural policy. In general, the production technology progress of enterprises can boost output in all scenarios, and household consumption, wages and investment will increase accordingly. As expected, a temporary positive productivity shock causes enterprises' marginal costs to fall, thereby increasing their output. At the same time, it raises the interest rate on capital and labor wages, which in turn stimulates household consumption and investment. However, enterprises will use temporary productivity gains to replace labor factors, thereby causing negative response of labor factors. Because environmental

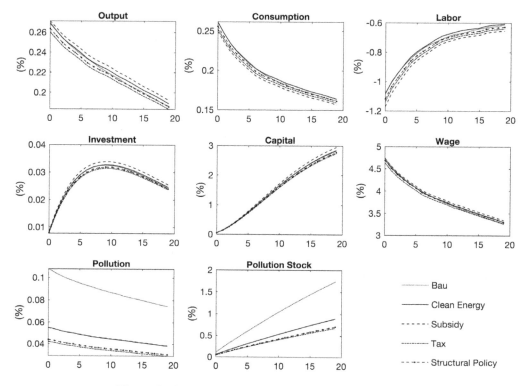

Figure 5. Response results of 1% positive TFP shock.

quality is directly affected by the output of polluting enterprises, at the current energy transition of 15.3%, the increase in output will further deteriorate environmental pollution. This impact is most obvious in the case of a single fiscal subsidy, and the weakest in the case of a single carbon tax, and structural policies are somewhere in between.

5.3.2. *Shock of government expenditure*

Government expenditure is an essential means for fiscal regulation and one of the critical structural shocks (Smets and Wouters, 2003). So, it is necessary to study its impact on the environmental economy. Figure 6 shows the shock response of a 1% increase in the proportion of government expenditure. In general, the increase in government expenditure directly raises the total output of enterprises, but the impact of government expenditure shock is weak as compared with the TFP shock. Consumption, investment, wages, and capital stock all decline to varying degrees yet labor rises slightly. As expected, this impact leads to the crowding out of private consumption and investment by higher government expenditure as well as a decrease in private consumption and investment. Increased government spending makes agents feel poorer because there are fewer resources available for private use. The increase in labor implies that agents have to work harder to offset the fall in interest rates on investment, wages and capital resulted from the shock of government spending. In terms of

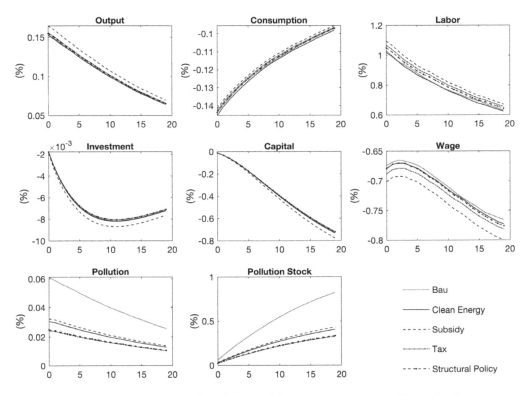

Figure 6. Response results of 1% positive government expenditure shock.

environmental quality, the increase in government expenditures not only increases the output of enterprises, but also increases the pollution emissions to a certain extent. In terms of environmental policies, carbon tax has a better effect on pollution reduction, and clean energy subsidy has a better effect in boosting enterprise output than in other scenarios. Structural policy is somewhere in between.

5.3.3. *Shock of clean energy technology*

The progress of clean energy technology is an essential factor in reducing emissions and promoting sustainable development (Shao *et al.*, 2016). This section analyzes the dynamic effects of carbon emission reduction policies in clean energy technology shock. Figure 7 shows the response results of the positive shock of 1 unit of clean energy technological progress. The impact of clean energy technology mainly drives the overall output by improving the output of clean enterprises, and its influence mechanism on the main economic indicators is similar to that of TFP. Advances in green technology raise overall output by lowering production costs for cleaner firms. Research and development of clean energy technologies stimulate consumption and investment while raising return on investment and capital. Different from the total factor progress, the progress of clean energy technology makes polluting enterprises gradually transform to clean enterprises and also promotes the increase of labor force.

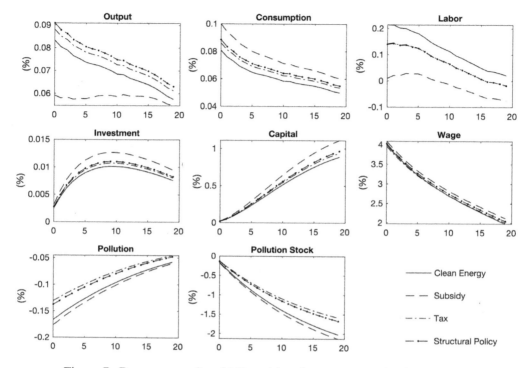

Figure 7. Response results of 1% positive clean energy technology shock.

It is worth mentioning that because clean enterprises produce no GHGs in the production process, they can increase production without causing more environmental pollution. Under the clean energy technology shock, the increase in environmental pollution at time 0 is much smaller than that under the TFP shock, which further verifies the importance of introducing clean energy and enterprise energy transition.

5.3.4. *Analysis of the output of heterogeneous enterprises*

This section compares the outputs of clean and polluting manufacturers under three exogenous shocks. It can be seen from Fig. 8 that under the impact of TFP and government expenditure, the deviation of the output of clean enterprises is greater than that of polluting enterprises. Under the shock of clean energy technology, the output of clean companies deviates positively whereas that of polluting companies deviates negatively. This is mainly because the progress of clean energy technology can increase the production efficiency and output of clean enterprises and, at the same time, increase the ratio of clean output to total output. Correspondingly, the proportion of output of polluting enterprises declines, resulting in a negative deviation.

From the perspective of policy effect, clean energy subsidy has the most obvious driving effect, while the structural policy has the best boosting effect on the output of clean enterprises. The vigorous development of clean industries will impose market

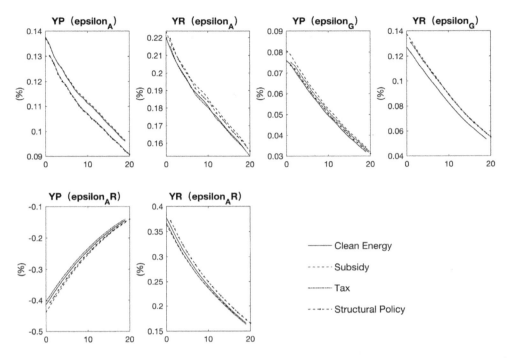

Figure 8. The impact of a 1% positive increase in TFP, clean energy technology progress, and government expenditure on the output of heterogeneous manufacturers.

competition pressure on polluting enterprises, which will induce a reduction in the output of polluting enterprises.

5.4. Sensitivity analysis

This paper aims to study the synergistic effect of clean energy subsidy and carbon tax. The degree of energy transition introduced in this paper is a parameter profoundly affects environmental quality and variables related to enterprise heterogeneity. Thus, this paper selects the degree of energy transition as a variable to test the robustness of the model and to further explore the dynamic effects of policy at different transition levels.

There are four degrees of energy transition in this paper: (1) Tranban = 0.153 (base degree), (2) Tranl-m = 0.2 (low transition degree), (3) Tran-m = 0.3 (medium transition degree), and (4) Tranm-l = 0.4 (high transition degree). Table 5 shows the steady-state values and change ratios in the four policy scenarios and transition levels.

In the four policy scenarios, as the degree of energy transition increases, variables such as output, consumption, investment, and capital all show a nonlinear upward trend, while labor and wage levels decline. The environmental quality has been improved to a certain extent, and the pollution stock and pollution equivalent have been significantly reduced.

Table 5. Sensitivity analysis of the degree of energy transition under various policy scenarios.

Scenarios Variable/ transition degree	No policy t = 0.153	t = 0.2	t = 0.3	t = 0.4	Clean energy subsidy t = 0.153	t = 0.2	t = 0.3	t = 0.4	Carbon tax t = 0.153	t = 0.2	t = 0.3	t = 0.4	Structural policy t = 0.153	t = 0.2	t = 0.3	t = 0.4
C	0.12	0.16	0.24	0.32	0.11	0.15	0.23	0.31	0.11	0.15	0.23	0.31	0.11	0.16	0.24	0.32
I	0.01	0.02	0.03	0.05	0.01	0.02	0.03	0.05	0.01	0.02	0.03	0.05	0.01	0.02	0.03	0.0 = 5
K	3.41	3.79	4.55	5.29	3.54	3.90	4.64	5.36	3.28	3.64	4.36	5.08	3.32	3.69	4.44	5.18
L	1.93	1.53	1.11	0.89	1.99	1.57	1.13	0.90	1.96	1.55	1.12	0.90	1.95	1.54	1.11	0.89
M	674.57	673.69	668.09	659.86	675.76	674.60	668.56	660.07	665.32	664.54	660.11	653.73	666.85	665.99	661.26	654.52
W	4.39	3.76	2.96	2.51	4.41	3.77	2.97	2.52	4.31	3.69	2.92	2.48	4.36	3.74	2.96	2.52
Y	0.43	0.48	0.57	0.67	0.45	0.49	0.59	0.68	0.43	0.47	0.57	0.66	0.43	0.48	0.57	0.67
Z	0.09	0.08	0.07	0.06	0.09	0.09	0.07	0.06	0.07	0.07	0.06	0.04	0.07	0.07	0.06	0.04
YP	0.22	0.21	0.18	0.14	0.22	0.22	0.19	0.14	0.21	0.20	0.17	0.13	0.21	0.20	0.17	0.13
YR	0.36	0.41	0.53	0.65	0.37	0.43	0.54	0.65	0.36	0.41	0.53	0.64	0.36	0.42	0.53	0.65
KP	0.52	0.76	1.36	2.12	0.54	0.78	1.39	2.14	0.50	0.73	1.31	2.03	0.51	0.74	1.33	2.07
KR	0.52	0.76	1.36	2.12	0.54	0.78	1.39	2.14	0.50	0.73	1.31	2.03	0.51	0.74	1.33	2.07
LP	0.18	0.16	0.11	0.08	0.18	0.16	0.12	0.08	0.18	0.16	0.11	0.08	0.18	0.15	0.11	0.07
LR	0.29	0.31	0.33	0.36	0.31	0.31	0.34	0.36	0.30	0.31	0.34	0.36	0.30	0.31	0.33	0.36
WP	0.67	0.75	0.88	1.00	0.67	0.75	0.89	1.00	0.63	0.70	0.83	0.95	0.64	0.72	0.86	0.97
WR	0.67	0.75	0.89	1.01	0.67	0.75	0.89	1.01	0.66	0.74	0.87	0.99	0.67	0.75	0.89	1.01

In summary, as the degree of energy transition increases, the economic growth rate in the case of a single clean energy subsidy is higher than those in the other three cases. In addition, under the current constraints of China's fiscal expenditures, clean energy subsidies to enterprises will crowd out the expenditures on environmental protection and thus reduce the environmental quality. Comparatively speaking, the single carbon tax can improve the environmental quality to the greatest extent. With the increase of energy transition degree, the economy will grow at a relatively low rate. The structural carbon emission reduction policy attempts to reach a balance while taking into account the advantages of the other two policies. Compared with the single carbon tax or clean energy subsidy policy, the structural carbon emission reduction policy is conducive to alleviating environmental pollution while maintaining economic development speed, which further verifies the synergistic effect of the structural environmental policy.

6. Conclusions

This paper constructs a small closed heterogeneous E-DSGE model that includes clean intermediate product manufacturers. After considering China's current progress in energy transition and the impact of clean energy technology advances on productivity, this paper explores the pollution accumulation and economic growth under the effects of carbon taxes and clean energy subsidies. Moreover, the synergy effects of structural environmental policy are comparatively analyzed. The major conclusions of this paper drawn are as follows:

First, the promotion of clean energy to alleviate China's dependence on fossil energy can bring double dividends of carbon emission reduction and sustainable economic development. The heterogeneity analysis results show that the positive effects of structural environmental policy increase with the promotion of clean energy and the progress of clean technology.

Second, structural carbon emission reduction policy has synergistic effects and can well balance the relationship between energy demand and economic growth. The results of scenario comparative analysis show that the single carbon tax improves environmental quality by internalizing pollution cost. However, due to China's over-reliance on fossil energy at present, sticking to the cost effect will lead to sluggish output growth and reduced social welfare. By contrast, clean energy subsidy has an obvious impact in boosting output, but it will result in losing control over polluting enterprises and further distortions of fiscal expenditure. Different from the other two policies, the structural carbon emission reduction policy has both the advantages of carbon tax in improving environmental quality and the direct driving effect of clean energy subsidies on the overall economy.

Third, distinguishing production technology and green innovation technology can better promote the development of energy-saving and environmental-friendly enterprises and improve the industrial structure. The analysis results of exogenous shocks show that TFP has the greatest impact on economic fluctuations, while government expenditure has the smallest. The impact of clean technology is more concentrated in improving enterprise production capacity and reducing environmental pollution. Structural carbon emission reduction policy amplifies the response of major economic variables to government expenditure and clean technology shocks.

In view of the above simulation results, the following discussions are made. First, enterprises continue to improve their technological level and use clean inputs, which is the most effective way to achieve economic growth and environmental quality improvement. Second, the government strengthens energy conservation and emission reduction by subsidizing clean enterprises with carbon tax revenue, which is conducive to carbon peaking and carbon neutral. Third, both total factor technology progress and clean energy technology progress can significantly improve enterprise output, while the latter has a more significant effect on environmental improvement. Therefore, the top priority of enterprises is to enhance their environmental protection technology and emission reduction consciousness.

It should be pointed out that the model proposed in this paper assumes that international climate policies and conventions will not affect the national environmental economic system in a closed economic environment. However, climate change is a global issue. In-depth research should be conducted on the carbon emissions of the countries and sectors in the world to fully understand the growth of carbon emissions and its influencing factors. Policy simulation under bilateral climate model is a key direction in further research.

Acknowledgments

We gratefully acknowledge the financial support from the National Natural Science Foundation of China (Research on the Environmental Management Policy Evaluation Method and its application Based on High Dimensional Panel Data, grant no. 71673078).

References

Acemoglu, D, P Aghion, L Bursztyn and D Hemous (2012). The environment and directed technical change. *American Economic Review*, 102(1), 131–166.

Alper, A and O Oguz (2016). The role of renewable energy consumption in economic growth: Evidence from asymmetric causality. *Renewable and Sustainable Energy Reviews*, 60, 953–959.

An, S and F Schorfheide (2007). Bayesian analysis of DSGE models. *Econometric Reviews*, 26(2–4), 113–172.

Angelopoulos, K., Economides, G., Philippopoulos, A., (2010). What is the Best Environmental Policy? Taxes, Permits and Rules under Economic and Environmental Uncertainty, CESifo Working Paper series 2980, CESifo Group Munich.

Angelopoulos, K, G Economides and A Philippopoulos (2013). First-and second-best allocations under economic and environmental uncertainty. *International Tax and Public Finance*, 20(3), 360–380.

Annicchiarico, B and F Di Dio (2015). Environmental policy and macroeconomic dynamics in a new Keynesian model. *Journal of Environmental Economics and Management*, 69, 1–21.

Annicchiarico, B, L Correani and F Di Dio (2018). Environmental policy and endogenous market structure. *Resource and Energy Economics*, 52, 186–215.

Argentiero, A, CA Bollino, S Micheli and C Zopounidis (2018). Renewable energy sources policies in a Bayesian DSGE model. *Renewable Energy*, 120, 60–68.

Argentiero, A, T Atalla, S Bigerna, S Micheli and P Polinori (2017). Comparing renewable energy policies in EU-15, US and China: A Bayesian DSGE model. *The Energy Journal*, 38 (KAPSARC Special Issue), 77–96.

Blackburn, K and GP Cipriani (2002). A model of longevity, fertility and growth. *Journal of Economic Dynamics and Control*, 26(2), 187–204.

Çebi, C (2012). The interaction between monetary and fiscal policies in Turkey: An estimated new Keynesian DSGE model. *Economic Modelling*, 29(4), 1258–1267.

Chan, YT (2020). Are macroeconomic policies better in curbing air pollution than environmental policies? A DSGE approach with carbon-dependent fiscal and monetary policies. *Energy Policy*, 141, 111454.

Chen, K, F Zhao, H Hao and Z Liu (2018). Synergistic impacts of China's subsidy policy and new energy vehicle credit regulation on the technological development of battery electric vehicles. *Energies*, 11(11), 3193.

Cherni, A and SE Jouini (2017). An ARDL approach to the CO2 emissions, renewable energy and economic growth nexus: Tunisian evidence. *International Journal of Hydrogen Energy*, 42(48), 29056–29066.

Del Negro, M, F Schorfheide, F Smets and R Wouters (2007). On the fit of new Keynesian models. *Journal of Business & Economic Statistics*, 25(2), 123–143.

Doda, B (2016). How to price carbon in good times... and bad! *Wiley Interdisciplinary Reviews: Climate Change*, 7(1), 135–144.

Domeij, D and J Heathcote (2004). On the distributional effects of reducing capital taxes. *International Economic Review*, 45(2), 523–554.

Fischer, C and G Heutel (2013). Environmental macroeconomics: Environmental policy, business cycles, and directed technical change. *Annual Review of Resource Economics*, 5(1), 197–210.

Fischer, C and M Springborn (2011). Emissions targets and the real business cycle: Intensity targets versus caps or taxes. *Journal of Environmental Economics and Management*, 62(3), 352–366.

Fouqueta, R and PJG Pearson (2012). Past and prospective energy transitions Insights from history. *Energy Policy*, 50, 1–7.

Grimaud, A, G Lafforgue and B Magné (2011). Climate change mitigation options and directed technical change: A decentralized equilibrium analysis. *Resource and Energy Economics*, 33(4), 938–962.

Haken, H and R Graham (1971). Synergetik-die Lehre vom zusammenwirken. *Ernahrungs Umschau*, 6(191), 178.

Heutel, G (2012). How should environmental policy respond to business cycles? Optimal policy under persistent productivity shocks. *Review of Economic Dynamics*, 15(2), 244–264.

Khan, H, K Metaxoglou, CR Knittel and M Papineau (2019). Carbon emissions and business cycles. *Journal of Macroeconomics*, 60, 1–19.

Li, M, Y Weng and M Duan (2019). Emissions, energy and economic impacts of linking China's national ETS with the EU ETS. *Applied Energy*, 235, 1235–1244.

Li, X and X Yao (2020). Can energy supply-side and demand-side policies for energy saving and emission reduction be synergistic? A simulated study on China's coal capacity cut and carbon tax. *Energy Policy*, 138, 111232.

Linde, J (2018). DSGE models: Still useful in policy analysis? *Oxford Review of Economic Policy*, 34(1–2), 269–286.

Lintunen, J and L Vilmi (2013). On optimal emission control–Taxes, substitution and business cycles. Bank of Finland Research Discussion Paper, p. 24.

Nimark, KP (2009). A structural model of Australia as a small open economy. *Australian Economic Review*, 42(1), 24–41.

Nordhaus, W (2008). *A Question of Balance: Weighing the Options on Global Warming Policies*. Yale, Yale University Press, New Haven.

Pan, X, H Xu, M Li, T Zong, CT Lee and Y Lu (2020). Environmental expenditure spillovers: Evidence from an estimated multi-area DSGE model. *Energy Economics*, 86, 104645.

Panwar, N, S Kaushik and S Kothari (2011). Role of renewable energy sources in environmental protection: A review. *Renewable and Sustainable Energy Reviews*, 15(3), 1513–1524.

Pindyck, RS (2013). Climate change policy: What do the models tell us? *Journal of Economic Literature*, 51(3), 860–872.

Pizer, WA and R Kopp (2005). Calculating the costs of environmental regulation. *Handbook of Environmental Economics*, Vol. 3, Elsevier, North-Holland, pp. 1307–1351.

Pop, R-E (2017). A small-scale DSGE-VAR model for the Romanian economy. *Economic Modelling*, 67, 1–9.

Shao, S, R Luan, Z Yang and C Li (2016). Does directed technological change get greener: Empirical evidence from Shanghai's industrial green development transformation. *Ecological Indicators*, 69, 758–770.

Shmelev, SE and SU Speck (2018). Green fiscal reform in Sweden: econometric assessment of the carbon and energy taxation scheme. *Renewable and Sustainable Energy Reviews*, 90, 969–981.

Smets, F and R Wouters (2003). An estimated dynamic stochastic general equilibrium model of the euro area. *Journal of the European Economic Association*, 1(5), 1123–1175.

Wang, Z, J Wu, C Liu and G Gu (2017). The analysis for synergistic effect of policy of environmental tax with dynamic CGE in China. In *Integrated Assessment Models of Climate Change Economics*, pp. 73–88. Springer, Singapore.

Xiao, B, Y Fan and X Guo (2018). Exploring the macroeconomic fluctuations under different environmental policies in China: A DSGE approach. *Energy Economics*, 76, 439–456.

Xiong, B, W Chen, P Liu and W Xu (2016). Fiscal policy, local governments competition and air pollution control quality. *Journal of China University of Geosciences (Social Science Editorail)*, 1, 20–33.

Xiao, B, X Guo, Y Fan, S Voigt and L Cui (2020). Climate policies under dynamic international economic cycles: A heterogeneous countries DSGE model. ZEW-Centre for European Economic Research Discussion Paper, No.20-011.

Yu, P (2013). Research on efficiency of environment policy in the context of economic growth—based on empirical analysis of province panel data. *Finance & Trade Economics*, 4, 16–23.

Zhang, J and Y Zhang (2020). Examining the economic and environmental effects of emissions policies in China: A Bayesian DSGE model. *Journal of Cleaner Production*, 266, 122026.

Zhu, X and Y Lu (2017). Pollution governance effect on environmental fiscal and taxation policy: Based on region and threshold effect. *Chinese Journal of Population, Resources and Environment*, 1, 83–90.

© 2025 World Scientific Publishing Company
https://doi.org/10.1142/9789819812264_0009

A BOOTSTRAP ASSESSMENT OF THE SHADOW PRICES OF CO₂ FOR THE INDUSTRIAL SECTOR IN CHINA'S KEY CITIES[¶]

MIAN YANG[*,†], JIANGCHUAN XU[†], MENGHAN LI[†] and HONGBO DUAN[‡,§]

[*]*Center for Economic Development Research,*
Wuhan University, Wuhan 430072, P. R. China

[†]*Economics and Management School,*
Wuhan University, Wuhan 430072, P. R. China

[‡]*School of Economics & Management,*
University of Chinese Academy of Sciences
Beijing 100190, P. R. China
[§]*hbduan@ucas.ac.cn*

This study constructs a modified assessment model based on the bootstrap method to estimate the CO_2 shadow prices for 35 typical cities' industrial sectors in China from 2005 to 2018. Based on data from China's seven pilot regional carbon markets, we evaluate the current CO_2 trading price distortions. The empirical results indicate that during the study period, the average CO_2 shadow price for the target cities is 1915.86 yuan per tonne, decreasing to 1880.57 yuan per tonne when using the bootstrap method for bias correction. The overall trends of CO_2 shadow prices in most key cities are increasing given the strengthening of environmental regulations following the 11th Five-Year Plan. In addition, compared with the CO_2 shadow prices in this paper, carbon trading prices in pilot cities present significantly negative distortions, which may fail to reflect the real opportunity cost of carbon abatement. Based on the findings of this study, several policy recommendations are proposed.

Keywords: Shadow price; bootstrap method; carbon price distortion; abatement cost.

1. Introduction

Since its reform and opening up, China's economy has achieved rapid improvement. However, such long-term intensive economic development has brought about enormous challenges related to energy consumption (especially fossil fuels) and a substantial increase in CO_2 emissions. U.S. energy information administration (EIA) statistics show that China's total energy consumption has seen a considerable increase from 19.11 quad Btu in 1980 to 139.43 quad Btu in 2017, making China the largest

---

[§]Corresponding author.
[¶]This chapter was originally published in Climate Change Economics, Vol. 12, No. 4 (2021), published by World Scientific Publishing, Singapore. Reprinted with permission.

CO_2 emitter worldwide, with its CO_2 emission level experiencing a 5.3-fold increase (from 16.65 to 104.87 million tons).

In recent years, to eliminate the overreliance on energy input and curb excessive CO_2 emissions, the Chinese government has actively promoted steady economic growth while simultaneously seeking a low-carbon development path (Yang et al., 2020). Since 2006, indicators like energy intensity, CO_2 emission intensity, and total energy consumption have been considered necessary binding emissions standards in terms of the economic and social development plan. More recently, China has solemnly pledged to the world that it will adopt more vigorous policies and measures to peak its carbon dioxide emissions by 2030 and strive to achieve carbon neutrality by 2060.

Policymakers have developed different instruments, including command-and-control and market-based environmental regulation instruments (Liu et al., 2019), to meet emissions goals. Compared with the administrative order, market-based mechanisms, including carbon emission trading systems (ETSs) based on the Coase theorem and carbon taxes based on Pigouvian taxes, are more cost effective. China has adopted ETSs and launched eight regional pilots since 2013. On December 17, 2017, China further launched a national ETS covering the power sector for the first time, with trading beginning in 2021 officially and gradually expanding sectoral coverage.

In the process of establishing a national ETS, the shadow price of CO_2 (i.e., marginal abatement cost (MAC)) has important theoretical and practical implications. On the one hand, the scientific measurement of the CO_2 shadow price involves the fundamental work of judging the pressure and potential of regional carbon abatement and also provides benchmarks and a realistic basis for the initial allocation of total carbon allowances (Duan et al., 2016). On the other hand, differences between CO_2 shadow prices and the actual carbon trading prices can be adopted to determine whether a carbon market is operating effectively and whether the emission reduction targets are well achieved. Furthermore, distortions in carbon prices also reflect the inequality between income and carbon emissions (Huang and Duan, 2020). Regarding price theory, the optimal price of the carbon allowance should be equal to the shadow price of CO_2 in a perfectly competitive market. When the carbon allowance price is lower than the shadow price, enterprises are more willing to purchase carbon allowances in the market, instead of mitigating emissions themselves, leading to a lower emission abatement than expected.

Given the significant theoretical and practical applications of the CO_2 shadow price, many studies have measured it using alternative methods based on diverse datasets. However, most existing studies focus on the provincial or industry levels, while only few of them estimate the shadow price of CO_2 at the city scale. From a methodological point of view, shadow prices have mainly been evaluated via deterministic models, such as a parametric linear programming (LP) method, in the extant literature, which neither can overcome the influence of stochastic factors nor provide information for statistical inference. To fill these gaps, this paper attempts to estimate the bias-corrected CO₂ shadow price derived from the directional distance function (DDF) based on the industrial energy consumption by species and other input-output data of 35 key cities in China (that is, the CO₂ shadow prices calculated in this paper refer to those of urban industry). On this basis, we compare the estimated carbon shadow price with the actual carbon allowance price to further evaluate the effectiveness of the existing carbon trading systems. This paper contributes to the literature in the following three ways. First, to the best of our knowledge, the estimates of the up-to-date carbon abatement cost at the urban-industrial level are innovative, particularly dynamic from 2005 to 2018. Second, we utilize a more optimized bootstrap approach to correct the possible bias of the CO₂ shadow price associated with the effect of stochastic factors. Finally, this paper examines the distortions in carbon prices among the seven existing carbon trading pilots, providing an empirical basis for governments' carbon market management.

The remainder of the paper is organized as follows. Section 2 reviews the relevant literature. Section 3 describes the model used for modified CO₂ shadow price estimation. Section 4 introduces the data and variables. Section 5 presents the empirical results. Section 6 concludes the paper and provides some policy implications.

2. Literature Review

This paper reviews the existing literature in terms of both sample selection and the methodologies adopted. Regarding sample selection, existing studies examine CO₂ shadow prices by using country- (Boussemart *et al.*, 2017; Xie *et al.*, 2017), provincial- (Choi *et al.*, 2012; Du *et al.*, 2016; Ma and Hailu, 2016; Shen and Lin, 2017), industrial- (Jiahuey *et al.*, 2019; Lee and Zhang, 2012; Vardanyan and Noh, 2006; Xian *et al.*, 2020; Zhou *et al.*, 2015) or city-level data (Wang *et al.*, 2017a; Wu *et al.*, 2019). Theoretically, the CO₂ shadow price is the microconcept derived from revenue functions; thus, the more microscopic the data are, the better the estimates of shadow price reflect the actual abatement cost. Nevertheless, most existing studies have adopted the first three data levels, and few have measured the CO₂ shadow price at the city level, which is more likely to be the level at which piloting carbon trading occurs. In the few studies that measure the CO₂ shadow price at the city level (e.g., Wang *et al.*, 2017a; Wu *et al.*, 2019), energy-related CO₂ emissions are calculated using only three energy sources (electricity, coal gas, and liquid petroleum gas). However, this approach is considered inappropriate and inaccurate because the main sources of CO₂ emissions, such as raw coal, coke, and gasoline, are not included. In addition, some studies have measured the shadow price of CO₂ using firm-level data. However, due to the availability of data, such studies (e.g., Du *et al.*, 2016; Wang *et al.*, 2017b; Wei *et al.*, 2013) have generally used thermal power plants as subjects, for which only cross-sectional evidence is available, making it impossible to provide robust data support for a distribution dynamics analysis and allowing for a new perspective at the regional level. Accordingly, to reconcile the research level with the data availability, we compile a city-level panel dataset that had not been previously used in the extant literature. More importantly, these prefectural-and-above cities cover all existing carbon emission trading pilots in China, providing further useful references for analyzing distortions in carbon allowance prices.

In the absence of the actual price of CO_2 emissions, it is essential to evaluate the shadow price of CO_2 using a scientific approach. Currently, there have been two main approaches to evaluating the value of undesirable outputs: engineering and economic approaches. The engineering approach focuses mainly on investments and expenditures related to reduction technologies and evaluates the abatement cost for reducing one unit of undesirable output based on information on the expected reduction (Dunant et al., 2019). Although the engineering approach conveniently takes a technological perspective to define the MAC, it does not consider institutional barriers to the implementation of emission abatement and transaction costs, leading to "negative" shadow prices (Lee et al., 2014).

Differing from the engineering approach, the economic approach estimates the abatement cost of undesirable outputs based on economic models and historical input and outputs covering the entire production process. The shadow price in this approach is interpreted as the potential opportunity cost of the desirable outputs that were abandoned to reduce the number of undesirable outputs. In general, economic methods can be roughly divided into two categories in terms of modeling techniques: nonparametric data envelopment analysis (DEA) models and parametric models. A DEA model is applied by taking advantage of there being no need to set a specific function form (Wang et al., 2018). For example, Jiahuey et al. (2019) used the nonradial DEA method to examine the CO_2 shadow prices of the Chinese chemical industry from 1980 to 2013, showing that CO_2 shadow prices continued to rise during this period. (Boussemart et al., 2017) used a robust DEA model to evaluate CO_2 shadow prices in 119 countries. Choi et al. (2012) estimated the shadow price at the provincial level in China with the dual model of the slack-based DEA model. However, the nonparametric DEA model is less suited to evaluating shadow prices due to the construction of a piecewise linear combination of all observed outputs and inputs, which may lead to unsolvable model issues. Thus, parametric models with specific functions that can be differentiable anywhere have been widely used in the literature. In general, such models can be roughly divided into four categories according to different functional forms: production functions (Shen and Lin, 2017), cost functions (Carlson et al., 2000), Shepard distance functions (Hailu and Veeman, 2000; Ma and Hailu, 2016; Maziotis et al., 2020; Vardanyan and Noh, 2006; Zhang and Jiang, 2019) and DDFs (Bellver-Domingo et al., 2017; Duan et al., 2016; He et al., 2018; Ji and Zhou, 2020; Molinos-Senante and Guzmán, 2018; Xian et al., 2020). Overall, the DDF is more appropriate (Ma et al., 2019) in the presence of undesirable outputs such as CO_2 emissions. The reason for this is that unlike the radial model, the DDF can handle the expansion of desirable outputs and the contraction of undesirable outputs simultaneously. Two parametric methods are widely used to estimate the DDF: the first is stochastic frontier analysis (SFA), which takes the error term into account and can be used for the statistical inference of parameters (Aigner *et al.*, 1977). However, the SFA method generally requires a larger dataset and may not completely guarantee the monotonic properties of the DDF; in other words, the shadow price derived through the SFA method may be negative (Ma *et al.*, 2019; Wei *et al.*, 2013). The second is the parametric LP method, which can guarantee the monotonicity of the distance function (Aigner and Chu, 1968; Färe *et al.*, 2005; Hailu and Veeman, 2000). Nevertheless, the parametric LP approach is a deterministic frontier model and cannot deal with the influence of random noise and make statistical inferences. To the best of our knowledge, only Du *et al.* (2016) and Jiang and Zhang (2018) used the naive bootstrap method to obtain the standard errors of parameters, which may be unable to simulate the true parameter distribution. This paper adopts a more optimized bootstrap method, including a smoothing procedure while resampling to correct the deviation in the original parameter vector, and then obtains the bias-corrected CO_2 shadow price.

3. Methodology

In this section, we first define the DDF based on the production technology set. Then, the distance and profit functions are used to derive the shadow price of the undesired output. Next, the bootstrap method is used to obtain the bias-corrected CO_2 shadow price. Finally, we estimate the distortion of the actual emission price of CO_2 based on the estimated shadow prices.

3.1. *DDF and production technology*

Considering the production process, production unit i uses the following inputs: $\mathbf{x} = (x_1, x_2, x_3, \ldots, x_N) \in R_+^N$ produces desirable outputs $\mathbf{y} = (y_1, y_2, y_3, \ldots, y_M) \in R_+^m$, accompanied by undesirable outputs $\mathbf{b} = (b_1, b_2, b_3, \ldots, b_J) \in R_+^J$. The technology is represented by output set $P(x)$, where $P(x) = \{(x, y, b) : x \text{ can produce } (y, b)\}$. $P(x)$ is a bounded closed set, describing the mapping relationship between inputs and outputs. Moreover, according to Färe *et al.* (2005), the output set is assumed to satisfy the following: (1) if $(y, b) \in P(x)$ and $b = 0$, then $y = 0$, which means that undesirable outputs are produced together with desirable outputs, and (2) if $(y, b) \in P(x)$ and $0 \leq \alpha \leq 1$, then $(\alpha y, \alpha b) \in P(x)$. This assumption implies that the undesirable and desirable outputs satisfy joint weak disposability. In other words, any proportional reduction in the desirable and undesirable outputs together is feasible, and any reduction in bad outputs is costly.

The production technique can also be denoted by a DDF based on the output set, which is defined as follows:

$$\mathbf{D}(x, y, b; g) = \sup \{\beta > 0 : (y + \beta g_y, b - \beta g_b) \in P(x)\} \quad (1)$$

where $g = (g_y, g_b)$ is a directional vector. The DDF provides information on the maximum distance needed for (y, b) to move forward along the direction vector. If the value of the DDF of a production unit is equal to 0, then the production unit is on the boundary of the production frontier, and its efficiency score is 1. Therefore, the DDF can be used to measure the efficiency of production units. The larger the value of the DDF is, the farther away the production unit is from the frontier, i.e., the less efficient it is, and vice versa. According to Färe et al. (2005), the DDF inherits the following properties:

(1) Representativeness: $\mathbf{D}(x, y, b; g) \geq 0$, if and only if $(y, b) \in P(x)$;
(2) Monotonicity in y: $\mathbf{D}(x, y, b; g) \geq \mathbf{D}(x, y', b; g)$ for $(y', b) \geq (y, b)$;
(3) Monotonicity in b: $\mathbf{D}(x, y, b; g) \geq \mathbf{D}(x, y, b'; g)$ for $(y, b) \geq (y, b')$;
(4) Monotonicity in x: $\mathbf{D}(x, y, b; g) \geq \mathbf{D}(x', y, b; g)$ for $x \geq x'$; and
(5) Translation property: $\mathbf{D}(x, y + \alpha g_y, b - \alpha g_b; g) = \mathbf{D}(x, y, b; g) - \alpha, \alpha \in P(x)$.

3.2. Deviation in the shadow price

The shadow price can be derived from the duality relationship between DDFs and revenue functions (Färe et al., 2006). Suppose that $p = (p_1, \ldots, p_M) \in R_+^M$ represents the prices of desirable output and that $q = (q_1, \ldots, q_J) \in R_+^J$ represents the prices of undesirable output. Then, the revenue function based on the DDF is defined as follows:

$$R(y, b, p, q) = \max\left(py - qb : (y, b) \in P(x)\right). \tag{2}$$

The profit function characterizes the maximum feasible profit in the presence of undesirable output, which is the sum of the positive profit from desirable output and the negative profit from undesirable output.

Given the feasible directional vector, the revenue function can be rewritten as follows:

$$R(y, b, p, q) \geq \left(py - qb + p\mathbf{D}(x, y, b; g)g_y + q\mathbf{D}(x, y, b; g)g_b\right). \tag{3}$$

Rearranging (3), the DDF in terms of the revenue function can be represented as follows:

$$\mathbf{D}(x, y, b; g) \leq \frac{R(y, b, p, q) - (py - qb)}{pg_y + qg_b}. \tag{4}$$

By applying the envelope theorem twice to (4), the shadow price can then be estimated as follows:

$$q = -p\left(\frac{\partial \mathbf{D}(x, y, b; g)/\partial b}{\partial \mathbf{D}(x, y, b; g)/\partial y}\right). \tag{5}$$

The shadow price of an undesirable output can be generally interpreted as the opportunity cost of reducing one additional unit of undesirable output and the gain associated with an increase in the number of desirable outputs.

3.3. Bias-corrected estimate of carbon shadow prices

To strictly guarantee the monotonicity properties of the DDF with respect to inputs and outputs, the parametric approach is employed to estimate the technological efficiency of producers. The functional specification should be first defined through the parametric approach. Since the quadratic function form is twice differentiable and allows for the incorporation of the translation property, it is utilized to parameterize the distance function. In the case of N factors, M desirable outputs, and J undesirable outputs, the DDF of production unit i can be expressed as follows:

$$\mathbf{D}_i(x_i, y_i, b_i; g) = \alpha_0 + \sum_{n=1}^{N} \alpha_n x_{ni} + \sum_{m=1}^{M} \beta_m y_{mi} + \sum_{j=1}^{J} \gamma_j b_{ji}$$

$$+ \frac{1}{2} \sum_{n=1}^{N} \sum_{n'=1}^{N} \alpha_{nn'} x_{ni} x_{n'i} + \frac{1}{2} \sum_{m=1}^{M} \sum_{m'=1}^{M} \beta_{mm'} y_{mi} y_{m'i}$$

$$+ \frac{1}{2} \sum_{j=1}^{J} \sum_{j'=1}^{J} \gamma_{jj'} b_{ji} b_{j'i} + \sum_{n=1}^{N} \sum_{m=1}^{M} \delta_{nm} x_{ni} y_{mi}$$

$$+ \sum_{n=1}^{N} \sum_{j=1}^{J} \eta_{nj} x_{ni} b_{ji} + \sum_{m=1}^{M} \sum_{j=1}^{J} \mu_{mj} y_{mi} b_{ji}. \qquad (6)$$

According to Färe *et al.* (2005), once the functional form is determined, the parameters of distance function (6) can be estimated by solving a deterministic LP model (Aigner and Chu, 1968), which seeks to minimize the sum of the deviations in all production units from the target frontier with specific constraints of the distance functions (i.e., properties like representativeness, monotonicity, and translation).[1]

$$\text{Min} \sum_i [\mathbf{D}_i(x_{ni}, y_{mi}, b_{ji}; 1, -1) - 0],$$

s.t. (i) $\mathbf{D}_i(x_{ni}, y_{mi}, b_{ji}; 1, -1) \geq 0, \quad i = 1, 2, \ldots, I,$

(ii) $\dfrac{\partial \mathbf{D}_i(x_{ni}, y_{mi}, b_{ji}; 1, -1)}{\partial x_{ni}} \geq 0, \quad i = 1, 2, \ldots, I; \quad n = 1, 2, \ldots, N,$

(iii) $\dfrac{\partial \mathbf{D}_i(x_{ni}, y_{mi}, b_{ji}; 1, -1)}{\partial b_{ji}} \geq 0, \quad i = 1, 2, \ldots, I; \quad j = 1, 2, \ldots, J,$

(iv) $\dfrac{\partial \mathbf{D}_i(x_{ni}, y_{mi}, b_{ji}; 1, -1)}{\partial y_{mi}} \leq 0, \quad i = 1, 2, \ldots, I; \quad m = 1, 2, \ldots, M,$

(v) $\sum_{m=1}^{M} \beta_m - \sum_{j=1}^{J} \gamma_j = -1, \quad \sum_{m=1}^{M} \beta_{mm'} - \sum_{j=1}^{J} \mu_{mj} = 0,$

---

[1] Although both SFA and parametric LP methods can be used to calculate shadow prices, the latter is adopted due to the fact that the former generally requires a larger dataset and may not completely guarantee the monotonicity properties of the DDF; in other words, the shadow price derived with SFA may be negative.

$$\sum_{j'=1}^{J} \gamma_{jj'} - \sum_{m=1}^{M} \mu_{mj} = 0; \quad \sum_{m=1}^{M} \delta_{nm} - \sum_{j=1}^{J} \eta_{nj} = 0,$$

$$(vi) \; \alpha_{nn'} = \alpha_{n'n}; \; \beta_{mm'} = \beta_{m'm}; \; \gamma_{jj'} = \gamma_{j'j}.$$

(7)

The shadow price derived from function (5) can be estimated with the parameters obtained from LP (7). The first set of constraints is used to model the representation property of the DDF. The second set of inequalities implies that the DDF is monotonically increasing with respect to the inputs. Similar logic is reflected in (iii) and (iv). The fifth set of constraints imposes homogeneity of one degree in the output vector, and finally, the symmetry of the trans-log function parameters is implemented by (vi).

However, the DDF in (7) is calculated based on the deterministic frontier model, which cannot overcome the influence of stochastic factors and be statistically inferred. Therefore, we utilize an optimized bootstrap method that was created by Simar and Wilson (1998) and developed by Wei and Zhang (2020) to correct the deviation in the parameters.

Then, the modified estimate of the CO_2 shadow price can be obtained through the following five steps:

(1) Calculate the estimated value of $\hat{D}_i(x_i, y_i, b_i; g)$ based on original parameter $\hat{\theta}$.
(2) Estimate the distribution of $\hat{D}_i(x_i, y_i, b_i; g)$ by the kernel density method, and re-sample from the initial $\hat{D}_i(x_i, y_i, b_i; g)$ based on the density distribution to obtain a bootstrap sample $\hat{D}_{ir}(x_i, y_i, b_i; g)$.
(3) Generate bootstrapped sample data according to $\hat{D}_{ir}(x_i, y_i, b_i; g): x_{ir}^* = x_{ir}, y_{ir}^* = y_{ir} + g_y(\hat{D}_{ir} - \hat{D}_i)$, and $b_{ir}^* = b_{ir} - g_b(\hat{D}_{ir} - \hat{D}_i)$.
(4) Calculate parameter θ_r^* in the DDF based on the "pseudo" sample data.
(5) Repeat steps (2)–(4) R times (2000 times in this paper), and derive the modified parameter estimates and standard error according to the following formula: $\tilde{\theta} = 2*\hat{\theta} - \bar{\theta}_r^*$, $\text{se}_{\text{boot}}(\hat{\theta}) = \sqrt{1/(R-1)\sum(\hat{\theta} - \bar{\theta}_r^*)}$ and $\bar{\theta}_r^* = 1/R \sum \theta_r^*$.

3.4. Distortion of actual carbon allowance prices

Due to the differences in production technology, industrial structure and factor endowment, significant heterogeneities exist in MACs among production units. In the presence of carbon emission trading markets, participants with lower MACs can obtain net income or reduce abatement costs by meeting certain carbon quotas. When the MACs of all participants are at the same level, the carbon emission trading market reaches equilibrium. In this section, with the formula derivation provided below, we show that once the MACs of all participants are the same and equal to the carbon trading price, the total cost of achieving a given emission reduction target is minimized.

Consider the following abatement cost minimization issues for a given total emission reduction:

$$\min C = \sum_i C_i(v_i),$$

$$\text{s.t.} \sum_i v_i = V, \tag{8}$$

where C is the total abatement cost of all participants, and C_i represents the abatement cost of participant i depending on actual emissions v_i. V is the total abatement target at the national level. The Lagrange operator can be used to solve the cost minimization issue

$$L = \sum_i C_i(v_i) - \lambda \left(\sum_i v_i - V \right) \tag{9}$$

Then, the minimization problem is transformed to solve the following set of equations:

$$\begin{cases} \dfrac{\partial L}{\partial v_i} = \dfrac{\partial C_i}{\partial v_i} - \lambda = 0, \\ \dfrac{\partial L}{\partial \lambda} = \sum_i v_i - V = 0. \end{cases} \tag{10}$$

When the MACs of all participants are equal, the costs under the emission reduction target can be minimized. The MAC is the optimal price of CO_2 emissions at this point. However, the MAC of each participant may differ in reality, and a gap may exist between the MAC and carbon emission price. Thus, the following distortion factor Δ_{it} is defined to estimate this gap:

$$\Delta_{it} = \frac{\text{MAC}_{it}}{P_{it}}, \tag{11}$$

Δ_{it} where represents the absolute value of the ratio of the MAC (shadow price) to the actual emission price of CO_2 for participant i, reflecting the degree of distortion in carbon emission prices. A larger value of Δ_{it} illustrates a higher degree of distortion in the carbon emission price, and thus, the actual total abatement costs are expected to be larger, and vice versa.

4. Data

The sample of this paper is the input and output data of 35 key cities in Mainland China from 2005–2018, collected mainly from the China Statistical Yearbook, City Statistical Yearbook, and Statistical Yearbook of each prefecture-level city. We consider a case of three inputs — labor, capital and energy — one desirable output — gross industrial product — and one undesirable output — CO_2 emissions.

Labor is represented by the sum of employees in three major industrial sectors: manufacturing, mining, and the production and supply of electricity, gas, and water.

Given that there is no database or statistical information that publishes capital stock data in prefecture-level cities' industrial sectors, we use a perpetual inventory method to estimate the capital stock based on the original value of fixed assets, accumulated depreciation and total fixed assets, as well as some other indicators. The relevant datasets come from prefecture-level cities' statistical yearbooks. The actual formula is $K_t = I_t + (1 - \delta_t)K_{t-1}$, where K_t and K_{t-1} represent the capital stock at times t and $t-1$, respectively. I_t is the total volume of investment in fixed assets at time t, calculated based on the original value of fixed assets two years before and after. δ_t is the depreciation rate at time t. Note that capital stock is converted to the 2005 constant price. Regarding the energy factor, although total energy consumption has not been published by prefecture-level city governments, most report that of industrial subdivision varieties. Considering the availability and comparability of data, the total energy consumption in prefecture-level cities in this paper is calculated based on the following nine energy sources: coal, washing coal, coke, crude oil, gasoline, kerosene, diesel, oil and natural gas. Each kind of energy is converted into standard coal to ensure the additivity of different energy sources based on the conversion factor in the China Energy Statistical Yearbook (2017).

The desirable output is expressed in terms of gross industrial product, which is converted to the 2005 constant price with the industrial producer price index. Regarding CO_2 emissions, existing studies usually use indirect methods to estimate industrial CO_2 emissions at the city level due to the absence of monitoring data on CO_2 emissions at that level. Some studies (e.g., Wang et al., 2017a; Wu et al., 2019) estimated CO_2 emissions based on only three types of energy consumption, while other studies based their estimates on energy intensity at the provincial level. Both methods are considered inappropriate because of the large gaps between estimated and actual emissions. Referring to Chen et al. (2019) and Zhou et al. (2018), we choose the above nine kinds of energy that are mostly used in industrial production to estimate urban-industrial CO_2 emissions. The formula for calculating CO_2 emissions is $CO_2 = \sum \text{energy}_i \times CF_i \times CC_i \times COF_i \times \frac{44}{12}$, where energy$_i$ denotes the energy consumption of fuel I; CF_i is the average net calorific value; CC_i is the carbon content,

Table 1. Overall descriptive statistics of input and output data, 2005–2018.

Variable	Unit	Obs	Mean	Std. Dev.	Minimum	Maximum
Labor	10^4 people	490	51	46	4	261
Capital	10^8 yuan	490	2120	1890	83	9190
Energy	10^4 tec	490	2292	2435	7	15,210
CO_2	10^4 tonne	490	6753	6511	12	39,754
Output	10^8 yuan	490	5710	5990	227	28,800

Notes: Std. Dev. = standard deviation; tec = tonne of equivalent coal.

denoting the level of carbon content per unit of heat; COF_i is the carbon oxidation factor; and the fraction of carbon oxidized based on fuel type i, 44/12, shows the molecular weight ratio of carbon dioxide to carbon (kg/kg).

Based on the above data verification process, the descriptive statistics for each input and output are shown in Table 1.

5. Results

5.1. *Parameter estimates*

Before estimating the parameters in the DDF, we normalize all input and output variables by dividing them by their mean values to overcome the convergence problem. The parameters in the DDF from the parametric LP are estimated by MATLAB 2018a. Then, this paper utilizes the optimized bootstrap approach to overcome the impact of stochastic factors by correcting parameter estimate biases. The modified estimates of CO_2 shadow prices are shown in Table 2.

By viewing the estimated values, it can be seen that gaps exist between most of the original and bias-corrected values of the parameter estimates, which implies that if the effect of stochastic factors is not taken into account, then the parameter results are

Table 2. Estimated parameters of the distance functions.

Parameter	Variable	Original estimate	Bias-corrected estimate	Standard. Dev.
α_0	cons	−0.029	−0.027	0.001
α_1	l	0.468	0.457	0.016
α_2	k	0.718	0.672	0.041
α_3	e	0.001	0.003	0.001
β_1	y	−0.867	−0.834	0.019
γ_1	c	0.133	0.166	0.019
α_{11}	ll	−0.169	−0.173	0.004
α_{12}	lk	−0.047	−0.041	0.005
α_{13}	le	0.034	0.040	0.005
δ_{11}	ly	0.137	0.139	0.005
η_{11}	lc	0.137	0.139	0.005
α_{22}	kk	−0.236	−0.215	0.012
α_{23}	ke	0.040	0.047	0.005
δ_{21}	ky	0.072	0.057	0.010
η_{21}	kc	0.072	0.057	0.010
α_{33}	ee	0.039	0.043	0.004
δ_{31}	ey	−0.041	−0.048	0.004
η_{31}	ec	−0.041	−0.048	0.004
β_{11}	yy	0.003	0.008	0.004
μ_{11}	yc	0.003	0.008	0.004
γ_{11}	cc	0.003	0.008	0.004

Notes: k, l, e, y, c denote capital, labor, energy, gross industrial product, and CO_2 respectively.

biased, affecting the accurate measurement of CO_2 shadow prices. Nevertheless, we find that the first-order undesirable output parameters represent the expected negative sign, as any increase in sulfur dioxide emissions increases the value of the distance functions, regardless of whether the parameters are corrected. The estimated values of $\alpha_1, \alpha_2,$ and α_3 are greater than zero and represent the positive monotonicity in inputs. Additionally, the DDF is required to be monotonically decreasing in desirable output and monotonically increasing in undesirable output, with β_1 being less than zero and γ_1 being greater than zero. In addition, associated standard errors allow us to justify whether or not the effect of the undesirable output and inputs on the distance functions is statistically significant. The results show that more than 2/3 of the 21 parameters estimated are significant at the 1% level, indicating that the quadratic form of the DDF defined in this paper is a good fit for city-level green production technology in China. The average environmental efficiency score of each city calculated based on the parameters in Table 2 is shown in Appendix A.

Once the parameters are estimated, CO_2 shadow prices can be evaluated through the above results. As shown in Table 3, the average industrial CO_2 shadow price in 35 key cities is 1915.86 yuan/tonne; after considering the effect of stochastic factors and adopting the bootstrap method for error correction, the corrected shadow price decreases to 1880.57 yuan/tonne. Table 3 compares the results in this paper with those of existing studies on shadow prices. For convenience of comparison, we transform all the shadow prices into RMB (yuan) according to the corresponding exchange rate. The results generally lie in a wide range depending on different data levels, research periods, distance functions, and estimation methods, varying from 0 to 18760 yuan/tonne. We can still find some basic facts and regulations from previous studies, for example, the shadow prices calculated with Shepard's input or output distance function

Table 3. Comparison with previous studies.

Relevant literature	Level	Time	Distance function	Approach	Shadow prices (yuan/tonne)
Wei (2014)	city	2001–2008	DDF	LP	967
Lee and Zhang (2012)	industry	2009	IDF	LP	0–133
Du et al. (2015)	province	2001–2010	DDF	LP	1300
Zhou et al. (2015)	industry	2009–2011	ODF	LP	394–1906
Duan et al. (2016)	province	2001–2010	DDF	LP	1000–2100
Jiahuey et al. (2019)	industry	1980–2013	DDF	DEA	10–610
Wu et al. (2019)	city	2002–2013	SBM	DEA	40–4719
Zhang and Jiang (2019)	firm	2005–2010	IDF	LP	8040–18,760
This study	city	2005–2018	DDF	LP + Bootstrap	1916 (original) 1880 (bias-corrected)

Notes: DDF, IDF, ODF, SBM, LP, DEA denote the directional distance function, input distance function, output distance function, slack-based method, linear programming, and data envelopment analysis, respectively.

(ODF; Lee and Zhang, 2012; Zhou *et al.*, 2015) being lower than those calculated with the DDF. The only exception is Zhang and Jiang (2019), which uses Shepard's input distance function (IDF). The reason behind this may lie in the fact that these authors utilize enterprise-level data to measure the CO_2 shadow price with higher heterogeneity. Compared with existing research, the results in the present paper are slightly larger. One possible reason for this is that we adopt the DDF with the current-level dataset. Moreover, we think that the DDF is more appropriate for measuring the shadow price of carbon emissions for the 35 cities than is the Shepard distance function since the dataset selected in this study includes data on the most developed city in each Chinese province, in which the abatement of undesirable output is accompanied by the improvement of desirable output with strict environmental regulatory constraints.

5.2. Intertemporal changes in shadow prices

Figure 1 shows the trends of average industrial CO_2 shadow prices in the key cities. Original CO_2 shadow prices are estimated from the actual data, while bias-corrected values are obtained from the bootstrap method. As demonstrated in Fig. 1, the parametric LP model without bootstrap correction tends to overestimate the real shadow price. In terms of the overall view, the trend of the CO_2 shadow price (bias-corrected) roughly experienced three periods. The first period was from 2005 to 2010, during which the shadow price of CO_2 increased steadily and continuously, increasing by 45.93%, from 812 yuan/tonne in 2005 to 1185 yuan/tonne in 2010. The second period was from 2010 to 2014, during which the CO_2 shadow price rose rapidly from a low point of 1185 yuan/tonne to 3954 yuan/tonne in 2014, for an increase of 233.67%. Similar results were also found in Choi *et al.* (2012), Du *et al.* (2015), Wang *et al.*

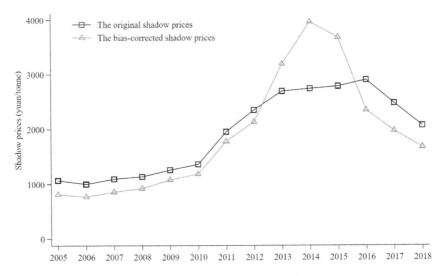

Figure 1. Trends in China's urban-industrial CO_2 shadow prices.

(2017a) and Wu *et al.* (2019), confirming that CO_2 emission abatement costs at the province and city levels exhibit an increasing trend during the 11th and 12th Five-Year Plans. During the first and second stages, the CO_2 shadow price experienced an obvious upward trend for the following two reasons: the first reason was the overall growth of the macroeconomy and the expansion of demand and prices of industrial products, while the second and more important reason was that during the 11th Five-Year Plan period, Chinese central and local governments implemented policies involving tremendous energy conservation and emission reduction actions, strengthening the restriction of environmental regulations. Finally, during the third period (2014–2018), CO_2 shadow prices reversed and showed a downward trend from 3954 yuan/tonne in 2014 to 1675 yuan/tonne in 2018, which was close to the price level in 2011. One possible reason for this is that the CO2 emission abatement threshold had decreased in recent years with the progress of technologies. Notably, since the desirable industrial outputs are deflated in this paper, the impact of price fluctuation on estimating CO_2 shadow prices can be excluded.

Figure 2 further investigates and compares different trends of industrial CO_2 shadow prices (bias-corrected) in 35 key cities, which show significant heterogeneities. The overall trends in CO_2 shadow prices of most cities are increasing, while the price trends show obvious transitions, to varying degrees, after 2015. The shadow prices of CO_2 in some cities (e.g., Fuzhou, Hangzhou, Nanjing, and Taiyuan) maintained a long-run growth trend during the research period, while other cities (e.g., Harbin, Shijiazhuang, Yinchuan, Xining, Kunming, and Lanzhou) experienced a decreasing trend.

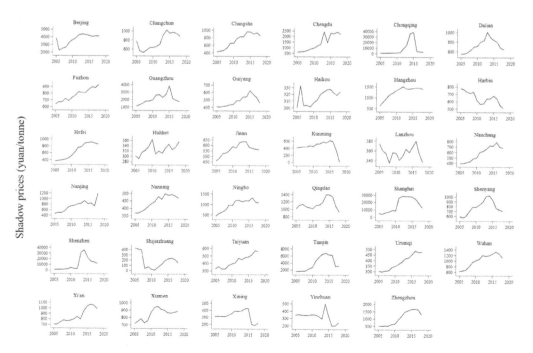

Figure 2. Trends of CO_2 shadow prices in different cities.

It is worth noting that CO_2 shadow prices are defined as the opportunity costs of desirable output due to the abatement of one unit of CO_2. Thus, the observed downward trend of the CO_2 shadow price means that the desirable output value required to reduce a unit of CO_2 emissions was reduced, and production technology was moving toward a "dirtier" direction, with all else being equal Jiang and Zhang (2018). Therefore, production technologies are shown to be "greener" in most key cities according to Fig. 2.

In addition, to test the equality of shadow price distributions across the eastern, central, and western regions simultaneously, a Kruskal–Wallis test is employed for the sample cities. The Kruskal–Wallis test yields a chi-square value of 88.67, with two degrees of freedom for the original shadow prices, and 90.48, with two degrees of freedom for the bias-corrected shadow prices, rejecting the null hypothesis of there being identical shadow prices for different regions, which means that there are significant differences between the mean value of estimated shadow prices for both types of measurements.

5.3. Regional differences in shadow prices and their influencing factors

This section explores the differences in industrial CO_2 shadow prices among different cities from a regional perspective. We calculate the average CO_2 shadow price in each city, as shown in Fig. 3. The average carbon intensity and energy structure value are

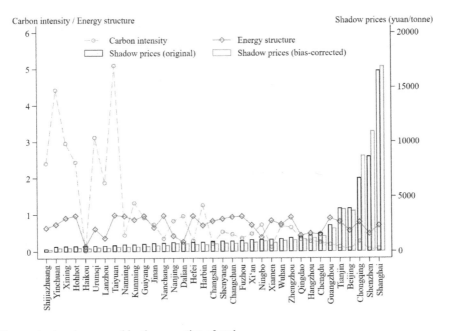

Note: Energy structure is measured by the proportion of coal.

Figure 3. Regional differences in carbon intensity, energy structure and industrial CO_2 shadow prices.

also added to explore the correlation among these three variables. As seen from the figure, the bias-corrected industrial CO_2 shadow prices by the bootstrap method in most cities declined to varying degrees, except for three cities (Chongqing, Shenzhen, and Shanghai). From the regional perspective, CO_2 shadow prices across cities show significant differences, with an unbalanced polarization distribution. As a whole, Shanghai, Shenzhen, Chongqing, Beijing, Tianjin, and Guangzhou, areas with relatively high levels of economic development, have higher CO_2 shadow prices and have, specifically, a cost of more than 2000 yuan paid per additional unit of CO_2 emission abatement. Moreover, the above six cities belong to the seven carbon emission trading pilots launched since 2013. Additionally, other cities have relatively small but still nonnegligible differences among CO_2 shadow prices, ranging from 183 to 1432 yuan/tonne. These results show that there is enormous potential emission reduction space in Chinese cities, which provides a scientific basis for introducing the national carbon emission trading market. Simultaneously, the evaluation of relative CO_2 shadow prices among cities provides a reference for the government to identify emission reduction targets and determine emission reduction costs.

Next, we explored the reasons for the significant heterogeneity in industrial CO_2 shadow prices among the cities from two aspects: energy structure (measured by the proportion of coal) and carbon intensity. First, compared with gas and various types of fuel oil, coal and coke have higher CO_2 emission coefficients. To generate equal heat, burning coal generates more CO_2. Therefore, regions with higher coal consumption can target carbon abatement by using more gas or fuel oil than coal. In comparison, regions with less coal consumption can achieve emission reduction targets only by reducing desirable output. In other words, regions with more coal consumption tend to have higher emission reduction potential and lower emission reduction costs. As shown in the figure, with the increase in CO_2 shadow prices, the proportion of coal in total energy consumption shows a declining trend. In addition, according to the basic principle of environmental economics, the MAC of CO_2 shows economies of scale, which is negatively related to carbon intensity. Figure 3 provides strong evidence of this pattern. Similar results are also found in the existing literature; with the implementation of emission reduction, the MAC of CO_2 increased rapidly, leading to more difficulty in further reducing carbon intensity. Additional statistical evidence is provided in Appendix B.

5.4. *Distortions in carbon prices*

Recall that the CO_2 shadow prices can ideally be regarded as the equilibrium carbon permit or allowance prices in carbon emission trading markets. This section compares the bias-corrected industrial CO_2 shadow prices with the actual carbon trading prices in the seven carbon trading pilot cities to investigate the distortion of carbon trading prices. The trends in the carbon prices of the seven carbon trading pilots are plotted in Fig. 4. In general, as the new carbon trading pilot is launched, the carbon trading price

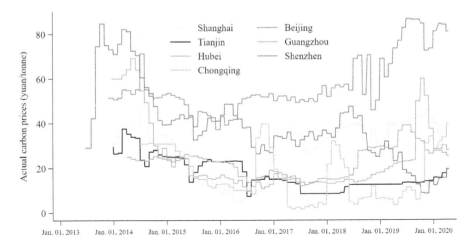

Data source: http://www.tanpaifang.com/tanhangqing/.

Figure 4. Monthly carbon prices in China's emission trading pilots 2013–2020 (yuan/tonne).

rises rapidly to a high level, reflecting market supply and demand. In contrast, the price curve remains relatively stable or declines slightly with few peaks and valleys in the following years. In Beijing, Guangzhou, and Shenzhen, carbon trading prices rise to their peak within a few months following the launch of carbon trading pilots, which varies from 78–86 yuan/tonne. However, after a short period of peaks, the carbon

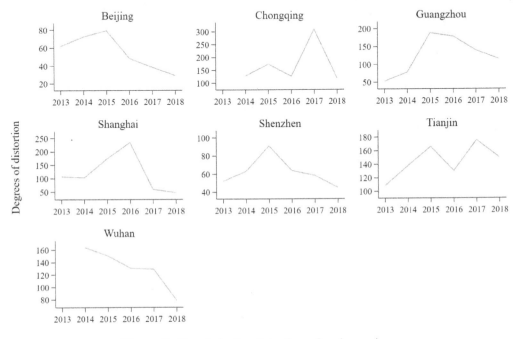

Figure 5. Trends in the distortion of carbon prices.

Table 4. Average distortion of carbon prices among the seven carbon trading pilots.

City	Beijing	Shenzhen	Shanghai	Guangzhou	Wuhan	Tianjin	Chongqing
Distortion	54.87	62.29	120.82	125.33	130.48	144.80	170.92

prices decrease and remain in the range of 40–60 yuan/tonne. In summary, regardless of the carbon trading pilot or time period, the carbon price does not exceed 100 yuan/tonne. Notably, the actual market price of carbon emission trading is much lower than the MAC of CO_2 emissions estimated in our study, which is 1880 yuan per tonne of CO_2 emissions, on average, during the sample period.

Table 4 presents the average multiple of differences between the observed carbon prices and estimated shadow prices. Regarding carbon price distortion, all carbon trading pilot markets exhibit significant carbon price distortion. Even in Beijing, with a minimal extent of distortion, there exists a 50-fold difference between the observed prices and the estimated shadow prices, while the multiple increases to 170 in Chongqing. The finding is in line with Ma and Hailu (2016) and Ma et al. (2019), who confirmed that the observed carbon prices in pilot markets are obviously lower than the estimated shadow prices and might not reflect the true opportunity costs of carbon abatement. Although the selected dataset can explain the overestimation of shadow prices to some extent, it appears to be impossible to attribute the differences between observed prices and estimated shadow prices to micro or macro sample periods. Therefore, this result reveals that current carbon trading prices are lower than the actual costs of carbon abatement because of relevant policy design, which discourages and constrains emission trading. Thus, appropriate reconciliation and rational interpretation are of immediate importance to make a useful contribution to better policy formulation as to this issue. The relatively low observed emission prices may be explained in the following ways. First, loose allocation leading to an emission trading quota is not scarce enough to incentivize enterprises to bid for emission rights. Second, the penalties for illegal discharge and overdischarge are relatively light; notably, the cost of law violation is relatively low compared with that of law compliance, leading to the unwillingness of enterprises to participate in emission trading markets. Finally, a low degree of marketization in carbon emission trading, insufficient coverage of trading objects, and prohibition of transregional trading jointly result in the low efficiency of the emission trading market and the relatively lower observed prices. It should be noted that the degree of distortion in carbon prices in most carbon pilot markets has decreased in recent years, except for that in Tianjin and Guangzhou, as shown in Fig. 5. This result indicates that most of the carbon trading pilots continue to make progress in efficiency improvement because of the distortion reduction in carbon prices.

6. Conclusions and Policy Implications

Against the backdrop of growing concerns about climate change and the commitments that China has made to peak its carbon emissions, it is urgent to explore realistic pathways to low-carbon development. The scientific evaluation of the CO_2 shadow price provides environmental policy guidelines, such as the risk hedging of the allowance price in emission trading markets and the setting of carbon tax rates for constant charge systems. To this end, this paper develops a modified evaluation model by using the parametric DDF and bootstrap method to estimate CO_2 shadow prices and the possible distortions in carbon markets.

The empirical results show that the average industrial CO_2 shadow price for target cities is 1915.86 yuan/tonne, compared to 1880.57 yuan/tonne when using the bootstrap method by taking stochastic factors into account. Given the enhancement of environmental regulations since the enactment of China's 11th Five-Year Plan, the overall trends in CO_2 shadow prices in most cities have been increasing, which indicates that the production technology in these cities is becoming "greener". The regional estimates indicate a great discrepancy in the cross-city shadow prices of CO_2, showing an unbalanced distribution of polarization. This finding reveals that enormous emission reduction space exists among Chinese cities, providing strong evidence for introducing the national CO_2 emission trading market. The CO_2 shadow prices in carbon pilots are significantly higher than those in nonpilot cities, which implies that the launch of carbon trading plays an important role in promoting the low-carbon transformation of urban-industrial production. Compared to cities with a lower proportion of coal, cities that consume relatively more coal can achieve lower emission reduction costs, and the CO_2 shadow prices rise sharply, with a gradual decline in carbon intensity. Most importantly, we find that the current carbon trading price cannot reflect the real opportunity cost of carbon abatement, and an enormous gap exists due to the differences in the allocation of carbon emission quotas, the willingness of enterprises to participate in carbon trading markets, and the degree of marketization of carbon emission trading. However, we observe a downward trend for carbon price distortion in most carbon trading pilot cities in recent years.

Several policy recommendations can be put forward based on the empirical results. First, the government should not only focus on the attainment of climate goals, such as the 2030 carbon-peaking target and the 2060 carbon-neutral target, but also take the MACs corresponding to these two targets as the direction of policy adjustment and raise the price of carbon through measures like buying back oversupplied quotas and reducing quota allocation. Second, the unequal shadow prices among cities denote the inefficient allocation of resources. One way to change this status is to use the shadow prices as a reference to reprice the carbon emission transaction among regions or industries and then achieve the equivalent assessment of environmental pollution with the invisible hand of the market. Finally, the higher CO_2 shadow prices in carbon trading pilots indicate that the government should actively promote the establishment of the national carbon trading market, expand the industry coverage of carbon trading markets, and improve the liquidity and marketization of carbon trading markets by introducing more market agents.

This study also has some limitations. For instance, due to the availability of data, the sample of this paper covers only 35 typical cities, leading the conclusions to be somewhat weaker than those in the case in which all the cities could be taken into account to estimate the MAC completely. Furthermore, the selection of the directional vector in the DDF may be controversial, and a variety of direction vectors or endogenous direction vectors can instead be selected.

Acknowledgments

We are grateful to the editor and anonymous referees for their valuable comments and suggestions. Financial support from the National Natural Science Foundation of China (Grant Nos. 72073105, 71874177, 71774122, 71874064, and 72022019), the National Key Research and Development Program of China (No. 2020YFA0608603), the Youth Innovation Promotion Association, CAS (No. 2021164), and Fund of University of Chinese Academy of Sciences, are greatly acknowledged.

Appendix A. Average Technical Efficiency Scores of Cities

The average environmental efficiency score (i.e., 1 minus the value of the DDF) for each city is reported in Fig. A.1. Overall, the DDF value captures the environmental efficiency score of each city well. For example, Haikou, a well-known tourism and low-carbon city, has the highest average environmental efficiency score, while many developed cities in the eastern and central regions (e.g., Ningbo, Shanghai, and

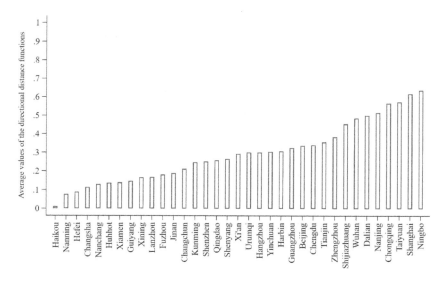

Figure A1. The average DDF values of the typical cities.

Taiyuan) have lower environmental efficiency due to higher energy consumption and carbon emissions.

Appendix B. Determinants of CO₂ Shadow Prices

To provide statistical evidence on the determinants of shadow prices, we test the correlation between shadow prices and carbon intensities as well as energy structures by using the following panel data model:

$$\ln \text{SP}_{it} = \alpha_0 + \alpha_1 \ln \text{CI}_{it} + \alpha_2 \ln \text{ES}_{it} + \alpha_3 \ln Y_{it} + \mu_t + \gamma_i + \varepsilon_{it}, \quad (A.1)$$

where SP_{it}, CI_{it}, ES_{it}, and represent shadow prices, carbon intensities, energy structures and gross industrial products, respectively. μ_t denotes year fixed effects (FEs) and represents the changing global environment over time. γ_i denotes city FEs, denoting all permanent unobservable influences across cities. ε_{it} represents the random error term. Subscripts i and t represent cities and years, respectively.

Table B.1 presents the results from pooled ordinary least squares (OLS), FEs, and random effects (REs) models. In all models below, almost all of the coefficients are statistically significant at the 1% level. Since the null hypothesis of nonsignificant individual effects can be rejected according to both the LM and F-tests, we conclude

Table B1. Determinants of CO₂ shadow prices.

Variables	(1)-OLS ln SP$_{it}$	(2)-FE ln SP$_{it}$	(3)-FE ln SP$_{it}$	(4)-RE ln SP$_{it}$
ln CI$_{it}$	−0.320***	−0.516***	−0.505***	−0.439***
	(0.024)	(0.054)	(0.054)	(0.044)
ln ES$_{it}$	−0.291***	−0.415***	−0.388***	−0.382***
	(0.055)	(0.065)	(0.064)	(0.061)
ln Y$_{it}$	0.498***	0.220***	0.161*	0.293***
	(0.029)	(0.056)	(0.094)	(0.065)
Constant	−2.034***	2.671***	5.350***	1.514
	(0.489)	(0.936)	(1.553)	(1.085)
Observations	490	490	490	490
R-squared	0.668	0.380	0.423	
City FE	NO	YES	YES	YES
Year FE	NO	NO	YES	YES
F-test		22.40***	23.25***	
LM(χ^2)				1105.78***
Hausman FE versus RE				14.50**

Notes: Standard errors in parentheses; ***$p < 0.01$, **$p < 0.05$, and *$p < 0.1$; the F-test tests the null hypothesis of nonsignificance as a whole of individual effects; the LM test has χ^2 distribution and tests the null hypothesis of nonrelevance of individual effects; the Hausman test provides evidence for choosing the fixed versus REs model; OLS is ordinary least squares; RE is random effects; and FE is FEs.

Table B2. Effect of the pilot carbon trading schemes on CO_2 shadow prices.

Variables	(1) $\ln SP_{it}$	(2) $\ln SP_{it}$	(3) $\ln SP_{it}$
$treat_i \times post_t$	1.649***	0.611***	0.397***
	(0.151)	(0.092)	(0.087)
$\ln CI_{it}$			−0.439***
			(0.055)
$\ln ES_{it}$			−0.386***
			(0.063)
$\ln Y_{it}$			0.159*
			(0.092)
Constant	6.564***	6.401***	5.571***
	(0.044)	(0.068)	(1.520)
Observations	490	490	490
R-squared	0.197	0.315	0.449
City FE	NO	YES	YES
Year FE	NO	YES	YES

Notes: Standard errors in parentheses; ***$p < 0.01$, **$p < 0.05$, and *$p < 0.1$.

that the pooled OLS estimator is not appropriate. Moreover, the Hausman specification test for fixed versus REs yields a p-value smaller than 0.05, suggesting that FE estimates are more efficient. Therefore, in this paper, we mainly focus on model 3 (the two-way FE model). The regression coefficients for both carbon intensity and energy structure are significantly smaller than zero, implying a negative relationship between them and shadow prices. Specifically, keeping other things equal, a 1% reduction in carbon intensity leads to a 0.505% increase in shadow prices, whereas a 1% reduction in the share of coal leads to a 0.388% increase in shadow prices. These results are consistent with our theoretical expectations in Sec. 5.3.

Furthermore, to investigate the relationship between environmental regulations and CO_2 shadow prices, we select the carbon ETS implemented in 2013 as an exogenous shock and use difference-in-differences (DID) models to examine the impact of environmental policy on shadow prices. The estimation of a standard DID model can be written as follows:

$$\ln SP_{it} = \beta_0 + \beta_1 (treat_i \times post_t) + \lambda Control + \mu_t + \gamma_i + \varepsilon_{it}, \quad (A.2)$$

where $treat_i$ equals 1 if a city belongs to China's six pilot ETS regions; otherwise, it equals 0. $post_t$ equals 1 for all years equal to or following 2013 (the policy period); otherwise, it equals 0. Item Control contains CI_{it}, ES_{it}, and Y_{it}. The other terms have the same meaning as the corresponding terms in Eq. (A.1).

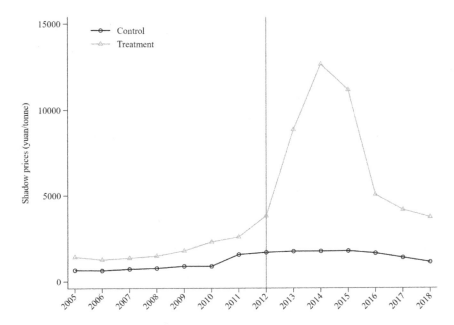

Figure B1. Illustration of parallel trend.

The regression results for Eq. (A.1) are shown in Table B.2. Here, we are interested in, which is significantly positive, indicating that the carbon ETS has a positive effect on CO_2 shadow prices. By the stepwise inclusion of FEs and control variables, three regression models are sequentially adopted. The result in column (3) of our main focus shows that the implementation of the carbon ETS leads to 39.7% average increase in CO_2 shadow prices.

The primary assumption of a DID approach is that the trends of the treatment group and the control group should be parallel over time. To test this hypothesis, we draw a diagram of their trends over time, as shown in Fig. B.1, according to which the treatment group and control group satisfy the parallel trend before the policy introduction, which shows that the identification results of the above models are quite reliable.

References

Aigner, D, CAK Lovell and P Schmidt (1977). Formulation and estimation of stochastic frontier production function models. *Journal of Econometrics*, 6, 21–37.

Aigner, DJ and SF Chu (1968). On estimating the industry production function. *The American Economic Review*, 58, 826–839.

Bellver-Domingo, A, R Fuentes and F Hernández-Sancho (2017). Shadow prices of emerging pollutants in wastewater treatment plants: Quantification of environmental externalities. *Journal of Environmental Management*, 203, 439–447.

Boussemart, JP, H Leleu and Z Shen (2017). Worldwide carbon shadow prices during 1990–2011. *Energy Policy*, 109, 288–296.

Carlson, C, D Burtraw, M Cropper and KL Palmer (2000). Sulfur dioxide control by electric utilities: What are the gains from trade? *Journal of Political Economy*, 108, 1292–1326.

Chen, S, H Jin and Y Lu (2019). Impact of urbanization on CO_2 emissions and energy consumption structure: A panel data analysis for Chinese prefecture-level cities. *Structural Change and Economic Dynamics*, 49, 107–119.

Choi, Y, N Zhang and P Zhou (2012). Efficiency and abatement costs of energy-related CO_2 emissions in China: A slacks-based efficiency measure. *Applied Energy*, 98, 198–208.

Du, L, A Hanley and C Wei (2015). Marginal abatement costs of carbon dioxide emissions in China: A parametric analysis. *Environmental and Resource Economics*, 61, 191–216.

Du, L, A Hanley and N Zhang (2016). Environmental technical efficiency, technology gap and shadow price of coal-fuelled power plants in China: A parametric meta-frontier analysis. *Resource and Energy Economics*, 43, 14–32.

Duan, H, L Zhu, G Kumbaroğlu and Y Fan (2016). Regional opportunities for China to go low-carbon: Results from the REEC model. *The Energy Journal*, 37, 223–252.

Dunant, CF, ACH Skelton, MP Drewniok, JM Cullen and JM Allwood (2019). A marginal abatement cost curve for material efficiency accounting for uncertainty. *Resources, Conservation and Recycling*, 144, 39–47.

Färe, R, S Grosskopf, DW Noh and W Weber (2005). Characteristics of a polluting technology: Theory and practice. *Journal of Econometrics*, 126, 469–492.

Färe, R, S Grosskopf and WL Weber (2006). Shadow prices and pollution costs in U.S. agriculture. *Ecological Economics*, 56, 89–103.

Hailu, A and TS Veeman (2000). Environmentally sensitive productivity analysis of the canadian pulp and paper industry, 1959-1994: An input distance function approach. *Journal of Environmental Economics and Management*, 40, 251–274.

He, W, B Wang, Danish and Z Wang (2018). Will regional economic integration influence carbon dioxide marginal abatement costs? Evidence from Chinese panel data. *Energy Economics*, 74, 263–274.

Huang, Z and H Duan (2020). Estimating the threshold interactions between income inequality and carbon emissions. *Journal of Environmental Management*, 263, 110393.

Ji, DJ and P Zhou (2020). Marginal abatement cost, air pollution and economic growth: Evidence from Chinese cities. *Energy Economics*, 86, 104658.

Jiahuey, Y, Y Liu and Y Yu (2019). Measuring green growth performance of China's chemical industry. *Resources, Conservation and Recycling*, 149, 160–167.

Jiang, W and S Zhang (2018). Robust estimates of industrial CO_2 shadow prices and emission reduction policies in China. *Management World*, 34, 32–49.

Lee, M and N Zhang (2012). Technical efficiency, shadow price of carbon dioxide emissions, and substitutability for energy in the Chinese manufacturing industries. *Energy Economics*, 34, 1492–1497.

Lee, SC, DH Oh and JD Lee (2014). A new approach to measuring shadow price: Reconciling engineering and economic perspectives. *Energy Economics*, 46, 66–77.

Liu, Y, S Wang, Z Qiao, Y Wang, Y Ding and C Miao (2019). Estimating the dynamic effects of socioeconomic development on industrial SO_2 emissions in Chinese cities using a DPSIR causal framework. *Resources, Conservation and Recycling*, 150, 104450.

Ma, C and A Hailu (2016). The marginal abatement cost of carbon emissions in China. *The Energy Journal*, 37, 111–127.

Ma, C, A Hailu and C You (2019). A critical review of distance function based economic research on China's marginal abatement cost of carbon dioxide emissions. *Energy Economics*, 84, 104533.

Maziotis, A, A Villegas and M Molinos-Senante (2020). The cost of reducing unplanned water supply interruptions: A parametric shadow price approach. *Science of the Total Environment*, 719, 137487.

Molinos-Senante, M and C Guzmán (2018). Reducing CO_2 emissions from drinking water treatment plants: A shadow price approach. *Applied Energy*, 210, 623–631.

Shen, X and B Lin (2017). The shadow prices and demand elasticities of agricultural water in China: A StoNED-based analysis. *Resources, Conservation and Recycling*, 127, 21–28.

Simar, L and PW Wilson (1998). Sensitivity analysis of efficiency scores: How to bootstrap in nonparametric frontier models. *Management Science*, 44, 49–61.

Vardanyan, M and DW Noh (2006). Approximating pollution abatement costs via alternative specifications of a multi-output production technology: A case of the US electric utility industry. *Journal of Environmental Management*, 80, 177–190.

Wang, J, K Lv, Y Bian and Y Cheng (2017a). Energy efficiency and marginal carbon dioxide emission abatement cost in urban China. *Energy Policy*, 105, 246–255.

Wang, K, L Che, C Ma and YM Wei (2017b). The shadow price of CO_2 emissions in China's iron and steel industry. *Science of the Total Environment*, 598, 272–281.

Wang, W, X Hualin, N Zhang and D Xiang (2018). Sustainable water use and water shadow price in China's urban industry. *Resources, Conservation and Recycling*, 128, 489–498.

Wei, C, A Löschel and B Liu (2013). An empirical analysis of the CO_2 shadow price in Chinese thermal power enterprises. *Energy Economics*, 40, 22–31.

Wei, X and N Zhang (2020). The shadow prices of CO_2 and SO_2 for Chinese coal-fired power plants: A partial frontier approach. *Energy Economics*, 85, 104576.

Wu, J, C Ma and K Tang (2019). The static and dynamic heterogeneity and determinants of marginal abatement cost of CO_2 emissions in Chinese cities. *Energy*, 178, 685–694.

Xian, Y, K Wang, YM Wei and Z Huang (2020). Opportunity and marginal abatement cost savings from China's pilot carbon emissions permit trading system: Simulating evidence from the industrial sectors. *Journal of Environmental Management*, 271, 110975.

Xie, H, Y Yu, W Wang and Y Liu (2017). The substitutability of non-fossil energy, potential carbon emission reduction and energy shadow prices in China. *Energy Policy*, 107, 63–71.

Yang, M, Y Hou, Q Ji and D Zhang (2020). Assessment and optimization of provincial CO_2 emission reduction scheme in China: An improved ZSG-DEA approach. *Energy Economics*, 91, 104931.

Zhang, N and XF Jiang (2019). The effect of environmental policy on Chinese firm's green productivity and shadow price: A metafrontier input distance function approach. *Technological Forecasting and Social Change*, 144, 129–136.

Zhou, C, S Wang and K Feng (2018). Examining the socioeconomic determinants of CO_2 emissions in China: A historical and prospective analysis. *Resources, Conservation and Recycling*, 130, 1–11.

Zhou, X, L Fan and P Zhou (2015). Marginal CO_2 abatement costs: Findings from alternative shadow price estimates for Shanghai industrial sectors. *Energy Policy*, 77, 109–117.

Lightning Source LLC
Chambersburg PA
CBHW080635150625
28081CB00007B/33